PENGUIN B

CRICKET'S GREATEST SCANDALS

Ever since Ken Piesse was given a brand new copy of the 1965 *Wisden Cricketers' Almanack* and memorised most of its 1066 pages, cricket has been his cornerstone and the Melbourne Cricket Ground his second home. Memories of double centuries in searing heat by Grahame Thomas and Jack Potter at Sheffield Shield level are as enduring a memory as the Test wicket-taking bursts by Graham McKenzie, Dennis Lillee and Shane Warne. While only a modest player himself, Ken did tour England with the Crusaders and in one memorable lead-up match against the Politicians at the MCG caught the then Prime Minister Bob Hawke in front of Bay 13. 'First time I've been caught out by a journalist in 25 years,' Hawke told the assembled media. *Cricket's Greatest Scandals* is Ken's 25th cricket book. In between manuscripts he's working on his leg-break.

Cricket books by Ken Piesse

Great Triumphs in Test Cricket (1979)

Prahran Cricket Club Centenary History (1979)

Cricket Digest Annual (ed.) (1980)

Cricket Year Annual (ed.) (1980–83)

Calypso Summers (with Jim Main) (1981)

The Great Australian Book of Cricket Stories (1982)

The Golden Age of Australian Cricket (ed.) (1982)

Duel for Glory: England Tours of Australia 1861–1982 (with Jim Main) (1982)

Donald Bradman (Famous Australians series) (1983)

Cartoonists at the Cricket (ed.) (1983)

The A to Z of Cricket (1983)

Bradman & The Bush (with Ian Ferguson) (1986)

Hooked on Cricket (with Max Walker) (1988)

Match Drawn (ed.) (1988)

Simply the Best: The Allan Border Story (1993)

Warne: Sultan of Spin (1995)

Cricket Skills & Secrets (1995–99)

One Day Magic (1996)

The Big Australian Cricket Book (1996)

Wildmen of Cricket Vol. 1 (with Brian Hansen) (1998)

TJ Over the Top (with Terry Jenner) (1999)

The Taylor Years (1999)

Steve & Mark Waugh (2000)

The Complete Shane Warne (2000)

Mahanama Retired Hurt (with Roshan Mahanama) (2001)

CRICKET'S GREATEST SCANDALS

Ken Piesse

PENGUIN BOOKS

Penguin Books Australia Ltd
487 Maroondah Highway, PO Box 257
Ringwood, Victoria 3134, Australia
Penguin Books Ltd
Harmondsworth, Middlesex, England
Penguin Putnam Inc.
375 Hudson Street, New York, New York 10014, USA
Penguin Books Canada Limited
10 Alcorn Avenue, Toronto, Ontario, Canada M4V 3B2
Penguin Books (NZ) Ltd
Cnr Rosedale and Airborne Roads, Albany, Auckland, New Zealand
Penguin Books (South Africa) (Pty) Ltd
5 Watkins Street, Denver Ext 4, 2094, South Africa
Penguin Books India (P) Ltd
11, Community Centre, Panchsheel Park, New Delhi 110 017, India

First published by Penguin Books Australia Ltd 2000
This revised and updated edition published by Penguin Books Australia Ltd 2001

10 9 8 7 6 5 4 3 2 1

Cover designed by David Altheim, Penguin Design Studio
Text designed by Leonie Stott, Penguin Design Studio
Typeset in Minion and Shannon Book by Post Pre-press, Brisbane, Queensland
Printed and bound in Australia by McPherson's Printing Group, Maryborough, Victoria

National Library of Australia
Cataloguing-in-Publication data:

Piesse, Ken.
  Cricket's greatest scandals.

Includes index.
ISBN 0 14 029912 2.

1. Cricket – Australia. 2. Cricket players – Australia.
3. Scandals in mass media. I. Title.

796.3580994

www.penguin.com.au

Contents

Introduction

Many people far more learned than me are pessimistic about cricket and its future. They worry that the game no longer has its integrity. Many feel a number of elite cricketers possess egos as inflated as their salaries and are dismissive of standards and tradition.

As galling as it has been to see cricket dragged through the gutters by captains of the game and others who have lost focus and fallen ingloriously rather than being protective of the greatest game of all, cricket has a charm and an in-built resilience that no erring individual can harm.

Bans have been implemented, security updated and lessons learnt. In time, after all the current inquisition and disappointment, the on-field action will again take centre stage. We will again revel in the awesome talents of Sachin Tendulkar, the impossible-to-ignore passion of Shane Warne and the joyous sight of Brett Lee bowling as fast as anybody, Thommo excluded, in the history of the game.

More countries will follow the Australian lead of cap presentations for debutants. They, too, will invite old players to share in the moment, not only on the morning of a game, but at the pre-Test dinners once the province only of the selected XII.

Cricket will always produce its mavericks and outlaws, and refreshingly so. And it will always have its past, both good and bad. As this book shows, cricket has been triggering controversy for more than 150 years. The very biggest scandals, such as match-fixing, are outlined in depth as part of our 'first XII', which also features Dean Jones' sacking, the crucifixion of Ian Meckiff and the Chappell underarm, through to the cash gifts accepted by the now-more-worldly Australian pair Shane Warne and Mark Waugh. Our 'second XII' also includes some of the most controversial moments, such as Don Bradman's strike at the start of the Bodyline summer, the watering of the wicket in Melbourne and Mike Gatting's furious toe-to-toe with a Pakistani umpire.

New scandals will emerge in the years ahead, triggering outrage and despair. But it doesn't mean the game is coming to an end. The game of cricket is simply too good to ignore.

If the new generation of emerging champions can remember that they are ambassadors and keepers of the game, it will soon enough flourish again despite the disgrace and dishonour triggered by the minority, who will forever be remembered for all the wrong reasons.

FIRST XII

*The constant habit of betting will
take the honesty out of any man.*
**Rev. James Pycroft, *The Cricket Field*,
first published 1851**

1. Satan claims a white knight: Hansie Cronje

Ali Bacher, for years the face and inspiration of South African cricket, was staying at the Pinda Game Reserve in northern Natal when he was woken by the telephone. It was Hansie Cronje. 'I'm sorry, Doc,' he began. 'I haven't been honest with you.' Cronje said the weekend's press conference had been a sham, one long lie. The lies were eating him up; he had accepted money and gratuities from bookmakers. He had been greedy, foolish and manipulative.

Bacher was aghast. Here was betrayal of the highest magnitude. He had trusted Cronje implicitly, giving him powers far beyond those of any captain in 111 years of South African Test cricket. He saw Cronje as the face of the game in the Republic, a squeaky-clean ambassador and inspiration to millions. However, within 12 hours he had ordered Cronje's dismissal as captain, suspended his one-year contract and sought government intervention.

As Bacher and the cricket world were soon to learn, 30-year-old Cronje had been on the take for years. His admissions at the King Commission in Cape Town confirmed long-held suspicions that the thriving billion-dollar illegal gambling industry had claimed insiders of the highest rank and repute. Cricket was crooked.

CAPE TOWN'S CENTRE for the Book, an elegant, wood-panelled 100-year-old library featuring the very finest in Edwardian architecture, had never seen anything quite like it. There, for ten and a half hours over three days, disgraced captain Wessel Johannes Cronje emerged from his private hell, revealing his double life and a litany of bribes and ill-gotten gains going back years. He'd taken up to US$100 000 (A$170 000), smuggled it undeclared into the country and hidden much of it around his Bloemfontein home. By associating with the cricket underworld, contriving results and implicating others, he had brought infamy on himself and his family and irreparably disgraced the game's good name. 'In a moment of stupidity and weakness, I allowed Satan and the world to dictate terms to me,' he said. 'The moment I took my eye off Jesus my whole world turned dark.'

Those who were crammed into the semicircular first-floor viewing gallery shook their heads in bewilderment. Many had sympathised with Cronje and simply refused to believe the charges of corruption brought against their hero by the New Delhi police. For these fans, it had been a shocking smear campaign. But now Cronje was confirming that he was not the paragon most people thought him to be – and that other icons of the international game had also succumbed to temptation. The web of deceit was global. Cricket had never known a lower moment.

If not actually revelling in the notoriety of his country's greatest sporting scandal, Cronje wasn't as contrite as his shocked supporters expected him to be. He showed little remorse, was flippant and occasionally even appeared arrogant. Several times he was admonished by Judge Edwin King and ordered to answer questions seriously, no matter how trite he thought them. Only at the end, when his face crumpled and he was assisted by two bodyguards from the courtroom, did the outside world first see his personal torment and inner demons emerge.

From the outset, Judge King, a former judge president of the

Western Cape, told Cronje he wasn't on trial. However, he reminded him that he must reveal all or, under South Africa's Corruption Act, jeopardise his chances of immunity from future prosecution. 'Mr Cronje,' the judge said, 'I know you're under strain. I want to know that you have my full understanding of your situation. I want you to be frank and honest with me. Before I swear you in, I would like to refer you to Chapter Eight, St John's Gospel: "The truth will set you free."'

Cronje's testimony was broadcast live via television and radio to millions throughout South Africa. In the inquiry room itself were testifying team-mates, United Cricket Board (UCB) officials, family, friends and three dozen journalists – none, ironically, from the subcontinent, the acknowledged hotbed of cricket corruption. Cronje confirmed his guilt and described how bookmakers had hounded him with up to 20 phone calls a day while he was on tour in India in 2000. In five years he had accepted bribes of almost US$100 000 and, in retrospect, reckoned he should have asked for more. He had also arranged to manipulate matches – without once, he said, fully following through.

Cronje told the inquiry his love of money bordered on a sickness. It had so enveloped him that he had lost touch with reality. Even declared annual salaries of 1.6 million rand (A$400 000) weren't enough. Satan was burning inside him. He had thought about jumping off a building but couldn't find one high enough. He had regrets that he would take to his grave.

The three-week investigation had worldwide repercussions. Cronje implicated former Indian captain Mohammad Azharuddin, who had always in the past vigorously protested his innocence. The already-banned Pakistani Saleem Malik was also damned. Cronje said his first contact with a bookmaker was in the person of a Pakistani or Indian man called John, whom he believed to be the same person who had approached Australian players Shane Warne and Mark Waugh only months earlier in Colombo.

Cronje told the Commission that before the 1995 Mandela Trophy in Cape Town he was approached by John with an offer of US$10 000 to throw the game. He said he would talk to the team about it. Having consulted only one member, Pat Symcox, he turned the offer down without reference to the remaining players. 'As I was walking onto the field, I was asked by [Pakistan's] Saleem Malik whether I had spoken to John,' Cronje said in his testimony. 'It was evident to me that he knew about the approach. I felt ashamed and embarrassed.' There was a further offer before the second final, which was also rejected. Cronje admitted that had Symcox not been so opposed to the idea, he would most probably have thrown the match.

'It's such a big temptation for a 26-year-old,' said Cronje. 'You're on the road and someone comes and offers US$10 000 for a little, tiny piece of information which can be helpful to him and all you have to do is supply him with a tiny piece of information which isn't going to affect the way you play, the way you captain or the outcome of the game. I probably gave him the wrong idea by saying: "Give me some time to think about it. Give me some time to speak to some of the team members about it." It was the worst thing I could have done. If I'd have said, "Forget it. Go jump off a building", it would have made my life so much easier.'

Throughout the 1990s allegations of match-fixing had been widespread, but suspicions had fallen only on players from the subcontinent. Now, for the first time, here was full-frontal evidence that the problem was global. One of cricket's greatest heroes, a committed Christian, was also corrupt. And others, too, might be, by implication.

IN ESSENCE, CRONJE'S double life had been discovered by sheer chance, via conversations secretly recorded by Indian police.

The tapes had been made by New Delhi police while the South

African team was staying at Delhi's Taj Palace hotel in mid-March 2000. The damning conversations between Cronje and a London-based bookmaker and garment manufacturer, Sanjeev (Sanjay) Chawla, were recorded, triggering the biggest hue and cry in South African cricket history.

The Indian police were investigating an extortion link said to involve Dubai gangsters and a notorious Mumbai underworld figure, Dawood Ibrahim. By sheer chance, while checking lists of regularly dialled international phone numbers, they tapped into room 346 at the Taj while Cronje was setting up a scam with Chawla. When they realised the conversation was about cricket, they kept listening – and recording.

The clipped Afrikaans accent of the foreigner was unmistakable. He was talking on a mobile phone and confirming other players said to be in on the deal: Herschelle Gibbs, Henry Williams, Nico Boje and Pieter Strydom.

CHAWLA: Is Strydom playing?

CRONJE: Yes, he is playing. Yeah.

CHAWLA: Boje?

CRONJE: Boje is playing.

CHAWLA: Yeah. Boje is playing – and who else is playing? Gibbs?

CRONJE: Gibbs and myself.

CHAWLA: Ya, what about anybody else?

CRONJE: No, I won't be able to get more.

CHAWLA: You won't be able to get more?

CRONJE: No.

CHAWLA: OK, just tell me, but you have only four with you and not anybody else?

CRONJE: No.

CHAWLA: Klusener and no one?

CRONJE: No, no. Impossible . . . The other guys are already angry with me because I have not received their money, you know.

CHAWLA: Tomorrow I can deposit the money in your account. It is not a problem because of time difference [between London and Delhi]. Tomorrow itself I can deposit the money.

CRONJE: OK.

In a later conversation, probably the next day, Cronje told Chawla of his progress in involving others in the match-fixing plan and confirmed the financial arrangements.

CRONJE: OK. I have spoken. Yes, everything is fine. Spoken to Gibbs, Williams and Strydom. Everything is fine.

CHAWLA: Already OK. And how many runs for Gibbs?

CRONJE: Less than 20.

CHAWLA: Less than 20?

CRONJE: Yeah.

CHAWLA: OK, so everything is according to plan. They have to score at least 250.

CRONJE: Yeah.

CHAWLA: And if you score 270 it is off?

CRONJE: OK. And financially the guys want 25. They want 25 each.

CHAWLA: All right. OK.

CRONJE: So that's 75 for those three and – what can you pay me? I do not know how much you pay me?

CHAWLA: You say.

CRONJE: If you give me – 140 for everybody.

CHAWLA: 140 altogether?

CRONJE: Yeah.

CHAWLA: OK, that's fine.

CRONJE: OK.

CHAWLA: And we will sort something out for the previous one as well.

CRONJE: OK, sure.

CHAWLA: Yeah?

CRONJE:　All right. So we definitely are on.

CHAWLA:　OK and one last thing. I want to ask you – you know just in
　　　　　case India bats first and if they get out for less than 250 and
　　　　　when you come to bat in the second innings, is it possible
　　　　　that you could ask Gibbs to [inaudible] his wicket? We will
　　　　　score him out and try and score slowly and not so fast so that
　　　　　you know – maybe we can get out of it.

CRONJE:　OK, I'll tell him.

Cronje initially denied all knowledge of wrongdoing or of having
any dealings with bookmakers. He said he would open his South
African bank accounts to prove this. Ali Bacher was equally
indignant, shocked that South Africa's good name could be so
blackened again after the rebel tour controversies of the 1980s.
Describing the affair as a total fabrication, Bacher called an
immediate press conference at Durban's cricketing headquarters,
Kingsmead, where the Proteas were playing a friendly game against
Natal. But instead of clearing the captain's name, the press
conference only added to the intrigue. Rather than being dismissive
of the charges, Cronje was ill at ease. He refused to look questioners
in the eye and said he didn't even know if he had met Chawla or any
other bookmaker. 'We see 40 or 50 people a day asking for
interviews, autographs and pictures,' he said. He even claimed not to
have read the transcripts of the taped conversations. For a captain
called to answer the most serious charges in the 123-year history of
Test cricket, this was a staggering oversight.

　　Among the 30 journalists at the press conference were several who
were travelling with the Australian team. They reckoned something
wasn't right. Why was Cronje so defensive? Surely he would have been
trumpeting his innocence. Maybe he *was* involved after all? There was
a feeling that too much had been left unanswered, including two of the
most important questions: had Cronje ever met bookmaker Chawla?

And were the published transcripts of his alleged conversations with Chawla authentic?

A throwaway line made by Cronje just hours before the press conference in a meeting with the UCB's acting president Percy Sonn and other officials, including media liaison officer Bronwyn Wilkinson, was the first hint that he might, in fact, be implicated. Reviewing the affair in the Melbourne *Herald Sun*, Robert Craddock, one of five Australians present at Kingsmead, said, 'The captain's innocence wasn't even discussed because everyone knew he was innocent – except the man who was living the lie. When Cronje was asked whether any of the other accused players should attend the press conference, he said, "Yes, they are innocent – I never told them anything." For a paralysing second, the people in the room who heard the comment felt like used-car salesmen who had staked their reputations on their latest sale, then heard the sound of a spluttering engine as it disappeared around the corner.'

The initial sympathy for Cronje turned into a tidal wave of bewilderment and anger after his agonised, pre-dawn phone call four days later to Bacher. A copy of the captain's confession was faxed to UCB headquarters and to Pastor Roy McCauley from the church. In it, Cronje all but admitted the validity of the charges of criminal conspiracy brought against him by New Delhi police and said that by selling information, he had betrayed his family, his friends and his Christian faith. He blamed the devil for his downfall.

'If the bookmakers can get to Hansie Cronje, they can get to anybody in world cricket,' said a shocked Bacher. 'He is definitely not looking for any escape hatches,' said Pastor McCauley, a long-time friend and confidant. 'His letter to me was written in very personal, spiritual terms and made it clear that he wanted to come clean with all concerned – his family, his team-mates, his country.' McCauley claimed that Cronje had merely been 'playing around' with the Indian bookmaker and that 'a joke gone wrong' had 'ruined his life'.

In the controversial, whistle-blowing game in question – an otherwise forgettable Pepsi Cup contest in Nagpur in mid-March during South Africa's 2000 tour of India – only Gibbs and Williams had in fact agreed to the fix. The bookmakers had lost heavily on earlier, 'clean' games and hoped that by bribing Cronje and the others they could fix the game and make one big 'kill', thereby wiping out their earlier debts. Cronje was under so much pressure from the bookmakers that he invented Boje and Strydom's involvement and planned to keep the extra money himself.

Gibbs opened the batting and made 74, accelerating the initial run rate so greatly that South Africa reached 320, a record score against India. Opening bowler Javagal Srinath conceded 65 runs from 11 overs. By lunchtime, all bets were off.

In sworn evidence, Strydom said Cronje had in fact approached him, but he thought his captain must have been joking. 'Hansie called me to his room the day before the match and said in a light-hearted way that he can get 70 000 rand [US$10 000] if we get less than 250,' Strydom said. 'I said no. If I had played 80 or 90 Test matches I might have agreed. I have always known Hansie as a practical joker. He did not put any pressure on to take the money and when I walked out of the room I thought I had passed a test by not taking a bet. I walked past him later. He nudged me and said how about 140 000 rand. I laughed and said no [again].'

Gibbs and Williams, however, had been more naive. Gibbs agreed to the fix because Cronje was not only his captain but his hero. 'I would do anything Hansie told me to,' said Gibbs, who at Cronje's request had previously repeatedly lied when questioned about the bribes. Pace bowler Williams had said yes because he was told Gibbs was involved. 'I was at first very nervous, but because Herschelle agreed, I agreed,' said Williams. 'I had a lot of respect for the captain. If he could do something like this, I could do it.'

As Cronje was to admit during his testimony, Gibbs and Williams agreed to accept US$15 000 each, rather than the US$25 000 Cronje had told Chawla was the players' demand. He was cutting himself in for an extra US$10 000 per player, as well as taking an overall fee. Had the fix worked, his take-home pay would have been a cool US$110 000.

AMAZINGLY, IT WASN'T until April 2000, when Cronje learnt that he was about to be charged for corruption in India, that he realised the impact of his deceptions. The Indian authorities were talking of a jail term of up to 10 years for Cronje and anyone else found guilty of criminal activity.

When he first read of the charges, he threw the mobile phone he had used to negotiate with Chawla into the dustbin. 'I got a huge fright,' he said. 'I was trying to get rid of all the evidence that I had any dealings with Sanjay.' Despite the hue and cry in Australia less than 18 months previously when it was discovered that Shane Warne and Mark Waugh had had dealings with illegal bookmakers, Cronje had not considered that what he was doing was wrong, or illegal, until he was in front of the firing squad.

Having been told that a full and honest testimony would exclude him from prosecution, at least in South Africa, he confirmed a series of scams he and others had been hiding for years. He said he had been approached by a variety of shady characters, all operating illegally, on a dozen occasions over a five-year period, in Dubai, in South Africa and especially in India – which, with a plethora of Tests and increasingly meaningless one-day internationals (ODIs) scheduled seemingly every second month, had become a virtual second home to the Proteas since their readmission into international cricket ranks. In total, the lures he made public at the inquiry totalled almost US$1 million. It was up to Justice King to decide if there were any others.

Forty players and officials were subpoenaed by the Commission, including the entire South African touring party to India in 1996 and all players and officials involved at international level from November 1998 to April 2000:

Ali Bacher	Derek Crookes	Makhaya Ntini
Daryll Cullinan	Fanie De Villiers	Andrew Hall
Herschelle Gibbs	Dave Richardson	Jonty Rhodes
Nico Boje	Andrew Hudson	Roger Telemachus
Pieter Strydom	Brian McMillan	Clive Eksteen
Henry Williams	Pat Symcox	Paul Adams
Shaun Pollock	Robbie Muzzell	David Terbrugge
Gary Kirsten	Goolam Raja	John Commins
Jacques Kallis	Craig Smith	Craig Matthews
Lance Klusener	Corrie Van Zyl	Dave Callaghan
Dale Benkenstein	Bob Woolmer	Steve Elworthy
Louis Koen	Graham Ford	Hansie Cronje
Mark Boucher	Mornantau Hayward	
Neil McKenzie	Charl Willoughby	

Judge King reminded witnesses that this was neither a court of law nor a witch-hunt, but was designed to uncover malpractice within the South African cricket team and, in due course, make recommendations to guard against further ill-doing. Those who did not fully cooperate could be fined or even imprisoned.

Gibbs was one of the first to give testimony. Until meeting with a team-mate, Mark Boucher, on the eve of the hearings, Gibbs had been prepared to swear his innocence, but when he was told he might be jailed if he lied, he admitted that the Indian tapes were authentic and that he had agreed to take money to score less than 20 at Nagpur. Once the game had started, however, he had concentrated only on his innings.

In another incident admitted by Cronje, he said that before the third Test in Kanpur during South Africa's 1996 tour of India, he was introduced to bookmaker Mukesh Kumar Gupta by Mohammad Azharuddin. 'Mukesh asked if we would give wickets away on the last day of that Test to ensure we lost,' he said. The bookie gave him US$30 000 and asked him to speak with the other players. Cronje led Gupta to believe he would, but didn't. South Africa lost the Test by 280 runs and Cronje kept the money, later describing it as 'money for jam'.

At the end of that tour, the Proteas agreed to a final, unscheduled one-day match in Mumbai as part of a benefit for Mohinder Amarnath, a game which was to be given full ODI status to accelerate ailing ticket sales and would also be Cronje's 100th ODI. Gupta offered him US$200 000 if the South Africans would agree to lose. Cronje asked for $300 000 and was told he could have $250 000. This time he discussed the offer with fellow players.

The scam was for South Africa to lose the match by between 70 and 90 runs. After an arduous six-week tour involving 23 internal flights, several in the team were ready to agree to throw the game. But Cronje said the vote must be unanimous and if there was any dissension at all, the deal would be off.

'For us it was a lot of money,' wicketkeeper Dave Richardson told the inquiry. 'There's always going to be some guy, a maverick who says, "Why not?"' Brian McMillan said the extra money was particularly appealing for older players like himself who were at the end of their careers. 'It's always a carrot,' he said. 'It's a lot of money. You think about this bit of extra cash, US dollars, keep it offshore or whatever you want to do. But you should always remember that you've got young and old people in the side. It's easier for the older players. They can think, "Great, good money." If the younger players get found out, they lose a career.'

Coach Bob Woolmer was angry that Cronje had even attempted to negotiate. In charge for five years, at a time when the South Africans were vying with Australia to be the finest team in the world, Woolmer said he had begged Cronje to disassociate himself from bookmakers before the match. 'He asked me what I thought [of the offer] and I said, "Don't even think about it." I told him match-fixing was one of the most heinous crimes in sport and he shouldn't consider getting involved.'

Woolmer said that the South Africans had had only seven fit men available for the game. At the time he thought Cronje was jesting and indulging in some by-play with the bookmaker. 'Hansie loves a practical joke,' he said. 'He would make a great poker player because you cannot tell what he is thinking behind that deadpan expression. I often used to tell him if he cried wolf, it would one day come back to haunt him. But he took money. Once he took that envelope it all changed and I can understand the fuss it has caused.'

Andrew Hudson, Daryll Cullinan and Derek Crookes were among those who had particularly strong objections. 'No, guys, it's bigger than you think,' Hudson said. 'You can't have anything to do with it.' After holding two meetings about the offer, the players finally rejected it – some reluctantly – on the morning of the match. Ironically they lost by 83 runs, within the bookie's original parameters. Cronje later admitted it was a missed opportunity.

While ODIs were usually the bookies' target, one Test match was also infamously affected. England won the fifth and final Test at Centurion, Pretoria, in 1999 in contrived circumstances after Cronje, on the take again, had convinced England captain Nasser Hussain that the waterlogged match could be opened up if they each forfeited an innings. England won by two wickets, with Cronje's generous declaration at 8/248 stunning team-mates young and old. Little did they know that the skipper had pocketed 50 000 rand and a leather jacket for helping to ensure a result.

Cronje also received other bonus money, most notably during India's 1997 tour of South Africa, where his earnings were indexed to those of Gupta. After South Africa won the first two Tests, in Durban and Cape Town, Gupta paid him US$50 000 for previous information and offered US$300 000 for the South Africans to lose the final Test. Cronje refused and the match was drawn. He claimed this was the last contact he had with bookmakers or punters for two years until England's visit in 1999.

After the Commission's revelations, Cronje's coordination of a private tour of India involving South Africa's best players, planned for 2000 with only the tacit approval of the UCB, was abandoned. The Indians placed an immediate ban on him and three others who were also said to be on the take, and his four major personal sponsors all withdrew their support.

His father, Ewie Cronje, attended the hearings on the opening two days but left after Gibbs' damning testimony. He was shocked at the revelations and at how little of the truth his son had divulged.

During his confession, Cronje said he regretted involving others in his deals, especially Gibbs, one of world cricket's emerging young players, and that they should not be damned for his follies. The UCB disagreed. After admitting his guilt, Gibbs was immediately stood down for an indefinite period, as was Williams.

HOW COULD A man with such a deeply moral, religious background and so much good old-fashioned integrity besmirch his and cricket's good name in this way?

Born and raised a proud Afrikaaner, a product of the famous Greg College and possessor of a Masters degree in business management, Cronje had been feted for years as South Africa's number one sporting son. Becoming a born-again Christian – a decision he made after he accidentally knocked down and killed a six-year-old black girl while driving in poor visibility on Natal's North Coast Road – had given new direction to his life. Grief-stricken, he swore off alcohol, lost 10 kilograms by training harder than ever before, and grew closer to his girlfriend, physiotherapist Bertha Pretorius, who invited him to attend Bible classes and prayer meetings. Their marriage prompted front-page headlines.

Despite occasional captaincy glitches – such as in Adelaide when he angrily rammed a stump through an umpire's door, in Sydney when he deliberately stepped on the ball, and in Cape Town when he was fined half his match fee after placing the umpires under undue pressure to use the third umpire to adjudicate on a dismissal – UCB officials felt Cronje had no peer as an ambassador for South African cricket.

It seems he gradually started to believe the billboards and adulation and began to consider himself untouchable. He threatened to resign his captaincy when it was suggested that a quota of black and coloured players be included in South Africa's best XI as proof of the nation's new multiracial policies. Cronje said he wanted only the best team, be the players black or white.

Those closest to him saw changes in his personality and lifestyle. The clean-cut college boy became complex and moody, with one critic even describing him as 'dangerously unstable'. He grew fond of the finer things in life. Far from being the intense, humble man who had first taken office as South Africa's captain in 1994, he started to flaunt his affluence, wearing expensive Italian suits and gold jewellery beyond the income of most people. He became increasingly arrogant and aloof. He capitalised on real estate and the stock exchange, had at least two foreign bank accounts, hoarded expenses and freeloaded on the generosity of friends and major sponsors. Speaking engagements netted him up to A$5500 per speech. He even had his own clothing label in India.

While others in world cricket may have had larger total incomes (such as the elite Australians and Indian champion Sachin Tendulkar), Cronje's annual earnings, starting at 1.5 million rand (A$375 000), were absolutely top notch by South African standards. He and Bertha were able to build an A$800 000 dream holiday home in the prestigious Fancourt Estate, a luxury golf and beach retreat on South Africa's striking south-western cape near George and home to many of

South Africa's rich and famous, including golfer Ernie Els. Cronje's net worth, said to be at least A$3 million, had been embellished by four major sponsors, all of whom withdrew after his admissions.

Cronje told friends he had agonised over his double life but, once tempted, had been powerless to say no. He had been greedy and 'lost the plot'. He knew he must be punished. His announcement that he was finished with cricket would once have been greeted with great sorrow – after all, he was just 30 and seemingly at the height of his career – but instead there was hardly a murmur. Rather than being a paragon, he had become a pariah.

HANSIE CRONJE'S RECORD

Int. debut	Tests	As captain	ODIs	As captain
1991–92	68	53	188	138

I was not involved in fixing or manipulating the results of cricket matches. I always played to win.   **HANSIE CRONJE**

2. Cricket's greatest villain: Saleem Malik

On the subcontinent, cricketers are bigger than movie stars. The game is the cornerstone of many people's life and elite players often earn 10 times the basic wage. After five years of regular Test and one-day cricket, almost all of Pakistan's best players are millionaires. Despite comparatively modest educational levels, even after their cricket careers are over most ex-players find well-heeled jobs with banks or airlines, guaranteeing continuing prestige and security for life.

Such is the adulation for their performances that some players form inflated opinions of their own worth – so much so that they openly flout the laws of the land. For the disgraced Saleem Malik, the inheritance of Pakistan's cricketing throne from Wasim Akram in 1993–94 confirmed his presence as one of the subcontinent's all-powerful cricketers and led to dangerous underworld liaisons.

IN HIS VERY first game in Pakistani colours as an impressionable, wide-eyed 18-year-old seated on the old players' balcony at the WACA ground in Perth, Saleem Malik saw the seamier side of cricket. As part of Pakistan's Test XII in the opening Test in 1981–82, he witnessed his captain Javed Miandad's infamous altercation with Dennis Lillee, in which Javed responded to an ankle tap by wielding his bat at the Australian in a mock gesture of striking him.

While Lillee was to be suspended for two one-day games, the agent provocateur, Javed, escaped without even a reprimand. It was a damning example for young Saleem to see cricket's integrity so openly flouted, with not even a 'please explain' demanded of his skipper. If Saleem's captain could so misbehave – and get away with it – why shouldn't the younger player?

Few were to love the limelight more than the cool, calculating, corrupt Saleem. Even under siege from the courts and the media he seemed to revel in the crossfire, just like on the field, where he was gritty enough on one occasion to face up left-handed to the West Indian pace attack to protect his left wrist, broken on a brute of a wicket at Faisalabad in 1986–87.

Imran Khan, Saleem's long-time team-mate, called him a 'flat pitch bully' – a damn fine player and as hard as anyone in the world to dislodge so long as the conditions were favourable. Imran also considered him untrustworthy and greed-driven. As early as 1992, before Saleem had become Pakistan's captain, the two were at loggerheads over bonus money that Saleem believed should have been directed to the team rather than towards Imran's cancer crusades.

Imran's dissatisfaction with self-interested players such as Saleem hastened his own exit from the game. Wealth, or the lack of it, was never an issue for the Oxford-educated supremo Imran, the most lordly of cricketers, who came from the upper middle classes of Lahore.

Saleem didn't enjoy anything like the same birthright or position of privilege as Imran. Like Javed, he'd been a street scrapper, learning the rudiments of cricket during matches played in city side streets from dawn to dusk. At 18 he became the youngest Pakistani to score a century on his Test debut and was hailed as a next-generation star, someone capable of taking over from Javed and Imran and leading the country to new heights. Unfortunately for Saleem, his passion for cricket became clouded and corrupted as he fell in with illegal book-makers and became the first genuine 'name' player to be outlawed for life by his own Board in the match-fixing scandal of early 2000.

He had his moments of greatness, such as in 1991 while playing for Essex, when his aggregate neared 2000 runs despite a brief holiday back in Lahore in mid-season; or in 1994–95, when in three Tests against Mark Taylor's Australians he played Shane Warne as well as anybody, anywhere, any time, on his way to 557 runs. But for every moment of inspiration there were inexplicable blimps, like the incon-gruous Test losses to New Zealand and Zimbabwe, and the mid-tour walkouts by two of his players who believed that the team's integrity revolved around Saleem's whims and wagers.

From the time he became captain, Saleem began to sully cricket's good name, attempting to fix Tests and one-day games both at home and away. Specific allegations of match-fixing involving Saleem concern the Test and one-day international (ODI) matches in Christ-church, New Zealand in 1993–94, and in 1994–95 the Singer Cup in Sri Lanka, the Test series at home against Australia and the Mandela Trophy in South Africa.

So notorious was Saleem at the coin toss that, in 1994, the Inter-national Cricket Council demanded the presence of a match referee as an on-the-spot observer. In his first Test as captain, at Auckland in early 1994, Saleem's call was virtually inaudible. Before the opposing captain, New Zealand's Ken Rutherford, could act, Saleem, first to the coin, blurted, 'You bat, we'll field.' By bowling first, Pakistan exploited the best of the conditions and Wasim and Waqar Younis took 15 wickets between them. The match ended in less than eight sessions.

The first time Saleem captained Pakistan at home, in 1994–95, he tried to bribe Australian trio Shane Warne, Tim May and Mark

Waugh. His threats to sue Australian newspapers for their reporting of the affair were never activated.

ALLEGATIONS OF SALEEM'S hotline to the gambling fraternity were rife during Australia's visit and became a major talking point as he led Pakistan on a three-month tour of South Africa and Zimbabwe in 1994–95. The Pakistanis made the final of the Mandela Trophy only to perform abysmally, with Saleem's preference to bat second in both matches puzzling onlookers and triggering major divisions within the team. After an evenly fought opening final in Cape Town – in which Saleem was run out – the Pakistanis crashed to a 157-run loss in the second final in Johannesburg, where South African legend Jackie McGlew accused Saleem of 'a blunder in generalship'.

Describing the losses as 'shambolic', Wasim approached Saleem and told him that players were starting to quarrel over the validity of the bribery rumours. 'I asked Saleem point blank about the rumours and he told me he knew absolutely nothing about the matter,' Wasim said in his autobiography. 'I persisted and said, "Come on, we can't just ignore it. What's going on?" and again he denied all knowledge.'

The players were unsettled and, according to Wasim, 'two odd decisions by the captain led to even more chatter in our dressing rooms. We knew that local knowledge always recommended fielding last at these two venues, because the ball boomerangs about later in the day. All the players were asking openly why we were fielding first after winning the toss and I could only say I didn't know the reason.' (Leading into the Trophy play-offs, sides batting second had won four and lost five ODI matches between the two countries.)

Wasim reckoned Saleem too reserved to be an inspiring leader. The captain's refusal to adequately explain his decisions fuelled talk that bookmakers must be paying him off. Neither did Saleem enjoy the total support of his vice-captain, wicketkeeper Rashid Latif, who was keenly involved in the dressing-room politics.

Leading into the one-off Test, also at the Wanderers in Johannesburg, in which the Pakistanis were thrashed to headlines such as PAKISTAN BUTCHERED IN THE BULLRING, there was an uproarious team meeting. Wasim and others walked out. 'Players were squabbling openly in the room and nobody was listening to the captain,' Wasim said. 'Someone then shouted, "What's all this about the toss and bets?", a clear reference to Saleem's two costly decisions in the preceding one-day matches. We all looked at each other and wild accusations started to fly around. I couldn't take any more and I stood up to say, "This is the worst team meeting I've ever been in. Where are the manners?"

'And I walked out. Others followed me leaving us in total disarray. Our manager Intikhab [Alam] realised he had to try to pull things together, otherwise the fallout would be spectacular and very public. No side goes down the plughole as quickly as Pakistan when we start rowing in the dressing room . . . "Inti" produced the [Holy] Koran and suggested we all swear on it that no one had been involved in betting in any of our matches. To a Muslim the Koran is hugely important and everyone in that room took the oath.' Later it was claimed by Waqar that Saleem and Rashid had come to blows.

The Test finally began in bizarre circumstances with Saleem starting with only 10 players. Fast bowler Amir Nazir, who had been sent as a reinforcement for the injured Waqar, arrived at the airport just an hour before the scheduled start and didn't make it onto the ground until after eight overs had been bowled. He repeatedly cramped on the opening day, adding to the farce. The Pakistanis were lax and disinterested in the field. 'It was almost as if they had chartered their own destruction,' said Jackie McGlew in the *Cricketer International*. He also made stern comment about 'some strange bowling changes' by Saleem. For his part, Wasim was thunderstruck that Amir was played ahead of Ata-ur-Rehman, a member of the original touring squad.

By the time the team arrived in Zimbabwe, dissatisfaction against Saleem's leadership had intensified. The opening Test in Harare began in extraordinary circumstances, with International Cricket Council referee Jackie Hendriks demanding a second toss. On the first, Saleem called 'Bird' (the national symbol on one side of the Zimbabwe coin), but Hendriks insisted he had heard no such call. When they tossed again, Andy Flower won and elected to bat. His team went on to a massive innings victory, their first-ever win at Test level.

Pakistan hit back to win the second and third Tests amidst Zimbabwean accusations of racist sledging and, in the series decider in Harare, an extraordinary charge laid by Saleem against local umpire Ian Robinson of deliberately tampering with the ball. Hendriks expressed amazement and 'extreme disappointment at the involvement and attitude of the Pakistan captain, a player of great stature and repute'. Saleem was fined half his match fee and given a two-Test suspended sentence. Opening batsman Aamer Sohail was also severely reprimanded. Adding further fuel to the most controversial of African tours, Rashid and specialist batsman Basit Ali flew home early, saying they wanted to dissociate themselves totally from Saleem and would not continue while he was in charge.

If Saleem was distracted by the on-field troubles, his focus was further affected in the series decider by the allegations of his attempted bribery of Warne, Waugh and May becoming public. He reacted angrily, as did Wasim, who refused to believe that the charges were authentic. 'I was astonished,' Wasim said later. 'There had been no allegations when they toured Pakistan a few months earlier. Why had it taken so long for the three Aussies to make public their charges?'

Saleem was stood down as captain and played no cricket for eight months while an independent inquiry proceeded, officials saying the 'ill discipline' on the tour of South Africa and Zimbabwe was also a factor in his suspension. Aamer and Saleem's brother-in-law, Ijaz Ahmed, were fined 25 per cent of their tour fees for misbehaviour.

Afterwards, Aamer was quoted as saying: 'If I was not bound by the code of conduct I could name so many players in the Pakistan team who have been bribed to lose matches. It is getting so bad that it is also getting all the guys who don't do it a bad name.'

Through his lawyer, Saleem called the charges against him 'viciously false and unfounded'. In a letter to Arif Ali Khan, the chief executive of the Pakistan Cricket Board (PCB), which also circulated to the press, Saleem's advisers said, 'The charges have been made five months after the alleged event. There is absolutely no explanation for the delay. Our superior courts have laid down in a long and consistent chain of authorities that a delay of even a few hours is fatal for the prosecution if no satisfactory explanation is forthcoming for such a delay.

'The Australians were our guests for several weeks after the alleged event. There was contact made more than once with their cricket authorities after their departure and before the accusation against our client. Did our client's accusers inform their own cricket authorities immediately after the alleged event? If so, why did the Australian Cricket Board [ACB] remain silent for months on end?

'Our client is reliably informed that the accusations against him were brought only after they were aired in some newspaper articles. This strongly suggests that the ACB was unconvinced of the veracity of whatever they had (or had not) been told by their own cricketers and reacted only to appease the Australian press. You are well aware of the scurrilous manner in which our leading cricketers have been lampooned and libelled, time and again by the press in Australia and one or two other countries. For them a Lillee and a Marsh who confessed to betting against their own team and whose team then lost the match can be excused, as can Atherton who had dirt in his pockets, but not a Miandad who raised his bat to defend himself.

'We are informed that the unsigned statements sent earlier by the Australian accusers have since been supplemented by statements signed before the equivalent of public notaries in Australia. According to our laws this makes no difference whatsoever. The veracity or otherwise of accusations such as those made against our client can be established only in a properly conducted judicial inquiry in which our client is given time and opportunity to confront his accusers, to cross-examine them and to lead evidence in his own defence. We understand that the PCB has offered to pay the travel expenses of our client's accusers and to meet their lodging expenses if they come to Pakistan but they have not done so. In these circumstances there is no legal or factual basis to keep our client in limbo. We hereby make a request on his behalf that the PCB issue a statement exonerating our client and dropping the inquiry against him. Our client reserves all legal rights in this matter.'

With the ACB blocking permission for the three Australian players, all key witnesses, to travel to Pakistan for cross-questioning – the option of a neutral London hearing having been disregarded by the Pakistanis – the charges against Saleem were unproven and thrown out by retired Justice Fakhruddin G. Ebrahim on the eve of the 1995–96 tour of Australia. Saleem was reinstated, but not as captain. Rashid and Basit both renounced their retirements and were also named for the tour, having paid fines of 50 000 rupees (approximately A$1750) for breaches of their African tour contracts.

Saleem was also chosen, but he had an unhappy tour, arriving late, falling for a duck fourth ball to Shane Warne in Brisbane and then cutting his hand and missing the second Test in Bellerive. The Australians had made a pact to ignore him, even off the field. They shook hands and chatted with the other Pakistani players, but were totally cold towards Saleem.

SALEEM MIGHT HAVE been relieved to be exonerated by Justice Ebrahim and happy to see him accuse Warne and Co. of being 'concocters', but the match-fixing issue simply would not die. Not only was Saleem still under suspicion, but so were now-captain Wasim, fast-bowling legend

Waqar and even the bright and bubbly Mushtaq Ahmed, one of the world game's most popular personalities. When a further Commission of Inquiry was established at Lahore's High Court in September 1998, all of Pakistan's on-field champions found themselves under intense fire. The inquiry's mandate was to:

- probe into the allegations regarding betting and match-fixing against members of the team
- determine and identify the persons, including members of the team, responsible for betting and match-fixing
- recommend such actions as might be appropriate
- suggest measures to avoid future incidents.

IF EARLIER INQUIRIES had lacked substance and skirted around the issues, this one was different from day one, with all observers – even journalists – being searched for weapons at the entrance to the court. There was steel in the judge's manner and questions which his predecessors had lacked. A former club batsman and keen cricket fan, 50-year-old Judge Malik Mohammed Qayyum was determined to find the truth. Midway through Waqar Younis' testimony, the judge interrupted him and said, 'Waqar, you are lying. Go away and sort yourself out and return on Saturday and tell the truth. I warn you I can charge witnesses with perjury and I will do so if need be.'

At one point Judge Qayyum called journalists Mark Ray from the Melbourne *Age* and Peter Deeley from London's *Daily Telegraph* into his office and said how pleased he was to have some 'foreign' reporters present. He told them: 'There is so much conflicting evidence here that some people are definitely lying. It is difficult to find out the truth but I am going to try.'

The ACB remained reluctant to fly their star witnesses to Lahore, so the inquiry came to them. Warne, Waugh and May gave evidence in Melbourne which effectively damned Saleem's evidence and sullied his reputation once and for all.

The Pakistani players, officials and bookies questioned were, in order:

1. Sarfraz Nawaz	18. Rashid Latif
2. Yawar Saeed Butt	19. Intikhab Alam
3. Arif Ali Khan Abbassi	20. Saleem Pervez, alias Paijee
4. Javed Burki	21. Khalid Mahmood
5. Basit Ali	22. Saeed Anwar
6. Haroon Rashid	23. Mushtaq Ahmed
7. Saleem Malik	24. Inzamam-ul-Haq
8. Ijaz Ahmed	25. Imran Khan
9. Rameez Raja	26. Javed Miandad
10. Aaqib Javed	27. Majid Khan
11. Ata-ur-Rehman	28. Saqlain Mushtaq
12. Dr Amir Aziz	29. Moin Khan
13. Dr Zafar Altaf	30. Shahid Afridi
14. Aamer Sohail	31. Azhar Mahmood
15. Dr Dan Kiesel	32. Akram Raza
16. Wasim Akram	33. Zahid Fazal
17. Waqar Younis	

Journalists interviewed included Fareshteh Gati-Aslam, Kamila Hyat, Imtiaz Sipra and Shahid Sheikh.

The accusations against Saleem began with the earliest testimonies. Former Test fast bowler Sarfraz Nawaz accused him of openly fixing even domestic matches. He said it was natural for Saleem to have an interest in gambling, as his brother was a bookie. The second person called – the well-informed Gati-Aslam – claimed that Saleem was not the only match-fixer: Ijaz and Wasim were also guilty. She believed that Wasim, after discussions with the Pakistani team physiotherapist, had feigned injuries and illness. He had also allegedly made cash offers to fellow players.

Haroon Rashid, a former player and coach, claimed that Saleem had sought his assistance in trying to fix a Sahara Cup match in India and expressed doubts about how hard the Pakistan players had tried during the Asia and Sahara cups in 1997. PCB chairman Javed Burki reported that Saleem and Mushtaq had been seen at the house of illegal bookmaker Khalid Ghitti during a rest day in the series in Colombo in 1994.

The most explosive exposé, however, was from Rashid Latif, the deposed wicketkeeper. He said that before the fifth ODI in Christchurch in 1993–94, Saleem had asked him to his room and offered him 10 lakh (A$32 350) to throw the match. According to Rashid, there were five others in the room at the time. He had refused the offer. Rashid also alleged that later that year, in Colombo, he saw a bag belonging to Saleem which contained up to 50 000 Sri Lankan rupees. Rashid claimed that Saleem had tried to bribe Saeed Anwar during the tournament, which was won by Pakistan 4–1. He said that, during one of the games, he had never seen so many mobile phones being used simultaneously in the rooms. He named Saleem, Waqar and Wasim as having had numerous phone conversations. He also produced audio cassette recordings containing conversations detrimental to Ata-ur-Rehman's initial evidence at the Qayyum inquiry.

Saleem Pervez, a bookmaker and former opening batsman with the National Bank team, admitted to being directly involved with leading players. It was he who had directly handed Saleem and Mushtaq US$100 000 to throw an important match against the Australians in Sharjah. He claimed that the players had asked for more but had eventually settled on the original figure. He named a whole host of games he believed had been tainted, from a Mandela Trophy match to a World Cup quarterfinal.

In his own much-awaited sworn testimony, Saleem said he had been exonerated once, and despite the mountain of evidence he was blameless in the whole affair. He admitted there had been a disagreement with his vice-captain Rashid in South Africa over who should bat first, but said that, as captain, he had the right to make his own choices and fashion the team tactics. He was amazed at Sarfraz's claim that Saleem had fixed the final between the National Bank and the Habib Bank in 1994 and repeated that Shane Warne had made his allegations only because he was nursing a grudge.

Ijaz said he was linked to Saleem only because of his marriage to Saleem's sister. He denied knowing or having any association with two bookies, Hanif Cadbury and Khalid Gitti. Ata-ur-Rehman, who was also later to be banned, claimed that Wasim had given him 100 000 rupees to bowl badly in a one-day international during a tour of New Zealand. He said he had changed his story later for fear of reprisals.

Wasim denied all charges of betting and links with bookmakers. He accused the PCB chief executive Majid Khan of trying to sabotage his reputation in a conspiracy. Later, in a *Four Corners* interview on Australian television, he said, 'I always play unless . . . I have been diabetic and am still playing at this level and never complained and have never come out [withdrawn] from a game.'

During the hearings it was revealed that a failed business venture involving Saleem may have triggered his bookmaking involvements. Three colleagues also implicated had fled Pakistan, leaving Saleem under significant financial pressure.

After the interviews were completed, Judge Qayyum ruled that Saleem was the main offender and had a clear case to answer. He believed Saleem should be banned for life from cricket, an inquiry should be held into his assets and criminal charges should be laid. Wasim was also not above reproach and should forfeit the captaincy. The judge recommended a A$10 000 fine. He believed that Ata-ur-Rehman's testimony was tainted and that he had clearly perjured himself. Like Saleem, he should be banned for life. He was fined A$3350.

Penalties against national heroes Mushtaq (A$10 000), Waqar, Inzamam-ul-Haq, Akram Raza and Saeed Anwar (all A$3350) were also recommended, Judge Qayyum saying that Pakistani players should have to declare their assets annually from the time they began playing first-class cricket. A zero-tolerance level against match-fixing should immediately be implemented by the PCB. Government intervention had delayed the release of Judge Qayyum's report by 12 months, but the judge insisted that if anything was withheld, he would go public.

After years of stonewalling, stand-offs and multiple inquiries, the PCB finally implemented all of Judge Qayyum's recommendations, running Saleem out of the game and into the criminal courts. Imran was just one of many Pakistanis who favoured a jail term for his disgraced ex-team-mate

History will accord Saleem few of the platitudes normally reserved for a player of his longevity and dynamic scoring ability square of the wicket, or as a captain whose success rate in 1994 made Pakistan the most successful Test and one-day team for that calendar year. Instead, he will be remembered as an openly smug, renegade captain who harboured and promoted corruption in and around his team.

One of the most sickening aspects of the whole affair is that he seemed to love every crooked, brazen moment. A fine of one million rupees (A$32 350) for disgracing the game and himself was like being thrashed with a feather. That he cannot hold any official position again in cricket is a relief.

SALEEM WAS SEEN as having such little credibility that his cries of indignation and innocence were deemed invalid even by his countrymen. London's *News of the World* claimed that Saleem had confessed everything to two of their reporters acting undercover as go-betweens for big gambling interests. The story made enlightening reading, but what was fact and what was fiction?

The journalists taped their interviews and conversations. There is no doubt that the third voice on the tape belongs to Saleem. But was he joking when he said, 'It will be very easy for me to fix a match. The players will agree. We've done it all before. It's better than dealing drugs'?

Saleem insists the tape is all a total fabrication. 'This is the computer age,' he told the ABC's *Four Corners* reporter Liz Jackson. 'They can do anything.'

In June 2001, a Pakistani court dismissed Saleem's challenge against his life ban, saying it had been validly imposed by the Pakistan Cricket Board. The dog had had his day.

The accusations [against Saleem] are a sham, absolutely ridiculous which have been cooked up by a defeated team with the sole aim of upsetting victors who continue their tale of international success.

EHTESHAMUL HAQ, sports liaison officer to the Pakistan Prime Minister

I have never attempted to throw a cricket match and have never even considered such a thing for a second. I also have no knowledge of any Pakistan player taking money to influence events on the field. That is a slur that just won't go away in Pakistan cricket and it claimed Saleem Malik when he was sacked as captain. Saleem has always protested his innocence and I have no reason to doubt him.

Former Pakistan captain WASIM AKRAM

It may be that he [Saleem] was offered a sum of money that may have been five times more for one game than he may well have earned for the whole year. That's the problem.   **Former Australian spinner TIM MAY**

In Pakistan . . . one can only be honest if one can afford to be. If one sets up a business, one has to make allowances in the costing of bribes.   **IMRAN KHAN**

Saleem Malik has officially usurped Douglas Jardine as the greatest villain in cricket history.   ***Age* cricket writer GREG BAUM**

ILLEGAL BETTING IS massive business on the subcontinent and an accepted part of the sporting culture. In India and Pakistan it is estimated that at least 10 times as much money is wagered on cricket as on horse racing. Business has so ballooned with increased telecommunications that many racing bookies now also double in the cricket industry. Limited-overs cricket has particular appeal and turnover, as matches last no more than seven hours.

The mid-1990s saw an explosion in betting. 'The betting network on the subcontinent is as elaborate as it is complex, extending across the Arabian Sea to Sharjah and Dubai,' said Andy O'Brien from *Sportsworld* magazine. 'Scratch the surface and you find that your bet is accepted by a small-time bookie in an anonymous side street in Bombay or Karachi, whose office consists of a table and chair, a few slips of paper, a pen and a telephone.'

The Karachi Stock Exchange comes to a virtual standstill when a match involving the Pakistani national team is in progress. For years the exchange has doubled as the centre for organised gambling in the city. In Mumbai (Bombay), the financial capital of India, there are thousands of illegal betting shops, which are allowed to exist via police and organised crime pay-offs. One haven for illegal bookmaking is Dulal Street, opposite India's biggest stock exchange.

Sharjah is also a central base for the gambling syndicates. On match days at the UAE Stadium the main grandstand resembles a stock exchange floor, with hundreds of fans armed with mobile telephones making their bets. So perturbed did Indian officials become about the integrity of some of the one-day internationals held in Sharjah that they boycotted the Sharjah tournament for three years. India's long-time captain Mohammad Azharuddin was accused of collaborating with the Pakistani team and the Sharjah organisers after his team repeatedly lost important matches to Pakistan.

Mumbai police are said to have been in possession of telephone tape recordings of match-fixing incidents stretching back to 1995. Five players in particular were implicated: Azharuddin, Ajay Jadeja, Nayan Mongia, Manoj Prabhakar and Nikhil Chopra.

When the Indian Government implemented a tax amnesty scheme in 2000 promising that those with ill-gotten gains could declare them without penalty, several cricketers are understood to have come forward. A senior Indian tax official, who was suspended soon afterwards for speaking too freely in public, said one of the cricketers, Azharuddin, had a personal fortune of US$50 million.

3. Fallen hero: Mohammad Azharuddin

When India's Mohammad Azharuddin made his stunning entry into Test cricket with an unprecedented three centuries in a row, he was unassuming and unpretentious, and owned little more than the clothes on his back and an old hand-me-down bicycle. Sixteen years later, having amassed a record 433 appearances for his country, he was banished from the game, his name blackened – yet another Test icon to yield to temptation and associate with the cricketing underworld.

Taxation investigators raided Azharuddin's Mumbai apartment and walked into a veritable Aladdin's Cave. Apart from the antique furniture, original paintings, expensive appointments and a hidden cupboard containing a treasure trove of more than 120 chic designer watches worth A$150 000, Azharuddin's luxury apartment included a spiral staircase leading to an apartment immediately above – which, unbeknown to the inland revenue authorities, he'd bought and converted.

'We've raided top politicians and movie stars but seen nothing quite like it,' said one of the taxmen talking about Azharuddin's split-level palace. 'For a while we all just stood and looked because it didn't seem right to disturb anything. It was so beautiful.'

In the area beside the front door was a near life-sized photograph of

Azharuddin fondly embracing an opposition player after a tournament in Sharjah. The player? Seedy Pakistani Saleem Malik.

BEFORE THE ARRIVAL of Sachin Tendulkar as India's pre-eminent player, Mohammad Azharuddin was the most exalted sportsman on the subcontinent, humble, generous and revered alongside India's most-celebrated film stars and leaders of state.

From the time the artistic 20-year-old made 226 on his Duleep Trophy debut and was dubbed God's gift to Indian cricket by the ageing legend Sunil Gavaskar, the baton was passed and Azharuddin became the new darling of all India. His thin frame, drooping shoulders and gawkiness belied a wristy, delicate and joyous batting style which thrilled millions in the most cricket-obsessed country of them all.

The eldest of seven children from a lower middle-class family, Azharuddin was raised by his maternal grandfather Mohammad Vajehuddin and attended Hyderabad's All Saints high school and Nizam College where he graduated with a commerce degree. Deeply religious and very private, the young Muslim had initially regarded money as inconsequential compared to the honour of representing his country. But in five astonishing weeks from December 1984 to January 1985, his life changed forever. In a series of majestic command performances against David Gower's Englishmen, he amassed 439 runs at an average of 109.75 – and became the young starlet of world cricket and India's most in-demand cricketer, on a pedestal with World Cup hero and India's national captain, Kapil Dev.

As millions were saluting cricket's graceful new on-field phenomenon, dozens of others looked to exploit his profile. New business opportunities abounded, most legitimate, but some questionable, plunging him into some dangerous liaisons, including several with men said to have direct links with India's underworld.

From the time he'd earned 25 rupees as the shyest of all models back in 1984, he'd found the lucrative extra-curricular monies irresistible, and as India's international program doubled and trebled into the mid-90s, handsome salaries on and off the field saw Azhar's net worth soar like no other Indian cricketer's before him.

Like his South African counterpart Hansie Cronje, Azharuddin *was* Indian cricket, his face emblazoned on billboards throughout the subcontinent. The visible trappings of wealth and materialism saw him donning expensive suits and designer shoes. In London he spent lavishly on clothes and in places such as Sharjah he indulged in gold bracelets, exclusive watches and fine jewellery. It was almost as if Azhar had a money tree back in southern India.

The failure of several business ventures, including a partnership in a Bangalore hotel and a stake in a Pepsi bottling franchise, were but minor setbacks in the big picture. The monies squandered were soon replenished as the Board of Control for Cricket in India, enjoying an unprecedented injection of funds via satellite and cable television rights, bankrolled its leading players.

By the mid-90s, Azharuddin was a millionaire in western terms, living a life of plenty and enjoying celebrity status.

He talked of setting up a cricketing school in Hyderabad and was known to stop at traffic lights and give money to beggars. India's leading cricket commentator, Harsha Bhogle, penned Azharuddin's biography and claimed Azhar, circa 1994, to be the fairest and most decent cricketer he'd ever met.

Significantly, however, Azharuddin told Bhogle he wanted to use cricket as a crutch to assist in his long-term security. 'I wanted to play well and knew that if I did, the money would come,' he said. 'I knew that to become rich, I had to stay in the team and so that had to be my first objective.'

It was at the Taj Palace hotel in Delhi in 1995 that Azharuddin and his second wife, model, actress and former Miss India Sangeeta Bijlani, were alleged to have been introduced to a match-fixer, former bank clerk turned jeweller Mukesh Gupta, by the sometime-Indian international Ajay Sharma. It was the beginning of an association that senior Indian police claim netted Azharuddin as much as A$85 million over a five-year period.

Gupta, one of the most prominent of eight illegal southern Delhi operators named in the Indian Central Bureau of Investigation (CBI) report, claimed to have initially paid Azharuddin 90 lakh rupees (A$400 000) for information. Far from satisfied with Azharuddin's predictions, he'd asked for his money back and expanded his operation via Indian all-rounder Manoj Prabhakar, who introduced him to other captains of the game, such as Cronje. According to Gupta's admissions, Azharuddin repaid 30 lakh rupees (A$133 000).

Despite Azharuddin's denials, the liaison seems to have continued. India's Central Bureau of Investigation claimed the renegade ex-skipper had admitted to fixing at least two one-day internationals: a Titan Cup match in 1996 and a Pepsi Asia Cup game in Sri Lanka in 1997.

And Cronje, in sworn testimony to South Africa's King Inquiry, claimed it was Azharuddin who introduced him to Gupta in 1996, thereby starting a chain of corruption which was to blacken his name forever.

In July 2000, amidst reports of Azharuddin having accumulated wealth and property beyond the horizons of anyone bar Indian royalty and the megastars of business, tax investigators simultaneously raided Azharuddin's homes in Hyderabad and Mumbai, unearthing an unaccounted A$1.54 million in cash, jewellery, property investments and deposits.

In an exhaustive probe code-named Operation Gentleman, tax officials claimed Azharuddin had the mind of a serial criminal, constantly changing his mobile number and even having monies paid to a third party to avert suspicion. When confronted by overwhelming evidence of wrongdoing, he continued to proclaim his innocence.

When Indian authorities initially suspended and then placed a life ban on Azharuddin and Sharma – among a series of penalties aimed at punishing those with match-fixing links – outraged fans burnt effigies of Azharuddin and newspapers headlined ALVIDA (Farewell) AZHAR. The International Cricket Council's anti-corruption officer Sir Paul Condon even suggested that the records of those found guilty of match-fixing should be deleted from the august pages of *Wisden*.

Twenty-eight of the 30 Indian board delegates voted to impose a life ban, the exceptions being Azharuddin's home unit, the Hyderabad Cricket Association, and former Board of Control for Cricket in India (BCCI) chief Raj Singh Dungarpur, who said: 'So many people come up and speak to cricketers at airports, parties and other places. Some of them may be bookies, but how are the players to know that? Bookies do not have labels pasted on them. I would rather believe a cricketer who has served his country than a bookmaker.'

Dungarpur had been BCCI president when Azharuddin was first elevated to the captaincy.

Azharuddin was to issue legal proceedings in a civil court in Hyderabad, saying through his lawyers that the BCCI had not followed proper legal procedure in taking action against him. Furthermore, the Indian board had not acted fairly or in a transparent manner. He suggested that the affairs of some Mumbai-based ex-cricketers, including legendary 'Sunny' Gavaskar, should also be thoroughly investigated.

'I think people are jealous of me. I have had a successful career and have played for long,' he was quoted as saying to *Outlook* magazine.

'I deny all allegations as false, untrue, baseless and with no substance whatsoever. I say that no bookie has ever approached me or my team-mates to the best of my knowledge. I am a dedicated player and the game of cricket is my love and passion.'

As the legal wrangle continued and the cricket world maintained its outrage, Azharuddin and his wife emerged from months of seclusion in their luxury home in Banjara Hills in Hyderabad to announce a fashion show to raise funds for children left homeless in the earthquake-ravaged state of Gujarat. They said it would be the first of many planned fundraisers by their newly formed company Azhar-Sangeeta Management Services. Even those whom Azharuddin had once claimed as friends were cynical. One said Azhar may have been a rich man, but morally he was bankrupt and no amount of charity work could hide the dirty truth that he was just as corrupt and compromised as his Pakistani friend and rival, the disgraced ex-Pakistan captain Saleem Malik.

His move from the hostile environment of Mumbai back to his home city of Hyderabad eased the pressure on him, though his public appearances were only occasional. There were rumours that he and Sangeeta were enjoying the patronage of prominent cabinet ministers.

According to Harsha Bhogle, time has softened anti-Azhar opinion. The fact that he is banned from cricket is punishment enough. Many Indians are privately more scandalised by political and stockmarket frauds than by their hero selling the game out.

'He still maintains he is innocent and that the CBI made up charges,' Bhogle said. 'There is still a fair amount of goodwill for him, especially in Hyderabad . . . there are pockets of people who recall his cricket very fondly and still have a very soft corner for him.'

So CHARMED were cricket connoisseurs by Mohammad Azharuddin's fairytale first years in the national team that his imperfections were generally glossed over, even the accusations, in 1989, from his Caribbean tour captain Dilip Vengsarkar that he was scared of fast bowling. One of six to be banned for a year amidst a players' revolt over match fees, he was almost immediately pardoned, and in 1990 offered India's captaincy – probably because he was non-controversial and considered a conformist. At 26, he hadn't even captained Hyderabad.

His leadership reign was to be controversial and littered with highs and lows. Averaging just 10 for the series coming into the fourth Test against Allan Border's Australians in Adelaide in 1991–92, his 106 was acclaimed as one of the great Test innings of the 90s, his first 50 including 11 fours on his way to 80 from 103 balls in the middle session on the fifth day. He toyed with an attack including the belligerent opening pair Craig McDermott and Merv Hughes, the left-arm pace of Mike Whitney and the leg spin of Shane Warne, playing just his second game.

Set 372 to win, India went down with 333 in a gallant fight. Once again Azharuddin was his country's hero.

In 1993, he was dropped before scoring in the first Test against Graham Gooch's Englishmen in Calcutta and went on to make 182, the Indians winning the series 3–0.

Not only could Azhar bat, he was a wonderful fieldsman, either outriding or at slip. If his early captaincy years had been noted for their lack of authority and direction and a mediocre win–loss ratio, all was forgiven in 1993 and 1994, Azharuddin's stellar years, when he led India to victories against England, Zimbabwe and Sri Lanka. In a 20-month period, Azhar won nine matches with three others drawn in a period of unsurpassed success for Indian cricket. He developed a supreme confidence, and like Cronje began to believe himself truly untouchable.

With 14 Test wins, he remains India's longest-serving and most successful Test captain. In addition to his 99 Tests, he also played a world-record 334 one-day internationals and during his 16 years at the top, amassed the most ODI runs.

THE FALLOUT from India's Central Bureau of Investigation report saw others tarred too, from ex-internationals Manoj Prabhakar and Ajay Jadeja to team physiotherapist Ali Irani, who were given five-year bans for associating with bookies and bringing the game into disrepute.

Delhi off-spinner Nikhil Chopra was withdrawn from the national squad after the CBI report which alleged he'd made at least four phone calls to illegal bookmakers.

According to the CBI, as much as A$100 million can be bet on a single one-day international and some select players had been on the take as early as 1992.

The Indian board of investigation headed by anti-corruption officer Mr K. Madhavan, a former CBI director and an investigator of 40 years experience, declared it ridiculous that 30-year-old Jadeja, like Azharuddin a key player at one-day level for years, would have received big monies just for weather reports and pitch information. 'It has to be surmised that no bookie or punter will pay money [only] for "information" which is very easily available on television and the word [information] is used for underperforming and match-fixing,' he said. 'Jadeja was not speaking the truth before me about his involvement with bookmaker Uttam Chand.'

Madhavan said the evidence against Jadeja 'clearly established he had been hobnobbing with a number of bookies and punters and had provided them information about cricket matches on payment of money'.

The investigation highlighted mobile phone conversations between Chand (and other Indian bookmakers) and Jadeja on the eve of India's home matches against New Zealand in October and November 1999.

Asked why Chand had so often phoned him, Jadeja said it was to inquire about his health. He had no idea how Chand had procured his mobile phone number.

Asked later if he had any regrets about his suspension, Jadeja said: 'Probably yes . . . I do have regrets and the biggest regret is that I'll miss playing cricket.'

Mr Madhavan had earlier interrogated Azharuddin for almost six hours in Hyderabad, who signed each page of his 12-page statement at the conclusion of the meeting and left without a word to waiting reporters.

Mr Madhavan said: 'Although he was tense initially, as he must have imagined me to be a beast or something like that, he was very relaxed later and at one stage even called me uncle [a term of deference for seniority]. He appeared to me a relieved man while he was leaving.'

At one point in the saga, the BCCI vice-president Kamal Morarka said the Central Bureau of Investigation's damning 162-page report read like a prostitute's diary. Many ex-captains were accused of malpractice, including New Zealand's Martin Crowe, England's Alec Stewart and Sri Lanka's Arjuna Ranatunga.

AZHAR IN 'QUESTIONABLE' INDIAN TESTS & ODIs

Year	Game	Venue	Type	Azhar captain	His scores	Result
1992–93	India v England	Calcutta	Test	✔	182	won
1992–93	India v England	Bangalore	ODI	✔	1	lost
1992–93	India v England	Gwalior	ODI	✔	74	won
1992–93	India v England	Gwalior	ODI	✔	95*	won
1993–94	India v Sri Lanka	Lucknor	Test	✔	47	won
1993–94	India v Pakistan	Sharjah	ODI	✔	29	lost
1994–95	Sri Lanka v India	Colombo	ODI	✔	25	lost
1994–95	India v West Indies	Kanpur	ODI	✔	26	lost
1995–96	India v Pakistan	Bangalore	ODI	✔	27	won
1996–97	India v Australia	Delhi	Test	–	17, 21*	won
1996–97	India v South Africa	Rajkot	ODI	–	9	lost
1996–97	India v South Africa	Mumbai	ODI	–	26	won
1996–97	India v South Africa	Ahmedabad	Test	–	35, 24	won
1996–97	India v South Africa	Calcutta	Test	–	109, 52	lost
1996–97	India v South Africa	Mumbai	ODI	–	22	won
1996–97	South Africa v India	Durban	Test	–	15, 8	lost
1996–97	South Africa v India	Cape Town	Test	–	115, 2	lost
1996–97	South Africa v India	Johannesburg	Test	–	18, 2	drawn
1996–97	West Indies v India	Bridgetown	Test	–	17, 9	lost
1997–98	India v Pakistan	Toronto	ODI	–	52	won
1997–98	India v Pakistan	Toronto	ODI	–	21*	won
1997–98	India v Pakistan	Toronto	ODI	–	67	won
1997–98	India v Pakistan	Toronto	ODI	–	7	won

Year	Game	Venue	Type	Azhar captain	His scores	Result
1997–98	India v Pakistan	Toronto	ODI	–	21*	won
1997–98	India v Pakistan	Toronto	ODI	–	50	lost
1997–98	Pakistan v India	Karachi	ODI	–	6	won
1997–98	India v New Zealand	Sharjah	ODI	✔	11	lost
1998–99	India v Pakistan	Jaipur	ODI	✔	1	lost
1999	India v Zimbabwe	Leicester	ODI	✔	7	lost
1999	India v Pakistan	Manchester	ODI	✔	59	won
1999–2000	India v South Africa	Bangalore	Test	–	9, 102	lost

* This list of matches, originally published in *Wisden 2001*, shows games which were mentioned in either India's Central Bureau of Investigation report or the Quyyum and King inquiries in India, Pakistan and South Africa.

MOHAMMAD AZHARUDDIN'S RECORD

Competition	Debut	Mts	Inns	NO	HS	Runs	Ave	100	50
Test	1984–85	99	147	9	199	6215	45.03	22	21
ODI	1984–85	334	308	54	153*	9378	36.92	7	58
All first-class	1981–82	229	343	38	226	15 855	51.98	54	74

EXCERPTS FROM THE CBI REPORT

- '. . . Azharuddin was paid a sum of 50 lakh rupees (A$220 000) as an advance with the arrangement that the initial amount would be adjusted against the matches he would "do" for MK (Mukesh Gupta). Azharuddin promised MK that he would provide the exact information as to when India would win or lose. He does not remember the exact number of matches which Azhar "did" for him during this period. MK went to Sharjah during an ongoing tournament and, through Asif Iqbal, met Jayasuriya. But Jayasuriya refused to "do" any matches for MK.'

- '. . . Azhar told MK to make future payments to him through Dr Ali Irani. According to MK, Azharuddin told him that the Ahmedabad Test would not end in a draw and India won that Test and MK recovered about 30 per cent of his previous losses.'

- '. . . MK also promises to pay him money equivalent to a Maruti Gypsy [car] which Manoj Prabhakar wanted to purchase, if he could provide useful information during the England tour. According to MK, Manoj Prabhakar gave him information about all aspects of the Indian team and he also underperformed in one of the Tests which ended in a draw.'

- '. . . Manoj Prabhakar promised to introduce MK to other international players against a payment of 50 000 rupees each and after dinner that night, spoke to Gus Logie of the West Indies over the telephone. However, Gus Logie refused to cooperate in any manner with him . . .'

- '. . . MK met Martin Crowe in 1991 in New Zealand and also had lunch at his house. MK added that Martin's wife, Simone, was also present during the meeting. MK had stated that he had paid a sum of US$20 000 (A$35 000) to Martin Crowe in exchange for information about the pitch, weather, team composition, etc. whenever the New Zealand team played.'

- '. . . Dean Jones promised to think about the offer. During that series, Manoj Prabhakar also introduced Brian Lara and Ranatunga to MK but they were not paid any money. In 1996 there was another tournament in Sri Lanka, the Singer Cup, in which India, Pakistan and Australia were playing. During that series MK rang Saleem Malik and requested him to do something for him. Saleem Malik gave him information that Pakistan would lose one particular match against Australia which came out true and he made good money on that.'

4. The big sting: Shane Warne and Mark Waugh

Shane Warne was in a beachside casino in Colombo, Sri Lanka, playing roulette – and losing. Red 23 wasn't proving as lucky as usual. He was down by as much as US$5000, which was serious money, even for a boom cricketer well on his way to his first million.

Then a man called John, whom Warne had earlier been introduced to at the tables by team-mate Mark Waugh, offered to cover his losses as a token of appreciation. Unaware that the man smiling back at him was an Indian bookmaker offering a deadly sweetener, Warne was initially hesitant before taking the envelope and shaking hands.

Warne was soon to become an informant to the illegal billion-dollar cricket gambling industry. But as well as this, within a month he was to be targeted for the biggest sting of all – the throwing of a Test match.

THE ADULATION RESERVED for Australian elite sportspeople is head-spinning, leaving only the very strongest truly unaffected. For megastars like Shane Warne, the most influential and charismatic cricketer of the 1990s, the rewards are boundless. Once an unknown kid at the Australian Cricket Academy who was sent back to Adelaide by bus for offensive behaviour around a Darwin hotel pool, Warne's meteoric rise into the national team as Australia's 350th Test player was *Boys' Own* fiction at its most irresistible.

From 1993 to 1995, Warne was the outstanding strike bowler in the world. Almost everything he touched turned to gold. He was the Blond from Black Rock, the Flipperman, the kid who could spin a cricket ball on ice. He suddenly had access to more money than he had ever dreamed about, or needed, and saw his name added to every important free list in Melbourne. Instead of driving around in his hotted-up old Cortina, he bought a blue Ferrari, and paid more than $900 000 for a house right on Brighton's exclusive Esplanade.

He was living his dream – playing cricket for his country, staying at the most luxurious hotels and mixing with the rich and famous. It was in September 1994, in this unreal atmosphere, a long way from home or reality, that he accepted a gift from a man he had met only 24 hours previously.

Warne said the little Indian told him he was wealthy and that Warne was his favourite cricketer. He had seen him lose heavily at the casino the previous night. Would Warne accept a token of his appreciation? It was an envelope containing US$5000 in greenbacks. 'No strings,' said John persuasively. 'I don't want anything in return.'

Warne's first reaction was to say 'Thanks, but no thanks', but when John said he would be personally affronted if Warne didn't take the envelope, he accepted it. So used had he become to the handouts and privileges accorded the world's most feted cricketers that he naively believed the money to be nothing more than a gift from a benevolent stranger who, like Warne himself, enjoyed a punt and had plenty of money. Warne shook John's hand, went back to the tables and blew the lot.

His new friend stayed in touch, ringing Warne two or three times before important matches asking for weather and pitch information and, on one occasion, the likely make-up of the team. In another call, he wished Warne a merry Christmas. The calls continued into the 1994–95 Carlton & United one-day series, as well as the short tour of New Zealand in early 1995.

While the Australians were in Colombo, John also gave Mark Waugh money: US$4000 in this case. The Australian owned race-horses, loved punting and dealt regularly with bookies. He saw no problem with providing pitch and weather information, but said selection was another matter altogether. During a five-month period, in five different countries, John rang Waugh on the eve of games at least 10 times. The calls stopped in Kingston, Jamaica, early in 1995, when Waugh told John they could no longer talk. By then, both Waugh and Warne had been interrogated and fined by the ACB.

At no stage in their liaisons with John did either Warne or Waugh divulge team tactics or policy. Nor did they suspect that he might have been involved in something as appalling as match-fixing.

COLOMBO WAS A prelude to Australia's next big tour – to Pakistan in September–October 1994 – and expectations were sky-high under new captain Mark Taylor. Although the first Test was to be played in Karachi, where Pakistan had been unbeaten since 1955, Australia seemed, at last, to possess the arsenal to win anywhere in the world, even on the subcontinent.

By the fourth night of the Test, at Karachi's National Stadium, the locals knew just how serious the Australian threat was. Having already conceded a first-innings lead, Pakistan was set 314 to win. At stumps they were 3/155, the pendulum having swung again in the final minutes with the dismissal of captain Saleem Malik by big fast bowler Jo Angel.

Saleem, with Saeed Anwar, had threatened to assume control of the game, so his dismissal was greeted joyously by the Australians. Saleem was one of the leading players of spin in the world and it was considered a huge plus to have him back in the pavilion rather than negating the dual wiles of Warne and Tim May on a fifth-day wicket.

Late that night, around 10.30, Warne and May were lounging around in their hotel room at the Pearl Continental when the phone rang. Saleem wanted to talk to Warne on a confidential matter. 'Wonder what he wants?' said Warne. 'Do you want to come too?'

'It's too late for me,' said May, who was dozing. 'I'm buggered. You go, Warnie.'

The Pakistanis were also staying at the Pearl. Curious and not wanting to offend, Warne went to Saleem's room. Known as 'The Rat' to the Australians because of his long face, Saleem had been a regular visitor to Australia and had played at Essex, the same English county club as Mark Waugh. Warne respected him as a player but thought him a little stand-offish. Why would Pakistan's cricket captain want to talk to him? And at 10.30 p.m.?

They talked about the intensity of the first four days and then Saleem looked at Warne directly and said that Pakistan couldn't afford to lose the match.

WARNE: Don't know about that, mate. We can still do it.

SALEEM: No, you don't understand. We cannot lose. Our pride is at stake. Everything is at stake. We can't lose this first Test.

WARNE: Well, mate, our pride is at stake, too. I'm sorry to tell you this, but we are going to whip you blokes tomorrow.

SALEEM: I don't think you understand what I am asking of you. What I want is for you and Tim May to bowl wide of the off stump and bowl poorly, so that the match is a draw, and for that I will give you and Tim May US$200 000. I can have it in your room in half an hour.

WARNE: What the hell is going on here? What do you mean? What are you talking about? I don't understand.

SALEEM: I am serious. You must get back to me.

Warne was amazed. Pakistan's captain, one of the finest cricketers in the world, was asking him to throw a game. And for huge money – twice Warne's then annual wage as an Australian cricketer and enough for him to pay cash for a double-fronted Victorian house back home in plush South Yarra.

'As far as I am concerned you can get &$#@ed,' he said, turning on his heel. 'But I'll tell Maysie ...'

Returning to his room, Warne was sheet-white. 'What did the Rat want?' asked May. When told of the bribe, May made a joke of it before telling Warne to ring Saleem back and tell him to &$#@ off. 'We'd heard rumours [of match-fixing] since the '93 tour of England, but had no idea how it worked,' said May recently. 'We'd thought at the time [in 1993] it was just a joke. Now we thought, shit, it really does happen. It was pretty scary stuff. You realised it wasn't just the local chicken shop behind it.'

Only days before making his offer to Warne and May, Saleem had called a press conference to denounce persistent rumours that his team was involved in gambling. Calling the rumours 'malicious', he had said it was a conspiracy against him and his team and was affecting performance and morale. 'The players are under tremendous tension,' he had said. 'The batsmen are afraid if they got out they would be said to have been bought by the bookies. The bowlers are afraid because if they have got hammered they will be labelled as bought by the bookies.'

Pakistan won the Test, but it was a titanic finish. With two runs needed to tie and three to win, Warne's dipping leg-break to an advancing Inzamam-ul-Haq all but bowled him. Instead it went for four byes, skidding straight through wicketkeeper Ian Healy. As Pakistani number 11 Mushtaq Ahmed fell to his knees, kissed the ground and thanked Allah, Healy looked back at the ball and the boundary, hung his head and furiously kicked the stumps. Pakistan's last two batsmen had scored a world-record 57 runs for the final wicket to steal a remarkable win. It was the closest any team had come to defeating the Pakistanis at the National Stadium and continued Australia's on-tour hoodoo on the subcontinent. On the podium Saleem hissed at man of the match Warne, 'You should have taken the money.'

After Taylor attended a post-match disciplinary hearing, Warne notified Taylor of the offer made by Saleem. Given the circumstances of Pakistan's extraordinary victory, he believed he had no other choice.

Australia's win in the subsequent Wills Triangular ODI tournament – which also involved Hansie Cronje's South Africans – was only some consolation given the spectre of match-fixing, which none of the Australians had ever experienced before. Halfway through the tournament, at a reception in Rawalpindi, Saleem again made an approach. This time it was to Mark Waugh, when Saleem offered him and three others a US$200 000 inducement to play badly. Given his own hard-line response to Saleem's first approach just weeks before in Karachi, Warne (who had been standing in a group with Waugh when the offer was made) was amazed at the temerity of the Pakistani captain as much as at the magnitude of the offer. After the Pakistanis won an extraordinarily fast-scoring match by nine wickets within 40 overs, Waugh, who had made a century, came into the rooms and flippantly declared, 'Ah, would've been better off taking the bribes, guys.'

At that stage only a few players – and coach Bob Simpson – even knew of the offers. Manager Col Egar didn't find out until the very last game of the tour, in Lahore a week later. 'Col, sit down. I've got something to tell you,' said Simpson. Egar listened in amazement and said, 'Righto, let's get hold of the match referee [John Reid] straight away and see what can be done.' The Australian players decided to say nothing publicly of the issue. Even Egar wasn't briefed by Taylor until they were back in Sydney. 'It was all very hush-hush,' said Egar later.

Having read about the ruthless practices of the subcontinental Mafia, some of the players feared physical reprisal and believed the bribery offers to be a matter for the ACB. Saleem, with a double-century and 143 in the last two Tests, had bullied Australia at every turn on the field and was central to Pakistan's 1–0 series victory. The Australians couldn't understand why a player so obviously gifted and at the height of his form could be so corrupt.

The scandal remained cricket's best-kept secret until the following February, when Phil Wilkins in the *Age* and the *Sydney Morning Herald* announced that an ICC inquiry was pending and that Waugh, Warne and May had all provided sworn statements to say that approaches had been made. As Warne said in *My Own Story*: 'Why would anyone make such serious allegations knowing they were false? Inventing something like that would cause more trouble for us than the accused.'

Having happily maintained a conspiracy of silence, the ACB immediately launched its own inquiry during the short tour of New Zealand, via team manager Ian McDonald. McDonald asked every player if he had had any dealings with bookmakers. Only then was the liaison between Warne, Waugh and 'John', the well-heeled Indian cricket lover said to come from New Delhi, uncovered. With the team about to depart for the West Indies, the ACB discussed the matter with visiting ICC officials, including president Clyde Walcott. They decided to keep the matter silent in the belief that it would be an enormous embarrassment for the players and a public relations disaster for the game given the fallout from the Saleem allegations and continuing doubt over the legitimacy of matches on the subcontinent. The Board did, however, fine both players heavily: on 28 February, 48 hours after Australia won the Centenary series in New Zealand, Warne was fined $8000 and Waugh $10 000.

It took four years for the cover-up to be unveiled. The story was told in intricate detail in the *Australian* by cricket writer Malcolm Conn and described on Melbourne radio station 3AW by former Test cricketer David Hookes, who had received a late tip-off while playing golf earlier that day. Conn had spent two months investigating claims that Mark Waugh had been involved with an illegal bookmaker. He had seen a letter – albeit unsourced – sent to the PCB's legal advisers during the Pakistan High Court inquiry conducted in Lahore during the springtime Australian tour to Pakistan.

'I didn't believe at the time that it could be true,' said Conn. 'But he [Waugh] was a punter so I didn't dismiss it completely. I was only thinking in terms of match-fixing.'

In Brisbane two days before the first Test against England in early November 1998, the ACB held their official launch of the Ashes tour. Later, a large group of media people, sponsors, officials and players went to Ian Healy's sports bar, Adrenalin. 'I mentioned Mark Waugh to an associate of mine involved in Australian cricket and he confirmed that Waugh had indeed been involved. I nearly fell over,' said Conn. 'He pointed out that it was not match-fixing but for giving information. He knew Waugh had been fined but couldn't be more specific. I rang many people to try and confirm it and went to Malcolm Speed [ACB chief executive] and put it to him. To each question, Speed, a former lawyer, said, "I can neither confirm nor deny."'

Conn knew that the story was 'on'. He checked and double-checked his sources and a few days later rang Speed to tell him he was writing what he knew and the ACB could comment if it liked. Speed said to give him an hour. When he rang back, he not only confirmed Waugh's involvement but said that another player was involved too: Shane Warne. Until then, Conn had had no inkling of Warne's involvement. But Speed's options had run out. He had no choice but to confess everything. The question 'Is there anybody else?' would undoubtedly have been asked.

The *Australian* ran the exposé as its front-page lead under a major heading: CRICKET STARS HUMILIATE NATIONAL GAME. The piece provoked extraordinary comment. It was the biggest cricket story since World Series and won Conn a Walkley Award, the highest award in Australian journalism.

Having been anything but transparent in the previous three and a half years, the ACB moved quickly. They held a press conference at the Adelaide Oval in December at which Warne and Waugh, looking like truant schoolboys, publicly admitted to receiving secret payments from illegal bookmakers. Their involvement, as innocent as it had initially seemed, seemed to be a prelude to a bigger sting. Both read prepared statements and refused to answer any further questions.

'I realise I was very naive and stupid. I've always strived to do the best I can for my country and I think that the way I play and conduct myself on the field shows I'm a cricketer with integrity who has never given anything but his best,' said Warne.

'In the period since I was fined the full implication of the possibility that I may be linked to actions much more sinister than those I innocently undertook in 1994 have become very clear to me. I realise and accept that my actions were naive and stupid,' said Waugh.

BAGGY GREEN SHAME headlined the *Sydney Morning Herald*, while the *Australian* said $11 000 PRICE OF DISGRACE. 'Their carefully worded but banal statements yesterday should have included words such as greedy and selfish,' said Patrick Smith in the *Age*.

Until that time, the Australians had been considered cleanskins in the match-fixing scandal that was bubbling away on the subcontinent and touching even white knights like Hansie Cronje. While the ACB was at pains to say that neither Warne nor Waugh was guilty of anything more than offering weather and pitch information, the Board's long-running silence – which almost certainly would have continued but for the inquiries of Conn and other journalists – was damning in itself and fuelled suspicions that there must be more to come. THE UNVEILING OF A DIRTY LITTLE SECRET, said the *Australian* the day after the press conference. The paper's Letters to the Editor column was full of the scandal. 'A new day, a new word: Hypocricket', said Philip Glaister from Brisbane. 'Naive and stupid, definitely, but they left out "greedy"', said Bruce Hogan of Cloisters Square, Western Australia. Ted Gallop from Kalamunda said, 'Memo Warnie: is the Australian Cricket Board pay so bad that you have to do a little moonlighting?', while Gareth Davies of Maylands lamented, 'I thought I'd never see the day where I would say "It's not cricket" about cricket.'

Cricket-loving Prime Minister John Howard was also straight onto the front foot. 'I would imagine, given the great passion Australians have for cricket, there's an intense feeling of disappointment about the whole issue,' he said. One of Don Bradman's Invincibles, Neil Harvey, said a two-year ban should be imposed on both Warne and Waugh. Richie Benaud was particularly appalled that the issue had been covered up for so long.

The ACB went to extraordinary lengths to keep the fines in-house. Certainly there was no mention of the scandal or the fines in its minutes. 'There was a majority decision taken to carry out the action which was carried out,' Malcolm Gray, current ICC chairman and then a Board member, told the ABC's *Four Corners* reporter Liz Jackson. 'It was wrong and it was silly . . . there's a totally different environment today.' The then ACB chief executive Graham Halbish said that the silence had been the decision of the entire board, not just one or two members. Furthermore, Walcott and David Richards, the ICC's executive director, had been informed.

It was widely felt that neither Warne nor Waugh should ever be allowed to hold any leadership role in the Australian team. However, most cricket lovers baulked at taking further action, as both players had already been fined four years previously.

The controversy weighed heavily. In the *Australian Women's Weekly*, Warne's wife Simone said, 'I told Shane to give up cricket. What he was going through, all the talk of bribery, wasn't worth it.' In the third Test, which started almost immediately after the press conference, Waugh was openly booed by sections of the large Adelaide Oval crowd while walking to and from the wicket on the opening day. Warne, still rehabilitating after shoulder surgery, was back in Sheffield Shield ranks representing Victoria against Queensland in Melbourne. Only 773 attended on the first day and it was impossible to truly judge the crowd's reaction to his latest impropriety. However, at nearby Jolimont Terrace, the home of Victorian cricket, receptionists were fielding irate phone calls demanding Warne's immediate resignation as state captain.

A few months later the ACB showed its hand when it officially ruled that past misdemeanours had no relevance and gave both players interim leadership roles. Warne, in fact, led the Australians for much of the one-day summer in January 1999 after Steve Waugh twice injured a hamstring and could play in only two of the 12 matches. With Taylor stepping down as captain on the eve of the West Indian tour, Warne was also made vice-captain behind Steve Waugh. For a player unsure if he would be able to play cricket again after shoulder surgery just nine months previously, it had been a traumatic, action-packed nine months. And more was to come.

Warne had wrestled with his form and his detractors all summer. Most were prepared to forgive and forget, but unfortunately for Warne, more misdemeanours were ahead – this time giving the conservative elements on the Board the extra ammunition they needed to act. By the 2000–01 summer, Warne's leadership ambitions had been shattered, with the administrators saying that his cricket genius would no longer override the ambassadorial faults and controversies ever-present in his life.

The pitch information would have just been the beginning, to get them on the hook so they could be played in. Someone tried the same game with me. It's a dirty game that starts with apparently harmless information and we know where it ends. Fixed matches. But with the Mafia involved it's a dangerous business and someone is going to get killed.   **Indian all-rounder MANOJ PRABHAKAR**

YOU CANNOT HAVE genius without faults. Shane Warne's focus on becoming the greatest-ever spin bowler has come at a price. He has struggled with living life in a goldfish bowl, his every movement monitored.

Not long after Warne and his family moved into a prestigious double-storey property on millionaire's row on Brighton's Esplanade, a bus pulled up outside. Warne started chatting to a man from the bus before bolting back inside when he realised he was one of a group of tourists on a sightseeing tour of the houses of the rich and famous. Like many great public performers, he needs an audience – but he also needs his space.

Warne has been labelled a larrikin who is undeserving of his sport's highest honour, the captaincy, because of what many regard as a carefree, do-as-you-please attitude. Purists say that the Australian Test captaincy should not only be a role for the best cricketer, but for one whose diplomacy skills and CV are flawless. However, those leading the push to disrobe the free-spirited, passionate Victorian as Steve Waugh's deputy captain were also among those who applauded loudest when Warne the showman consistently performed his big-spinning feats, despite stress-related surgeries that have threatened his very career.

When he was accused in June 2000, during his one-off season with English county side Hampshire, of harassing 22-year-old Donna Smith, a nurse and single mother from Leicester, Warne admitted the contact but denied anything more than some 'dirty talk' on the phone, which the woman had reciprocated. In a public relations gaffe he was to regret, he said that had the incident remained private, it would not have been a mistake.

'To me the journey of life is something you live and fully enjoy,' he told Channel Nine's *A Current Affair*. Warne confessed that the spotlight on high-profile international sportspeople made his life a soap opera. As had been proved in the past, he couldn't even light up a cigarette without creating a stir.

However, Warne has either ignored or somehow bypassed many of the everyday disciplines most people take for granted in their daily lives. Author Roland Perry compared Warne to a boy in a bubble, unaware of the fallout around him. A millionaire well before his 30th birthday, Warne simply didn't have to worry about issues such as his family's embarrassment at the 'SHAME WARNE' headlines in the *Daily Mirror* over the Donna Smith affair.

Asked what happened on the night he met Smith after Hampshire's match against Leicester, Warne said, 'She came up to me and said, "I heard you are famous. Can you sign my back?" She bent over in front of me and wanted me to sign her back. I said no. She tried to lift up my shirt and said, "Well, I'll sign your chest." [I said,] "No, I'm not doing that, thank you." She kept on trying.' Warne said his wife Simone was disappointed, but that like all married couples they 'had their ups and downs'.

The allegation that he had indulged in phone sex was the latest in a litany of incidents, starting with his expulsion from a youth tour of Sri Lanka and his subsequent premature exit from the Australian Cricket Academy. Other transgressions include:

- losing his temper and swearing at South Africa's Andrew Hudson in a Test match in Johannesburg in 1994, precipitating a heavy fine and worldwide censure
- in the West Indies in 1999, breaking an agreement with a nicotine-gum maker not to smoke but still pocketing almost A$200 000 for going without his beloved cigarettes for a short period
- cavorting on a balcony and making uncomplimentary gestures at rowdy English fans after Australia retained the Ashes at Trent Bridge in 1997
- impounding a bag belonging to a 15-year-old Wellington boy after the boy took a snapshot of Warne smoking a cigarette during a rained-out ODI at the smoke-free Westpac Trust Stadium in New Zealand in 2000.

Speaking on *A Current Affair*, Warne said that much of the publicity has been unwanted and the episode with the nurse is an example of how the media seem to delight in exposing his misdemeanours. 'In Australia unfortunately it [the publicity] was like a runaway train,' he said. He conceded that he virtually discounted himself from leadership responsibilities, a position confirmed soon afterwards by the ACB when it sacked him from the vice-captaincy and replaced him with Adam Gilchrist. For every 10 letters received by the ACB on the issue, nine were anti-Warne. He'd worn out his welcome.

5. Simply irresistible: Dennis Lillee

As tour pranks go, it was the grand-daddy of them all. But so irresistible were the 500/1 odds that Dennis Lillee felt compelled to have a slice, even if it did mean betting against Australia. It was just one of the many controversies to embroil the maverick fast bowler during a headlining career that knew few limits.

DENNIS LILLEE HAD never been anything but a small-time gambler. The son of a Perth truck driver, money wasn't for squandering. But like many of his Australian team-mates, the betting tents dotted around the Test and county grounds in England were a fascinating lure. You could bet on just about everything, from the smallest regional race meeting through to the game in progress.

At Bradford, during Lillee's first tour in 1972, most of the Australians donated to a team kitty, believing the 5/1 odds to capture five Yorkshire wickets before lunch was highly achievable. 'With about half an hour to go in the session we had our five wickets and Dennis was running around and jumping up and down with excitement,' said his best mate, wicketkeeper Rodney Marsh. 'He went to the tent to collect and the bloke explained that the session hadn't finished and if we got any more wickets it would be a lost bet. Dennis yelled out that we couldn't take any more and we all acknowledged the fact and proceeded cautiously. We had Bob Massie at fine leg who wasn't the best of fieldsmen at any time, but sure enough a few minutes before the end of the session this bloke hooked one and Ferg [Massie] took a screamer. We all raced down to kick his backside!'

In 1981, Kim Hughes' Aussies had taken such a stranglehold on the third Test in Leeds that betting agency Ladbrokes, looking to initiate some late-match interest, posted the extraordinary odds of 500/1 on a series-squaring English win. Dour Yorkshiremen dismissed the odds as ludicrous and went back to their fish and chips and Tetley's, wondering if the game would need a fifth day. In the Australian dressing room, however, Lillee couldn't believe his eyes.

On a high, having just broken the record for most wickets in Ashes Tests, he said, 'Have a look at that [scoreboard]. Five hundred to one! Surely those odds can't be right.' Reaching for his wallet, he said he'd have £50 on it and asked who else wanted to be involved. No one was keen, not even Marsh, who reckoned he was throwing money away. 'All right,' said Lillee. 'Have 10 with me then.'

Marsh was still reticent, but minutes later, as the Australians were re-taking the field, Marsh walked past the Australian bus driver, Peter Tribe, and with a raise of his hand indicated he'd have five. Spinner Ray Bright also said he was in, but just as quickly changed his mind. 'The punter in me told me you only have a bet if you have a chance of winning,' he said. 'Basically it was a giggle bet.'

At 7/176 in their second innings and still 51 behind, the Englishmen were facing another humbling defeat. Several of the England team – including Ian Botham, who was not out – had already booked out of their hotel on the fourth morning, believing there was little chance of the game going the distance. 'Most of us had given up the Test for dead,' Botham said in *The Incredible Tests 1981*.

I was sports editor at the *Sunday Observer* newspaper at the time, and when the seventh wicket fell with England still almost 100 runs behind, around midnight Melbourne time, we changed our front-page banner to ASHES COME HOME. We also ran the latest odds: 1/4 Australia, 5/2 the draw, 500/1 England.

The tea-to-stumps session remains one of the greatest in cricket annals, with the Englishmen scoring 175 runs from 27 overs. Most of these runs came from the inspired Botham, who bludgeoned the bowling, delighting in the nothing-to-lose situation. Before his match-saving onslaught, bus driver Tribe's initial reaction had been to keep the 15 quid and hand it back to Lillee and Marsh at the tea break, believing he'd be doing them a good turn. But in the end Tribe had gone around to the tent and laid the bet. Then he witnessed the amazing comeback, which saw Australia, in just 24 hours, forfeit a seemingly invincible position to narrowly lose the closest Ashes Test in more than 50 years.

Tribe said he felt sick in the stomach watching the Aussies capitulate. In cricket's most stunning turnaround, England won by 18 runs. It was only the second time in more than 100 years and 905 Tests that a side following on had won the match.

Lillee and Marsh collected a cool £7500 (A$15 000). Bright, who was rooming with Lillee, still remembers all the £1 notes in their hotel room and the many pints of lager the money helped to buy. 'Ladbrokes didn't have [all] the money at the ground,' he recalled. 'The rest arrived a few days later.'

There was no suggestion that either Lillee or Marsh had not played with their normal focus and ferocity. Lillee's fifth-day stand of 35 with Bright was the second highest in Australia's total of 111 all out. And one Test later, at Edgbaston, Marsh cried when Australia squandered another winning position to lose by 29 runs.

The hero of the greatest comeback of all was former England captain Botham, who, free of leadership responsibilities, played the most exhilarating cricket of his celebrated career, bullying the Australian attack in a savage display of power not seen from an Englishman since Ted Dexter was in his prime. With almost 200 runs and six wickets, Botham not only saved the match and the series, but established himself, once and for all, as one of the finest all-rounders in cricket history.

While there were rumours of a bet, details remained in-house until 12 months later with the release of the third of Lillee's autobiographies, *My Life in Cricket*, where Lillee candidly revealed the wager. The ACB was suitably embarrassed and immediately inserted a clause into their player match contracts, banning players from betting on games in which they were involved.

'I never lost a moment's sleep because of it,' said Lillee. 'I didn't regard it as betting against my team or my country. I just thought the odds of 500/1 were ridiculous for a two-horse race. I'd flatten anyone who ever suggested I threw a game. I have a completely clear conscience over it. I believe my integrity, as far as playing to win every game I played, is unquestioned.'

Marsh said both he and Lillee felt they were betting against the English bookmakers, 'trying to show the Poms how silly they were for offering such stupid odds of 500/1'.

'I couldn't see the harm in having a bet,' Marsh said. 'Nobody would have known or cared about the bet if we had won. It wasn't until after the game when someone said that we had won a quid that it dawned on us. But I don't believe we did the wrong thing because we didn't consider it a bet against Australia. That was never the intent.'

New South Wales captain and ex-Test batsman Rick McCosker believed that the bet reflected badly on cricket and was a poor example to young people. Former Australian batsman and one-time captain Neil Harvey went further, saying that Lillee should be banned from the game.

Bus driver Tribe was happy, though. For his part in the windfall, he received a set of golf clubs and a return air ticket to Australia.

DENNIS LILLEE'S RUN-INS with and growing dislike of administrators were second only to his hatred of opposing batsmen. He had a maverick streak and even blued at times with his captains, especially if they happened to give someone else the new ball!

While universally respected for his unyielding commitment and unsurpassed wicket-taking talents, Lillee is also regarded as Australian cricket's most notorious bad boy. From the time he knocked Geoff Boycott's cap from his head with his first delivery in an international against the 1970–71 Englishmen at the WACA Ground, Lillee generated news like few Australian cricketers before or since.

His spitfire speed from a rocking, energetic run-up was timed in excess of 90 mph, just fractionally behind the wild one, pace partner Jeff Thomson. Lillee's frank admissions that he bowled his short deliveries to scare and, if necessary, hurt opposing batsmen were part of his intimidating persona. He revelled in his role as Australia's spearhead and refused to slow down and become a change bowler. Ian Chappell said he had never met a cricketer with such an iron will, or such a love of running in fast.

As the all-star fast bowler of the 1970s, Lillee was feted virtually everywhere he went. He made such a remarkable recovery from his severe spinal injury of 1973 that officials, glad to have him back, allowed him to overstep authority even if it tweaked at the game's very fibre. Unwittingly, those who tended to forgive and forget and gloss over Lillee's indiscretions ultimately did him a disservice. Initially a shy man, bordering on introverted, Lillee developed a supreme ego. Had he been subject to discipline earlier, he may not have become quite as roguish a figure.

Purists point to Lillee's antics, saying that he defied authority too often. Central to their argument were his involvements in the Javed

Miandad kicking controversy in 1981–82, the aluminium bat affair, the Leeds betting furore, and the vandalism of a dressing room at Launceston's historic NTCA ground during his comeback half-summer with Tasmania in 1987–88.

Rarely before had there been a more provocative 10 seconds in Test history, or as open a display of on-field aggression, as in the infamous incident with cheeky Pakistani Javed Miandad at the WACA Ground in Perth. As Javed menacingly brandished his bat, having been ankle-tapped, Lillee clenched his fists and shaped up like an old-time bare-knuckle boxer. The cricket world held its breath.

From slip, Australia's captain, Greg Chappell, yelled 'Dennis!' and sprinted down the wicket to intervene. Umpire Tony Crafter had already stepped between the pair, trying to shepherd Lillee away. It was an extraordinary, never-to-be-forgotten display of petulance that resulted in a two-match ban for the West Australian.

In his book *Over and Out*, Lillee says this incident is the only one he truly regrets. 'Javed jabbed me in the rib cage with his bat, but nobody wanted to know about that,' he said. 'I'm not saying I was right in what I did, even though I gave him only a slight tap on the pad. I'm sorry thousands of kids saw it, but I'm also sorry the incident wasn't fully shown in television replays.'

THE FIRST WEEKS of the 1979–80 season – the first of the cricket compromise – were almost as stormy, with Lillee wearing charges of petulance and of interfering with the spirit of the game.

The first black mark came as the opening West Indian Test in Brisbane was petering out to a draw. Relegated on the final afternoon to first-change duties behind Thomson and Rodney Hogg, Lillee angered Chappell and wicketkeeper Marsh by deliberately sending down a bouncer while Marsh was standing over the stumps. Having seen Lillee bowl a slow off-break from just three paces, Chappell called to him, asking whether he was bowling fast or spin. 'Spin,' said Lillee, riled at the no-ball calls being made by umpire Robin Bailhache. Chappell changed the field to suit a slow bowler, thinking Lillee intended to finish his over, which was to stretch to 11 balls, as quickly as he could.

Instead, from just five or six paces, he delivered a short-pitcher at close to top pace. It whistled past an astonished Collis King and fairly thumped into Marsh's gloves. Marsh fumed and cursed at Lillee, who was already storming back to his mark without even half an apology. Chappell was clearly unimpressed and strode 60 metres from slip to near the members' pavilion to admonish his fast bowler.

Ten days later Lillee was headline news again, this time over his revolutionary Combat aluminium cricket bat in the opening Test against England at the WACA Ground. Lillee had first used the bat, without even a ripple of protest, in the Test in Brisbane, but given that he had batted just nine minutes and faced just seven balls without scoring a run, the lack of attention was hardly surprising. However, his continued use of the bat caused a furore and triggered action from the game's rule-makers, Marylebone Cricket Club.

In a bizarre start to the second day of the Test, Lillee, who was not out overnight, resumed with the bat he had been attempting to market into schools at two-thirds of the price of normal English willow. After four deliveries from Ian Botham, one of which Lillee drove through mid-off for three, England captain Mike Brearley complained to umpires Don Weser and Max O'Connell that the ball had been damaged.

An unscheduled 10-minute break in play ensued while Lillee argued over the legality of his bat. Australia's 12th man, Rodney Hogg, came out and offered Lillee a wooden bat but Lillee refused and marched back into the rooms with Hogg before re-emerging, still with the offending blade. 'I wanted to introduce the bat to the public,' Lillee said afterwards. 'We wanted the bat to get some exposure for Christmas sales. Mike Brearley stuck his nose in when he shouldn't have.'

Lillee was hooted by sections of his home crowd over his antics, which included hurling his bat 20 metres towards the pavilion in apparent anger. Many, like English wicketkeeper Bob Taylor, felt that Lillee was grandstanding and making a fool of himself. 'It was a totally theatrical performance for the benefit of the cameras and Lillee had the cheek to feign a loss of temper,' said Taylor.

The umpires refused to re-start the game until Lillee swapped bats, so Chappell ended the fiasco by taking a conventional Duncan Fearn-ley blade out himself. It was an extraordinary stand-off in which Lillee openly flouted the game's laws and the authority of the umpires. He escaped immediate censure when he produced a letter from the ACB saying it neither approved nor disapproved of the revolutionary bat. At the time, the laws of cricket did not demand that bats be made from wood.

The aluminium bat now takes pride of place among Lillee's array of memorabilia at his home in Perth. While Combat bats are now some-times auctioned, Lillee says he would never part with the original, which is signed by both teams and includes a message from Brearley: 'Good luck with the sales, Dennis.'

DENNIS LILLEE'S STANDING as the greatest fast bowler of all time is rarely questioned. He smashed opposing batting line-ups apart like a tor-pedo zeroing in on an unprotected frigate. Intimidation and passion were central to his on-field psyche. He bullied, taunted and berated batsmen. Some critics considered him headstrong and even callous; but no one dared say it to his face.

Lillee was also one never to be intimidated by formality. He said 'G'day' to the Duke of Edinburgh and during the Centenary Test in 1977, even asked Her Majesty the Queen for her autograph. Months later, a personally signed photo of the Queen arrived from Buckingham Palace!

Lillee's bowling partnership with Jeff Thomson in 1974–75 revived memories of Bodyline. It seemed inconceivable that any pair could have bowled faster. In response the MCC's team physiotherapist, Bernard Thomas, prompted the Englishmen to wear across their chests made-to-measure foam-rubber 'armour'. 'Never in my career have I witnessed so much protective gear applied to individuals before they went out to bat,' said captain Mike Denness. 'On the plane flying from Australia to New Zealand, the players were clearly more than relieved that they had all left Australia intact and without fatal injury.'

The recalled veteran Colin Cowdrey rated Lillee and Thomson the most difficult and unpredictable pair he had ever faced. He said they were ahead of the very best from around the world he had opposed in his prime years, from Lindwall and Miller and Hall and Griffith to the Springbok tearaways Adcock and Heine.

In the Sydney Test, Lillee's first ball to Dennis Amiss soared over Amiss' and Rod Marsh's heads before thudding one bounce into the sightscreen for four byes. Another bouncer, to tailender Geoff Arnold, just missed the batsman's ear and again soared out of Marsh's reach to the boundary. Even Lillee looked relieved that the ball had missed Arnold. The Englishman seemed frozen by fear and had hardly moved from out of his stance.

In the second innings, John Edrich, England's acting captain, had a rib broken by the first ball he faced from Lillee. With huge black storm clouds gathering and Lillee charging in to chants of 'Kill, kill, kill', the atmosphere was unforgettable. One hundred and eighty thousand people attended the five days of the game, an SCG record.

Few fast bowlers have had finer physique or temperament, or such a gloriously flowing action. He added edge to it; with a hostility to his opponents often theatrical and sometimes offensive. He would have been greater still without that. **JOHN ARLOTT**

Dennis was a captain's dream and a batsman's nightmare. **IAN CHAPPELL**

Dennis Lillee is very plainly the finest pace bower of my era, if not of any era. Lillee has everything. He frequently bowls well within himself for four balls of an over, slipping in two exceptionally quick deliveries from an action which scarcely seems to deviate from normal. He does exactly what he wants with the ball, swinging it either way but bowling the outswinger with control and consistency.

KEITH FLETCHER

Some say it is money that has caused this collapse in the ethics of the game, others that it is the reflection of a graceless age. In Australia, I am afraid, it is partly the result of weak government. For too long, the Australian Cricket Board have been over-tolerant of indiscipline and actions of dubious intent. True cricket lovers have been as sickened by Lillee's antics as they have been spellbound by his bowling.   ***Wisden* editor JOHN WOODCOCK**

Of all the great fast bowlers I have faced – Roberts, Holding, Hadlee, Marshall – I would have to place him as the best . . . Given the combination of his natural talent and a ferociously competitive nature, he was as complete a fast bowler as there can ever have been.   **DAVID GOWER**

Dennis Lillee was the complete fast bowler with a magnificent action and superb control and variation. He and 'Thommo' [Jeff Thomson] made a perfect combination.   **MICHAEL HOLDING**

At times he becomes a little hard to handle when he becomes too hot under the collar. When he 'loses his cool' Dennis is inclined to swear a bit and carry on towards the batsmen, but that's only because he is such a determined competitor.

ROD MARSH

He is a bowler of great endurance. He does so much with the ball and it is always a worry which way he is going to go and just what he is going to do next. Lillee is after you all the time.   **VIV RICHARDS**

As a competitor he was fierce. The sort of guy that, if the time came, would slit your throat with a smile on his face.

Former world champion sprinter and Lillee's fitness coach, AUSTIN ROBERTSON snr

It was Dennis' snarl and piercing, flashing glance which had the most effect. His statistics for wickets in Test matches cannot do justice to how he achieved them and in what circumstances.   **DIRK WELLHAM**

AUSTRALIA'S TOP SIX TEST WICKET-TAKERS

	TESTS	BALLS	RUNS	WKTS	AVE	BEST	5WI	10WM	BALLS/WKT
1. S. K. Warne	87	24415	10010	376	26.62	8/71	16	4	64.93
2. D. K. Lillee	70	18467	8493	355	23.92	7/83	23	7	52.01
3. G.D. McGrath	70	16784	7078	326	21.71	8/38	18	3	51.48
4. C. J. McDermott	71	16586	8332	291	28.63	8/97	14	2	56.99
5. R. Benaud	63	19108	6704	248	27.03	7/72	16	1	77.04
6. G. D. McKenzie	60	17681	7328	246	29.78	8/71	16	3	71.87

(To 1 July 2001)

6. Why a walking headline was dropped: Dean Jones

Sent to Siberia while still in his prime, Dean Jones hated life amongst the second-stringers. Troubled by selection frustrations and yearning for home, he cracked in faraway South Africa, announcing his international exit. No amount of back-pedalling, mega-scoring or popularity poll pressure in his home town of Melbourne could convince the national selectors that Victoria's best cricketer was anything but retired. Proud, brash and opinionated, Jones could play, but in cricket's inner sanctum his acceptance levels plummeted.

Were there reasons other than cricket for Deano's demise? For all the controversy he courted, thousands of adoring Melburnians think so. 'Bring back Deano' banners are still seen at the MCG, testament to the enduring respect for 'The Legend' – the nickname Jones penned himself.

NO AUSTRALIAN CRICKETER has made taller scores and been hero-worshipped by so many, yet offended so often, as Dean Jones. A stroke-maker who sprinted between wickets with daredevil flair, Jones' skill and adventure triggered fresh fortune for his teams. His double-century in cricket's second tied Test in Madras remains one of the all-time Test epics. Both his Test and one-day international averages are well above 40. Yet in a game renowned for its bonhomie and happy associations with its old stars, there is little love lost between Jones and many cricketing insiders, from former team-mates and administrators through to media people used to handing out, rather than receiving, the barbs.

From the time Jones retired as the highest runmaker in the history of Victorian cricket, he has never again been made particularly welcome in the Bushranger dressing rooms. And when he found himself in the same Australian Broadcasting Corporation media box as his former state deputy Darren Berry, with whom he had been warring for years, even the electronic scoreboard operator recognised the unease. Within seconds, up flashed the message: 'Temperature at the MCG: 30 degrees. Inside the ABC commentary box: 40 and climbing!'

Jones passed Paul Reiffel in the street one day, and when Reiffel didn't respond to his 'G'day', Jones exploded, wishing him a &#@*ing horror day. Even Merv Hughes, as benign now off the field as he was aggressive on it, has never forgiven Jones for deliberately belittling him in a scratch match one pre-season at suburban Frankston. 'We used to hang out together a lot, too,' said Hughes.

At the height of the Hansie Cronje cash-for-favours scandal in 2000, ABC television's Geoff Hutchison of the *7.30 Report* sought to interview Jones, but walked away when Jones asked that the camera angle include the sign outside his Port Melbourne restaurant. It caused quite a how-do-you-do, with the ever-quotable Jones later laughing at the irony of a reporter's deliberate retreat. As one of the ABC's frontline cricket commentators, surely the rules of protocol could have been bent just a little?

On the third morning of a match against Western Australia during his final interstate trip as a Victorian player, Jones sat out for the best part of an hour in the dressing rooms after an altercation with Berry and coach John Scholes, with a wide-eyed Shaun Craig acting as substitute.

Making friends and enemies, the champion player seemed to have a polarising effect on people. Long-time Test team-mate David Boon says Jones has a heart of gold and believed he was capable of playing many more Tests. Bill Lawry called him a saviour of international cricket, while Ian Botham said he would trust Jones with his life. Yet the door wasn't just shut on Jones' career – it was slammed.

For all his contradictions, Jones was a trailblazer. Not only was he the first to wear sunglasses, he made an art form of the boundary slide, pioneered the second run to fine-leg and loved to advance to even the fastest bowlers. Occasionally he also outraged, like the time in a one-day final in Sydney when he demanded that giant West Indian fast bowler Curtly Ambrose remove a white sweat band from his wrist. A fired-up Ambrose took 5/32 in an absolutely lethal spell, one of the fastest ever in a one-day game.

Jones played big shots on and off the field and cornered the news even ahead of emerging Victorian superstar Shane Warne. Often abrasive and outspoken, he became a walking headline, eventually wearing out his welcome. Even his long-time captain Allan Border admitted Jones had offended too many, too often. When Jones was dropped from Australia's one-day side for the series decider at Bloemfontein in early 1994, Border reckoned the stylish right-hander had lost his focus. Jones told old team-mate Boon that he simply wasn't prepared to be a nondescript any more. Let them pick younger men, even if they didn't deserve it.

He was also stripped of the Victorian captaincy and never recalled despite an outstanding run of centuries, including a peerless triple-ton against South Australia in the inaugural day/night Sheffield Shield match in Melbourne in 1994–95.

By rights, as Victoria's most distinguished player and one of Australia's all-time most-capped, he should have departed a hero and been given every good wish: Dean Jones, master runmaker, the leading one-day player of his time – thanks for the memories. But instead of free-flowing tributes, much of the copy was coloured. As formidable a player and personality as he was, the consensus from dressing rooms, from Derbyshire to his beloved MCG, was that Deano had shot himself in the foot. He had overstepped team boundaries, divided opinion and, for some, become unmanageable.

Jones' emotional farewell at VCA House in 1998 was an admission that he no longer held the numbers in the corridors of power. In reality he beat the axe only by days, the selectors having decided that, as good a player as he still was at 37, team harmony was as important as performance. Even institutions have a use-by date.

DEAN JONES IN TEST CRICKET

OPPONENT BY OPPONENT

Country	Mts	Inns	NO	Runs	HS	100s	Ave
England	17	28	2	1320	184*	3	50.76
India	8	13	2	681	210	2	61.90
New Zealand	5	8	1	171	99	–	24.42
Pakistan	6	10	2	291	121*	2	36.37
Sri Lanka	6	11	2	537	118*	3	59.66
West Indies	10	19	2	631	216	1	37.11
Total	52	89	11	3631	216	11	46.55

* denotes not out

GROUND BY GROUND

Venue	Mts	Inns	NO	Runs	HS	100s	Ave
Adelaide	6	11	1	603	216	3	60.30
Brisbane	5	8	1	121	38*	–	17.28
Hobart	1	2	1	121	118*	1	121.00
Melbourne	6	10	0	251	59	–	25.10
Perth	5	7	1	488	150*	2	81.33
Sydney	6	10	2	460	184*	1	57.50
Total	29	48	6	2044	216	7	48.66
Overseas	23	41	5	1587	210	4	44.08

BY BATTING POSITION

Position	Inns	Runs	HS	100s	Ave
3	28	1167	210	3	48.63
4	18	931	216	4	71.62
5	36	1317	157	3	37.63
6	5	163	118*	1	40.75
7	1	48	48	–	48.00
8	1	5	5	–	5.00
Total	89	3631	216	11	46.55

FIRST INNINGS v SECOND INNINGS

	Inns	Runs	HS	100s	Ave
First	51	2432	216	7	48.64
Second	38	1199	150*	4	42.82

No DRAMA IN Dean Jones' turbulent career rivalled his demotion to 12th man in the opening Test of the 1992–93 West Indian summer. In naming impressive 21-year-old West Australian Damien Martyn, the selectors chose to ignore Jones' highly commendable eight years at the top level and his series-topping efforts just months earlier in Sri Lanka. Martyn was a wildcard, but he had captained Young Australia and seemed as unaffected as any young batsman to enter Sheffield Shield ranks since the gifted Doug Walters.

The integrity of the selectors – West Australian Lawrie Sawle, Victoria's Jim Higgs, NSW's John Benaud and coach Bobby Simpson – was never in question, nor should it have been. As a panel they had made some extraordinarily far-sighted decisions, with Ian Healy's elevation from unknown stumper to his country's 'keeper and the fast-tracking of Shane Warne being absolute masterstrokes.

Some Victorians suggested that had a second national selector been Melbourne-based, Jones would have avoided the axe. But the two from NSW had for years been Jones devotees. It was Simpson who had suggested he should use a lighter bat in India in 1986–87, leading to Jones scoring an immediate double century. Twelve months earlier, Benaud, a skilled journalist, had ghosted Jones' best-selling first book.

Conspiracy theories were also floated, but Jones was simply a victim of circumstance, someone who for reasons beyond his own control had not had the same match practice as other top-order contenders leading into the Brisbane Test. As well, he had always struggled to make runs in Brisbane, where the humid conditions triggered more movement off the seam than at any other Australian venue. Only one of his 35 first-class centuries had been scored there. And in five 'Gabba Tests, his average was just 17.

The selectors also felt that a less predictable Australian front six could cause the West Indians problems. Jones might have played outstandingly well in Sri Lanka, but his performances the previous summer had been poor (bar an unbeaten 150 at the close of the summer in a 'dead' Test against an undistinguished attack).

The pro-Jones lobby points to his deeds in Sri Lanka as being indisputable evidence that their man was cut off at the knees. After all, it had been just 10 weeks since Jones' match-saving deeds in the inaugural Test at Colombo's Khettarama Stadium. On what was reclaimed marshland, Jones had made 77 and 100 not out, and was man of the match.

Had he been part of the second-innings collapse, which saw Tom Moody and Mark Waugh out to successive balls from 20-year-old debutant off-spinner Muttiah Muralitharan, Australia (after barely squeaking home in the first Test) could have been sorely embarrassed. Even the street-fighting Allan Border succumbed cheaply and left Australia at 5/149 in its second innings, an overall lead of just 138 with Jones the last remaining batting specialist. In scoring an unbeaten century, his 11th in 52 Tests, Jones was fortunate to survive two grassed catches; one a real soda. Despite this luck, in the context of a rain-affected draw it was an absolutely crucial knock.

He had been given more responsibility, too, at No. 4 after the selectors ruled that Border, while still inspiring, was not seeing the ball like he once did and should bat lower. Ever since the '89 tour of England, Jones had been Australia's virtual full-time No. 5. His promotion, and the use of West Australian giant Moody at the head of the order replacing fellow sandgroper Geoff Marsh, completed the team's biggest batting revamp in years.

Jones gladly accepted the challenge, having previously made three centuries and averaged 88 from No. 4. It was there that he made his mammoth career-best 216 against a triple-A West Indian attack including Malcolm Marshall, Patrick Patterson, Curtly Ambrose and Courtney Walsh in Adelaide in 1988–89.

In Sri Lanka, Jones averaged 55 and made more runs that any of Australia's batting specialists. While he missed out in the final Test at Moratuwa, so did Mark Waugh, who became the most notable batsman in Test history to score four ducks on end and for weeks, in an Olympic year, had to endure the nickname 'Rings'.

Jones had every reason to think he should remain one of Australia's first-choice batsmen, but the demise at age 33 of Border's long-time vice-captain Marsh earlier in the year left him uneasy. Jones was only two years younger. Clearly, the Academy kids such as Warne, Martyn, Michael Bevan, Justin Langer and Michael Slater were pushing through.

On the eve of selection, the legendary Dennis Lillee suggested in his syndicated Australia-wide column that the West Indies could be beaten without Dean Jones. Under a heading in the Melbourne *Herald Sun*, TIME TO LET DEANO GO, Lillee wrote, 'He [Jones] might be a fine one-day player, but that's perfect for him when there are no slips or gullies. He's the one to go if new blood is to be injected, which it should.'

Jones seemed vulnerable. An uncommonly wet Melbourne spring had seen hardly a ball bowled (other than indoors) during the entire month of October, and in his only two Sheffield Shield matches preceding the first Test in Brisbane Jones had missed out, scoring 24 runs in three digs. Conversely Mark Waugh, so out of sorts in Sri Lanka, had made a double-ton against the touring West Indians in Sydney, while Martyn started the season brilliantly with twin centuries against the Queenslanders at the 'Gabba.

Breaking with tradition, the selectors named an extra pace bowler in their XII and included a seventh batsman in Martyn, who they believed had the flair and inner confidence not to be intimidated by any pace attack, even if it did hail from the Caribbean, home of the world's most lethal speedsters. Most expected the youngster to be 12th man, but Jones wasn't so sure. Leading into the game he played golf with Allan Border and when he asked where he would be batting, Border was strangely noncommittal.

In his autobiography, *My Call*, Jones reported an 'animated discussion' between Border and coach/co-selector Simpson on match-eve. 'I don't know what was said but I sensed it was no good for me,' he said. 'At the team meeting, there was no discussion of the batting order, which was just ridiculous and very unprofessional. We were about to play a Test match, for goodness' sake.'

The Australian selectors felt the West Indians could be vulnerable without Viv Richards, Gordon Greenidge and Jeff Dujon and wanted to telegraph as few of their pre-match moves as possible, including the composition of their top order. At 10 p.m., Simpson rang Jones and asked if he could see him for a chat. When Simpson offered him a drink, Jones knew he was dead in the water.

'Dean was finding new ways of getting out, which suggested his powers of concentration were deserting him,' said Simpson in *The Reasons Why*. 'Concentration is the first thing to go, not eyesight, mobility or courage.'

As 12th man, Jones ensured he was far from forgotten, especially during a mid-match hailstorm when he sprinted onto the 'Gabba with an armful of helmets to protect ground staff from the hailstones, some of which were as big as golf balls. Only Deano would have done that.

As a 17-year-old, Dean Jones opened the bowling for a Melbourne mid-week team, the Plastic XI, and would curse and abuse the opposition, many of whom had been playing top-level club cricket for years. Even then he was a 'one-off', brazen and cocksure, with an unpredictability that amazed even his mates.

It mattered little to Jones that he consistently ignored protocol. So what if he used a mobile phone in the Victorian team bus or called himself 'Legend'? The public condemnation of his team-mates, however – among them Mark Taylor – was treated more seriously. Taylor hadn't played even one game on Australian soil as Australia's just-appointed new captain when Jones took aim, saying Steve Waugh was more suited to dual captaincy of the Test and one-day sides. 'My biggest problem with Mark is his fitness and whether he can bat 50 overs,' Jones said. 'And then I wonder if he's got the firepower at the death. I doubt whether he can hit big fours and sixes. He can probably say the same thing about me in the last couple of games. But at least I've done it – and I've never seen him do it.'

Jones played well for Melbourne and Victoria, but comments like these were never going to win friends or favour. In his column in the *Sunday Age*, he also went after some former Australian players who'd been critical of the team in newspapers, saying they'd 'forgotten how hard the game is'.

'In the Australian [one-day] team we've got to the stage of wondering who is next on the hit list,' he said. It was good provocative copy and spoken from the heart, but it led to lost friendships. The further his dream drifted of being picked again for Australia, the more outspoken he became.

Jones admits to mood swings and to calling a spade a bloody

shovel, but he says that goes with the territory. It is others who should have adapted. He had never wanted to be loved, only respected. Maybe he was too honest and passionate for his own good at times, but why should he apologise? If people were happy to applaud his hundreds, they could accept his warts, too.

Having seen his average slump to 31 in the season in which he was axed, it was to Jones' eternal credit that he bounced back so strongly, enjoying a succession of stunning years in the Sheffield Shield and fuelling Australia-wide support for his return. In scoring 16 centuries, he surpassed even the 100-making deeds of the mega-scoring Bill Ponsford, who collected runs with such rapidity that bowlers asked for his bat, 'Big Bertha', to be measured in case it was too wide.

No player with Jones' profile or sheer weight of runs has ever been snubbed for so long. Even those who toured South Africa with Kim Hughes' rebel teams in the mid-80s were soon forgiven. In five golden summers after being dropped from the national side, Jones made more than 4000 runs in a dazzling set of performances. 'I've always been a confidence player,' he said. 'When I get on a roll, it's hard to stop me.'

DEAN JONES' RUN BLITZ

Age	Season	Runs	HS	100s	Ave
32	1993–94	918	158*	4	76.50
33	1994–95	1251	324*	4	69.50
34	1995–96	974	145	3	51.26
35	1996–97	521	152	2	40.07
36	1997–98	896	151*	3	52.70

* denotes not out

Jones' age seemed inconsequential as he went on a phenomenal run spree, including his memorable triple-century in Melbourne's first-ever day/night Sheffield Shield match in 1994–95 – an awesome innings of power and nonchalance in which he made a South Australian attack which included two Test-standard spinners in Tim May and Peter McIntyre appear incompetent. SA wicketkeeper Tim Nielsen said he hardly had to take one ball, so dominant was Jones over the first day and a half of the high-scoring game. In four full sessions, using his favourite Super-Legend Kookaburra bat, he made 71, 83, 64 and 77 before declaring on 324 not out, the highest score at the MCG in 30 years.

In interstate cricket, only South Australia's Darren Lehmann and Queensland's Matthew Hayden were anywhere near as prolific – and neither had the same following as the publicity-pushing Jones, who combined playing cricket with radio commitments and a ghost-written newspaper column. The media work ensured his high profile but also miffed officials, several saying privately that Jones' campaign of self-promotion had become a bore. When he threatened to quit the captaincy in favour of a TV career he said was on offer, some on the executive were all for letting him go. They were further riled several months later when Jones broadsided the administration, saying they were responsible for the parlous condition of cricket in Victoria.

Jones' backers couldn't believe the different sets of rules the selectors applied for out-of-form captain Mark Taylor, who endured the worst streak of any batsman in Test history without being axed. Plenty of Jones' mates were prepared to back him. Australian ODI all-rounder Ian Harvey says his own first-class career was threatening to stall for good before he had a full-frontal dialogue with Jones in Perth in the mid-90s. Having played only 10 state games in three years, Harvey knew another failure against the Warriors would be final. 'There were still four or five games to go and Deano [then captain] told me I'd be playing no matter what. It was a big turning point for me. I went out and got 50 in the second innings [against Western Australia], 85 at Bellerive in the next game and then 136 against the Redbacks. Only then did Deano confess had I made a duck in that second dig, I would have been dropped! But it was his way of giving me some confidence to go out and play my natural game. I'm very grateful to him. If I'd got dropped after that game I might never have made it back.'

England fast bowler Devon Malcolm, whom Jones captained at Derbyshire for a year and a half until Jones' mid-season walk-out in 1997, said he may have been a harsh man-manager but that few possessed his spirit or mental toughness. 'Dean was a very hard man,' he said in his book *You Guys Are History!*, 'but he was still a fine batsman who led from the front. He'd never ask another batter to do what he couldn't manage and he won respect for his positive approach. Winning popularity contests didn't bother him as much as winning cricket matches . . . Jones and [Les] Stillman [Derby's Australian-born coach] kept boosting me throughout the 1996 season, telling me I was still the fastest bowler in England. Whenever I took a wicket, they'd say "That's another one for [Ray] Illingworth" [England's selection chairman].'

The conservatism inherent in cricket means that many are prepared to talk only 'in club' about the *real* Dean Jones. Bob Simpson called him frustrating, exciting, reliable, unreliable, selfish, unselfish, a mug lair and a team player, and ventured that Jones' unpredictability was an inherent part of his charm. Merv Hughes, once one of his closest friends, says a spat in a trial game spilled into training at St Kilda's Junction Oval a week later. According to insiders, punches were almost thrown. 'I thought he was trying to take me down,' said Hughes in *Merv: The Full Story*. The pair didn't speak again for three months and still rarely do. Another one bites the dust.

DEAN JONES IN ONE-DAY INTERNATIONALS, 1983–94

Mts	Inns	NO	Runs	HS	Ave	100	Strike Rate
164	161	25	6068	145	44.62	7	72
batting first	96	12	4108	145	48.90	5	76
batting second	65	13	1960	104	37.69	2	65

7. Sixty seconds of insanity: Greg and Trevor Chappell

Greg Chappell admits that everything got to him: the heat, the pressure, the schedule and especially the sight of strapping All Black Brian McKechnie striding to the wicket for one death-or-glory swipe. He admits that he was unfit to be Australia's captain late that steamy Sunday afternoon in Melbourne in 1980–81 when, in a moment of madness, he ordered his younger brother, Trevor, to bowl a shameful underarm.

Greg's decision ensured Australia a win, but violated the spirit of the game. So incensed was New Zealand's Prime Minister Robert Muldoon that he dubbed it 'an act of cowardice', and said it was further proof of his theory that Kiwis had higher IQs than Australians. Grandstanding he may have been, but for patriotic Australians the incident remains an indelibly black mark on Chappell's otherwise peerless career.

IT ALL BEGAN when burly tail-ender Wayne Daniel clubbed Mick Malone for a huge six at VFL Park, Waverley, to lift the West Indies to a fairytale final's victory from the penultimate ball minutes before midnight in January 1978. There wasn't a more exciting or memorable finish in the two years of the rebel World Series movement – and the scars were deep.

Greg Chappell had been involved in some stoushes and scandals – like the time he announced his abdication to Kerry Packer's World Series rebels while still captain of traditional Australia in 1977 – but none are as remembered, or have remained as publicly prominent, as the infamous win-at-all-costs underarm he ordered to end an unforgettable third one-day final against Geoff Howarth's touring Kiwis on 1 February 1981.

The best-of-five finals series was tied 1–1 coming to Melbourne. After an exhausting schedule of five Tests and 10 lead-up World Series games, Chappell didn't want to extend the finals any longer than was absolutely necessary. He was virtually out on his feet, desperate to get off the field and momentarily forget about cricket in a week which not only included at least one more World Series final, but yet another Test match.

Earlier, in Australia's innings, he'd been brilliantly caught in the outfield by Martin Snedden, but neither umpire could confirm the catch and Chappell went from 58 to 90, the bonus runs being all-important in the match fortunes. The Kiwis were livid, especially Mark Burgess, who had been close to the catch, and Snedden, who angrily clashed with Chappell. Lance Cairns, the bowler, said, 'It was the most brilliant catch I've ever seen . . . Greg watched it, then turned away. He simply did not want to believe his eyes.' But umpire Peter Cronin, at the bowler's end, wasn't absolutely sure if the catch had been taken. His partner, Don Weser, in one of his first internationals, had been watching the batsmen running between wickets. There was only one avenue open to Cronin: he ruled Chappell not out.

Thanks to opener Bruce Edgar's unbeaten century and some sloppy Australian fielding, the Kiwis clawed their way towards the 236-run target. As Trevor Chappell began the final over, 15 runs were still required. In the run-chase, Richard Hadlee and Ian Smith fell and with one ball remaining, seven were needed to win and six to tie. Greg Chappell sat down in the outfield, at the foot of the MCC's cigar stand, believing the game finally safe.

But as soon as he saw NZ's No. 10 McKechnie enter, picture-perfect flashbacks of Daniel's amazing swiped six in the same city three years earlier raced through his mind. Surely it couldn't happen again, could it? Forgetting his physical discomfort, he rose to his feet and started walking towards his brother, looking over his shoulder at the old manual scoreboard and double-checking the equation.

McKechnie, a rugby and cricket dual international, didn't have the air of a man who intended just to pat the last ball back to the bowler. He'd come to party. A first-ball six at the expansive MCG was a big ask, but he fully intended giving it a try. As he made his way from the players' viewing area and out of the shade down the race and onto the field, there was a roar of anticipation. Few of the world-record crowd of 52 990 had left. It had been a highly dramatic and entertaining game. Mathematically a glorious tie was still possible, even if the odds were astronomical.

As he was walking out, McKechnie was already focusing on the most likely area for hitting sixes. The huge square boundaries were out of the question. Even Lance Cairns with his trusty Excalibur bat would struggle to hit the east or west fences. Going straight was the answer. He reasoned that Chappell would try to bowl a yorker at leg stump and restrict the room in which to swing his arms. He would therefore step away at the point of delivery and swing as hard as he could, hoping to lift the ball over the mid-on fence and into the members – a hit of 85 metres from where he stood.

As he reached the centre square, the only players in his immediate vicinity were Rod Marsh standing near the stumps and the Chappell brothers at the far end.

'How are you at bowling your underarms?' big brother Greg was saying to Trevor.

'Oh, I don't know – why?'

'Well, you're about to find out. Don,' said Chappell, turning to umpire Weser, 'Trevor is going to bowl the last ball underarm.'

'I beg your pardon?'

'The last ball will be bowled underarm.'

'Hang on, I'll inform the batsman . . . and the other umpire.' Weser conferred with Cronin. When he told McKechnie, the New Zealander dropped his bat in amazement.

'It didn't enter my mind to say no,' said the younger Chappell. 'I actually didn't consider it to be a yes/no type of question. It was the captain of my team asking me to do something that was, at the time anyway, within the rules of the game. It seemed like a good idea.'

Hundreds of kilometres away in Adelaide, the Chappells' father, Martin, was watching on television. He instinctively knew what was happening. 'Trevor's going to bowl an underarm,' he told his wife, Jeanne. In the commentary box, Bill Lawry was incredulous. 'Would you believe it?' he said. Behind the wickets, Marsh was shaking his head. 'No, mate, don't do it,' he yelled, trying to be heard above the commotion. Trevor shrugged his shoulders, looked back at Greg at long-on and, from a two-step run-up, delivered a slow grubber. Even 'the Bradman of Bowls', Glyn Bosisto, would have approved of his style, but this was a cricket match. It had been almost 60 years since an underarm had been bowled at the MCG.

McKechnie blocked it, threw his bat up the wicket in disgust and stood in mid-pitch arms akimbo, defiantly glaring at Trevor. 'I thought to myself "They must be joking". I couldn't believe they'd stoop so low,' he said afterwards. At the non-striker's end Edgar stuck his two fingers up in a defiant gesture at the bowler before consoling McKechnie and, seeing the fans storming onto the field, running for the rooms.

Neither umpire had noticed that Dennis Lillee was outside the fielding limitation line and that technically it was a no-ball. An angry Howarth was one of the first to reach the harassed umpires. He was furious. 'Underarm bowling has been banned. You shouldn't have allowed the delivery,' he yelled, before giving the umpires a real serve. It wasn't until later that he learnt that the ruling applied only in England. In the VCA room, match referee Bob Parish was called to the phone. It was long-distance: Adelaide. Like everyone else, Don Bradman was incredulous.

If Greg Chappell could change one moment of his career, this would be it. If he had any idea of the furore the ball would cause, he would have backed down. But at the time, he was beyond reason. He had spent six and a half hours on the field and, as he told biographer Adrian McGregor, knew the action wasn't going to be well received. 'I expected a lot of people would say, "Tch, tch, not cricket", but quite honestly I didn't give a rat's tail. I was quite prepared for a rap over the knuckles if it saved us from an extra game.'

Umpire Weser said, 'He seemed the normal Greg Chappell to me. He didn't seem any different.'

The Australians sprinted off to widespread boos from all around the ground. Soft-drink cans and paper cups were thrown in their direction. One young girl ran at Chappell and said he had cheated. The Kiwi players stood at their open door, grim-faced, several spoiling for a fight. Watching from the Delegates' Rooms, a teary Sam Loxton, one of Bradman's Invincibles, made his way down the stairs and told Chappell it was a heck of a way to win a cricket match. 'You may have won the game, son, but you've lost a lot of friends,' he added.

No one spoke in the Australian dressing rooms. The silence was almost eerie and was broken only by the ringing of the telephone. 'Perth calling for Greg Chappell.'

'No, not here, you've rung the wrong place,' said Trevor, who was nearest.

Next door, in the New Zealand rooms, Burgess had hurled his cup and saucer against a wall and Howarth and manager Ian Taylor were hurriedly examining the tour conditions. If that was the way the Australians wanted to play it, they could have some of their own medicine in Sydney. Senior Australian Cricket Board officials Parish and Ray Steele moved among the New Zealand players, apologising profusely.

High in the Olympic Stand, where Richie Benaud and the Channel

Nine commentary team were based, Benaud was strong, eloquent and unequivocal. Benaud believed that Chappell must have miscalculated in the final hour; otherwise his No. 1 bowler Dennis Lillee, rather than Trevor Chappell, would have bowled the fateful last over. 'Now, you can have your own opinions about that [the delivery]. Let me tell you what mine is. I think it was a gutless performance from the Australian captain.'

Nor did other past and present players hold back their views. Tony Greig called for Chappell's resignation as captain. Keith Miller said one-day cricket had died and Chappell should be buried with it. 'Just how far does the lure of the lolly [money] go to deprive us of basic self-respect?' said the legendary Bill O'Reilly. 'Just goes to show you,' said Doug Walters, doing his best to defuse the tension in the Australian rooms, 'the game's not over until the last ball is bowled!'

'Just wait until the Poison Typewriter Club [the press] gets to you,' said Lillee. For once, someone else was in trouble.

THE PREVIOUS UNDERARM to be bowled at the MCG occurred in 1922–23. Victoria's Arthur Liddicutt bowled one shortly after the tea interval during a day-long partnership by MCC pair Geoffrey Wilson and Wilfred Hill-Wood. According to historian Ray Webster, the delivery was a one-off and was bowled purely out of frustration at the stonewalling tactics of the two Englishmen. Hill-Wood took more than three hours to make 50 and more than four hours for his 100.

AS HE WAS making his way back from the most acrimonious press conference of his life, Howarth was stopped by Marsh in the narrow passageway leading from the downstairs Delegates' Room into the player rooms.

'I don't want this to go any further because if the team hear that I'm saying it, it doesn't do the team situation much good,' Marsh said. 'But I want to apologise for what happened. It shouldn't have happened. I was not in agreement and told Greg so. Please accept my apologies.'

Looking to escape the spotlight, Chappell flew to Sydney that night along with Lillee, Len Pascoe and Walters. He didn't have to listen to the ABC to realise he had created a monster. The underarm led every news bulletin. He had told journalists afterwards it was within the laws of the game as they currently stood. What he didn't say was that he was at breaking point and not fit to be captain. That was to come later.

Awoken at midnight at his Wellington home by a journalist calling from the *Sydney Morning Herald*, NZ's Prime Minister Robert Muldoon exploded, calling it 'the most disgusting incident in the history of cricket'. He said canary yellow was a most appropriate central colour of Australia's one-day uniform. 'If the bloody Australians want it, they'll get it fair between the eyes,' he said.

The next morning, at Tullamarine and Kingsford Smith airports, there was an incredible commotion. 'It was as though we had assassinated the president of the United States,' said Allan Border in *An Autobiography*. 'There were camera crews, reporters, photographers, all trying to get somebody to say something.'

At the Sheraton Hotel in Sydney Chappell was also being besieged, his phone having first rung at 6 a.m. Amidst calls for his resignation, he said he had been hunted by all sorts of people. 'I fair dinkum expected somebody to crawl through the window,' he said.

GRUBBY END TO A GREAT GAME, said the *Age* in its editorial. 'Australian cricket is in disgrace and the country's reputation severely damaged.' Others were just as damning.

- 'It [was an action] which has since been described as shameless, spineless, disgraceful, churlish and gutless. The Australian sporting image has been tarnished as never before.' – *Australian*
- 'Greg reached an all-time low in win-at-all-costs gamesmanship.' – Melbourne *Herald*
- 'One ball dints Australia's image as a sporting nation.' – *Sydney Morning Herald*

- 'There could not be a lonelier man in the cricket world than Greg Chappell.' – London *Times*

In Wellington, a flag flew at half mast over the office of a big Australian insurance firm.

SOON AFTER THE underarm, Qantas ran an ingenious newspaper advertisement for a special $299 return airfare to New Zealand. The advertisement featured a picture of the underarm delivery along with the caption: 'NZ$299 return. Once again the opposition will accuse us of cheating.'

CHAPPELL WAS REPRIMANDED by the ACB and formally reminded of his responsibilities as national captain in upholding the spirit of the game. A telephone link-up of ACB delegates immediately outlawed underarm bowling. Those who wanted him to stand down accepted his carefully worded statement of regret: 'I have always played cricket within the laws of the game. I took a decision yesterday which, whilst within the laws of cricket, in the cool light of day, I recognise as not being within the spirit of the game. The decision was made whilst I was under pressure and in the heat of the moment. I regret the decision. It's something I'd never do again.'

Even his brother Ian asked, 'Fair dinkum, Greg, how much pride do you sacrifice to win $35 000?' According to biographer McGregor, Jeanne Chappell rang Ian and said that as Greg's brother he should have shown more loyalty. 'I'd never say anything against you if you did something wrong,' she said. 'I'd always support you even if you were on a murder charge.' Ian said he couldn't make a 'wishy-washy' comment. He told his mother that if that was the only mistake Greg made in his first-class career, he would go well.

The Board offices in Jolimont on the fringes of the MCG received more than 1000 letters, 90 per cent of them castigating Chappell. Within 24 hours, the *Sydney Morning Herald* had received more than

100 letters complaining of Chappell's action. At the *Courier-Mail* in his home town of Brisbane, however, letters were more plentiful in his defence.

Chappell was booed walking onto the Sydney Cricket Ground for the fourth final the following day. He was a little apprehensive coming to the wicket until opposing captain Howarth patted him on the backside and wished him good luck. On reaching 50, Chappell raised his bat defiantly to the Channel Nine commentary box. In a torrent of criticism, none had stung like Richie Benaud's. Chappell had been captain of Australia on and off since 1975. Richie, more than anyone else, should have realised the increased pressure and demands of the modern game. Chappell finished on 87 to spearhead an Australian win and be named Player of the Finals.

On his retirement three years later, he had led in 48 Tests and 49 one-day internationals, comprising more than 250 days play. Yet for many people, Greg Chappell's leadership is best remembered for those 60 seconds late on a cricket day that Melburnians still vividly recall as 'Black Sunday'.

'I shouldn't have been out there,' Chappell said in an interview with Sydney writer Mike Koslowski on the 15th anniversary of the incident. 'Mentally I was struggling to get through the season. I wasn't fit on the day . . . had I not been out there or had I been in a better frame of mind, it would never have happened.' He said his actions were 'indefensible' but that the captaincy demands were so intense and the schedule so exhausting that he had simply cracked. Soon afterwards, the ACB had appointed a full-time media manager to lessen the load.

'It wasn't something done in isolation,' Chappell told Koslowski. 'It was the culmination of years of frustration, anger and annoyance at the way we were being treated.' Marsh, who had opposed the underarm, said 'it was about 48 degrees' in the centre of the MCG and that Chappell 'was simply gone'.

McKechnie never played cricket for New Zealand again. Looking back, he said the incident should have been dead and buried the following day.

Asked how he would have reacted in a similar circumstance, English Test umpire Don Oslear said, 'I might have said, "Come on Greg. It has been a tremendous game. Let's bowl it up."'

THERE WAS A comical finale to the Chappell grubber, in Sydney in between finals. Doug Walters said if anyone tried to bowl at him underarm he would hit it for six. Allan Border was immediately sceptical and bet $10, with Rod Marsh acting as referee and stakesman.

After practice the trio went out to the SCG No. 2 oval and Border bowled an underarm. Walters waltzed out to meet it, flicked the ball up with his foot and hit it high over the boundary and onto nearby Driver Avenue! An incredulous Border appealed for lbw. 'Nar, not out,' said Marsh. 'He was too far down the wicket.'

The noise was so tremendous I doubt whether [Trevor] Chappell even heard Marsh. But no one went up to Chappell to point out the consequences.

New Zealand all-rounder LANCE CAIRNS

Greg Chappell brought a holocaust of criticism down on his head and his prestige as a sportsman was left in the dust. **NZ Test selector DON NEELY**

Many will remember Greg Chappell from his actions that day – I prefer to remember him for being one of the great batsmen.

NZ wicketkeeper IAN SMITH

To this day I have no idea why he did it . . . we were all under pressure but it would never cross my mind to do anything so blatantly stupid and unsportsmanlike. **NZ captain GEOFF HOWARTH**

It was a bloody stupid thing to do and I hope it will never happen again.

HAROLD LARWOOD

My main regret was that Trevor probably suffered more than anybody else. That was unfair. He didn't have any say in it. **GREG CHAPPELL**

Fifty thousand people left the MCG today feeling just like I did when I saw the movie The Sting; *they were shaking their heads asking: 'What the hell happened there?'* **DOUG WALTERS**

Chappell should perhaps have been praised rather than pilloried for exposing, albeit to his own advantage, a glaring loophole in the laws. **DENNIS LILLEE**

I felt like crawling into a big hole and wished I'd never played the game.

KEITH MILLER

The chance of my hitting a six must have been one in thousands.

BRIAN McKECHNIE

Yes, Greg Chappell, you may be a great man who doesn't sledge, never unnecessarily appeals when bowling and never shows disapproval of the decisions of umpires. But in a game surrounded by fine sportsmen intent only on playing the game, you dared to publicly display that you were prepared to win without actually cheating. You should have been more underhanded.

Brisbane journalist HUGH LUNN

TREVOR CHAPPELL SAYS New Zealanders have always treated him kindly and with respect since the underarm incident. 'Mostly the incident is taken in a light-hearted manner,' he says. 'There were certainly plenty of comments from the crowds at the cricket, but nothing more than at games I've been involved in back in Australia.' He has been invited to NZ three times directly as a result of the underarm, on the first occasion to play in a double-wicket competition. His partner? Brian McKechnie!

What particularly upsets Chappell is that the incident has been linked with bigger scandals such as the betting and match-fixing allegations which saw Saleem Malik, Mohammad Azharuddin and Hansie Cronje disgraced. 'Cricket is not the gentleman's game that it has long been made out to be,' he said. 'I have no problem accepting that the underarm was not in the spirit of the game and shouldn't have happened, but it wasn't cheating and it was nothing like the controversies of Bodyline or match-fixing.'

8. The ultimate raid: World Series Cricket

When Kerry Packer pirated the cream of the world's finest to form his rebel cricket troupe in 1977, it smashed an establishment monopoly, introduced exciting, entertaining innovations to a captive new television audience and ushered a fresh prosperity into the game.

In a masterstroke of bold, top-secret planning that changed the very dynamics of the game, the world's best players signed contracts guaranteeing them the security they had been denied for years. Establishment cricket was plunged into a bitter 23-month conflict with Australia's richest man, who was hell-bent on obtaining exclusive television rights for his Nine Network.

Packer's action also triggered some extraordinary moments, such as the time in the Australian rooms during the establishment's mega-event, Melbourne's Centenary Test, when World Series Cricket's Austin Robertson jnr handed an envelope containing a hefty sign-on advance to one of the star signees, Doug Walters, with a cheery 'Here's your theatre tickets, Dougie.'

NOT ONLY WAS the unforgettable Centenary Test cricket's ultimate week-long party, it was also the venue for Kerry Packer's coup de grâce, when the business tycoon knew that he had Australian cricket at his mercy. After the rejection of his $2.5 million offer for exclusive television rights, Packer went on a revenge mission with all of his renowned focus and ruthlessness.

Believing the ACB to be insular and ultraconservative, Packer said, 'We'll do all we can to cooperate with the Cricket Board and, if they cooperate with us, there is no reason why Test cricket as it is now will be affected. But if they don't, they'll walk straight into a meat mangler.'

Packer refined and expanded the embryonic World Series Cricket (WSC) concept into a brilliantly contrived, controversial assault on the game and its traditions. So successful was the raid on the establishment's finest that Packer's wish to underwrite a series of matches for his prime-time summer television audiences was transformed into a full-blown international triangular tournament involving the game's champion players.

It was just three years since Kerry's father, Sir Frank Packer, had died and passed on his flourishing newspaper and television empire to his son, a hard-nosed, domineering, sports-loving businessman used to getting his own way. As his intermediaries made contact with the very best players worldwide, Packer unearthed a wall of resentment that administrations had preferred to ignore for years.

In the game's biggest controversy since Bodyline, not only did world stars and Test captains such as England's Tony Greig and West Indies' Clive Lloyd turn renegade, so did every notable Australian player – including the major box office attractions the Chappell brothers, Dennis Lillee, Rod Marsh and, in the second year of WSC, the world's fastest bowler, Jeff Thomson.

In two seasons, Packer's expenditure ballooned to as much as $30 million – the actual figure has never been published – but he had gained 600 hours of television for his network. He was preparing to go again into a third season, too, with a Pakistani visit followed by a tour of India when the ACB, having accumulated heavy losses throughout the furore, brought an end to the impasse. A hush-hush meeting between Packer and Don Bradman was critical in the compromise.

The Board granted its arch-foe exclusive television rights for 10 years and totally reassessed its scale of player payments, including the provision for bonus prize monies. WSC players were allowed to re-enter official competition without prejudice or penalty, many having originally been turned away from even their long-time club teams. In Perth, the West Australian Cricket Association had banned them altogether. In Melbourne, the highest-available standard to rebels Ray Bright and Richie Robinson was suburban club cricket. Max Walker spent the early weeks of the season with Melbourne's Club XI.

Many of the players referred to Packer as 'The Godfather', someone who genuinely loved to dote on and mix with the sports stars he so admired. 'He kept every promise and then some,' said one leading 'Packerite', Ian Redpath. 'I snapped my Achilles in my second game and Packer came down by helicopter, landed on Kardinia Park and came up to see me at the Geelong hospital. He even organised a TV for me.

'Kerry Packer had the resources and the medium of his television network to do the experiments the ACB had never contemplated. In the end both learned from each other.'

Redpath earned more in two years of WSC than he did in six years with the ACB, without the heartaches. 'For the first time players had a financial base in which they could plan their lives,' he said. 'And Packer realised just how important cricket's traditions were. The cricket was hard and tough. And we went all over the place. But Packer himself was very, very good. I'd come back from playing every Test in the West Indies [in 1973] and didn't even get a game the following summer against New Zealand. I couldn't afford not to play [WSC].'

Not only did the ACB learn its lessons and restructure player conditions, it based many of its future financial projections around the day/night formulas which had so flourished under Packer. Even his establishment arch-rival Bob Parish freely concedes that cricket owes

Packer deep gratitude for its facelift, which ushered in fresh riches and followers and dramatically raised the profile of the game. 'He did the game a good turn,' he said. 'With the expense of all the court cases, some we won, some we lost, cricket was losing a lot of money.'

Day/night cricket has proved a veritable money tree for cricket boards. There has also been a considerable flow-on effect, with one-day fans also following Test match cricket. Until Packer stamped his imprimatur so boldly on the game, short-version cricket had been little more than an incidental for the ACB and the very first one-day international fixture arose purely by chance.

Before WSC, the only major grounds with lights were football stadiums. Now all Australian grounds are floodlit except cricket's southernmost citadel, Hobart's riverside Bellerive Oval. And at the bastions of traditional cricket – the Melbourne Cricket Ground and elsewhere – the Packer blueprint is now fashionable, with quality turf wickets being prepared in huge concrete bases off-site before cranes lift them into position at the start of each season. Equally important are other innovations such as coloured clothing, numerous television cameras that give fans the best seat in the house from both ends, on-field microphones and white balls with black sightscreens.

Packer changed the game's rules and the lives of not only the world's Test stars of the 1970s, but those who followed. He may have been brazen and abrupt – the ACB first found out about the rebel matches via the newspapers – but the new vigour and interest cricket enjoyed through dual tours and the World Series triangulars encouraged a captive new audience.

Pre-Packer, Australia's world-champion cricketers, including some of the game's most charismatic stars, were earning no more than $66 a day plus expenses. While their fees had ballooned by the time of the Centenary Test, the idea of an updated provident fund had floundered. So discontented was the influential elite that most couldn't sign quickly enough.

Lillee was one of the first to commit. According to his manager Austin Robertson, he was being paid 'fish and chip money'. With no base contract and ongoing physiotherapy bills to pay for a bad back sustained while representing Australia, what choice did he have? Lillee believed that starting salaries for the game's best cricketers should be $25 000 minimum. Under a rival promoter, he was to receive a guaranteed $35 000 a year for three years.

As others joined in the crusade, a bitter wedge was driven between the ACB and its leading players, with the Board too late to recognise the level of discontent. When it did act and agreed to lift match fees, the breakaway plans were already hatching.

In the 1990s champion cricketers threatened strike action to help their state-level peers win a bigger slice of cricket's thriving income streams. The high-profile frontliners of the 70s did the band of young, up-and-coming stars a financial favour by activating a set of lucrative salaries and contracts that form the basis of the game's growing professionalism into the new millennium. Today's champions can play well into their mid-30s, even at state level, whereas their predecessors would have long retired to re-enter private enterprise and work at reviving their cricket-deprived personal incomes. Bob Cowper, for example, one of the few to score 300 in a Test match, played his last Test match for Australia at 27 so he could pursue a career in international finance. The elegant Victorian Paul Sheahan was 26 and only just entering his prime years when he retired to concentrate on school teaching.

Even the best players were uncertain of ongoing selection and the modest rewards it brought. Graham McKenzie was never the same after his stunning omission as a 26-year-old in mid-series against the 1967–68 Indians, explained by the selectors as allowing them to experiment with pace back-ups with an English tour looming. McKenzie was the world No. 1 at the time – one journalist in Perth described him as 'more popular than Vegemite, more famous than the Swan River'. In his previous Test in Melbourne he had taken 7/66 and 3/85, part of an effort that saw the Indians at 5/25 shortly after midday on the opening morning in the most stunning start to an MCG Test in more than 50 years.

When Bob Simpson announced that he would be retiring at the end of the series against the touring Indians, having just captained Australia in a record 29th Test, he too was dropped, and like McKenzie missed a match fee. Morale-wise the non-selection was a public relations disaster for the Board and widened even further the gulf between the administrators and players. Soon afterwards, at the conclusion of an arduous six-month tour of Ceylon, India and South Africa, the idea of a fifth unscheduled Test match in Johannesburg was abandoned over the size of the extra fee to be paid to each Australian player. Vice-captain Ian Chappell and McKenzie led the dissenters when the Board offered an additional $200 per player (compared with an at-home match fee of $180). Chappell had wanted $500. He believed after such a long campaign that the Board owed it to the players to give them a decent bonus. 'We were sick of being pushed around,' he said in his book *The Cutting Edge*.

KERRY PACKER'S INTEREST in underwriting a rebel series and providing his network with hours of extra, potentially top-rating sport was fuelled by the game's 1970s boom period when the Australian XI under Ian Chappell revived and rose to world-champion status in front of huge, adoring nationwide television audiences.

During the 1970–71 Ashes series, for the first time viewers in the capital cities and most major country areas were able to watch virtually every ball via the ABC. The six Tests drew more than 600 000 spectators, while the daily television audience by the summer's climactic end was said to be around one million. Between 1974–75 and March 1977 and the fabulous Centenary Test, more than two million fans attended 16 Tests, with millions more watching on TV. In 1977 Packer's Channel Nine offered £150 000 – twice the asking price – for exclusive rights to the Ashes series in England.

Once Packer started his revolutionary day/night match coverage, his network reported even bigger ratings. The first match under lights, at the Sydney Cricket Ground in late 1978, was a runaway success, with Packer ordering the gates to be opened after the dinner interval. While the cricket itself was mundane, more than 50 000 attended the match.

Richie Benaud, leading the Channel Nine commentary team, said it was one of the most wonderful sights he had witnessed. In *Not Just an Autobiography*, he said, 'The Hill was packed, the outer was packed. The members' stands were packed . . . the attraction of the day/night match, the excitement of the lights and the wonderful atmosphere combined to make it an evening I'll never forget.'

Tony Greig had echoed these thoughts on the first night at VFL Park in Waverley 12 months earlier. 'Between innings, we took supper in the underground restaurant and the sight that greeted us as we walked up to pitch level again was one that will live with most of us for the rest of our lives. More than 22 000 were in the stadium and the big-powered lights beaming down onto the green turf created a tingling, expectant atmosphere. There is something about sport at night which touches the nerve ends and this was no exception. We knew at that moment that the battle was being won.'

In other capital cities such as Adelaide, the one-day games, non-partisan as they were, also captured the imagination. The very first WSC one-dayer at Football Park, West Lakes, attracted just 1690 fans, but the last, when local hero David Hookes hit West Indian Andy Roberts for 2 sixes in a row, drew almost 20 000.

World Series also made money on its tour of the West Indies in 1979. By comparison, the ACB lost heavily in 1978–79 despite the presence of its traditionally biggest drawcard, England, for six Test matches.

WORLD SERIES PRODUCED many underrated on-field moments in its two years. Most Supertest participants agreed that it was the toughest, most satisfying cricket of their lives, even if television ratings and gate figures favoured establishment cricket.

Some of the performances of the high-profile attractions such as Lillee, Viv Richards, Greg Chappell, Barry Richards, Andy Roberts and a young David Hookes were breathtaking. With winner-take-all prize-money, the habit of tail-enders batting without helmets disappeared as fast bowlers ignored tradition and peppered their counterparts with almost as many bouncers as the top-order batsmen.

The most intriguing aspect of WSC, however, was its very implementation. How could a private promoter so boldly usurp the ruling body and secretly sign the cream of its stars, many during their finest hour? Those responsible for the recruiting operation, Austin Robertson and John Cornell, still marvel at the ease of the strike.

Lillee was the initial go-between who made most of the introductions in the opening months of 1977. While most meetings were in dressing-room corners and hotels, others were in less salubrious surroundings. In Doug Walters' case, it was a dusty, out-of-the-way cement bunker at the back of Auckland's Eden Park. Waiting for Walters in the room, which had no chairs and a solitary light globe only just hanging from a thread from the roof, Cornell – alias 'Strop' from the TV comedy *The Paul Hogan Show* – couldn't help himself. 'Dougie,' he said, looking serious. 'Don't suppose you can lend me a couple of bucks!'

The Centenary Test in March provided the perfect forum to consummate the deals, not only with present players but with those like Redpath and McKenzie, who had retired but were attending the match as guests of the ACB. Eleven of the 12 Centenary Test Australians (all except Gary Cosier) had been earmarked by sole selector Ian Chappell. Most signed on the spot. While all of them knew they were risking long-term bans, the prospect of being part of 'The Best versus The Rest' breakaway matches was exciting, and the two- and three-year contracts guaranteed money only achievable in traditional ranks over a six- or seven-year period – *if* their form was good enough to keep them in the Test XI.

For the leading West Indians like Richards, Michael Holding and Co., their $25 000 a year salaries represented more than four times the money earned touring England with the official West Indian team the previous winter. Unlike the Australians, the WSC matches were unlikely to affect their international schedules. 'We weren't philanthropists. We had a job to do,' said Robertson. 'There was no "Ha-ha, this is behind everyone's back."'

Only a few of the Rest of the World squad rejected the advances, the most notable being England's Geoff Boycott, who was immediately replaced by Tony Greig as World XI skipper. Most players queued to join. Some who were uninvited were shattered, like the just-retired Australian leg-spinner Terry Jenner, who was playing suburban turf competition in Adelaide.

Packer had initially tried to deal with the Board, only to be told that broadcasting negotiations had already been completed with the ABC – and at a fraction of Packer's offer of $500 000 a year. 'C'mon now, we're all harlots,' Packer said in a meeting with the ACB's two most senior officials, chairman Bob Parish and treasurer Ray Steele. 'We all have our price. What's yours?' When told that only the formalities were to be completed for a new three-year deal, Packer said he'd offer $1.5 million over three years *after* the ABC contract had expired.

Until then, the ACB's annual sponsorship stream and surpluses had revolved around the corporate support of its No. 1 backer, the Benson & Hedges Company. Never before had an entrepreneur ever offered anything like the money Packer was talking. 'I could tell by their looks,' Packer said later in a court hearing. When Parish demurred and suggested it best for Packer to try again in three years, a collision course was inevitable.

By May, 35 of the world's finest players had signed with JP Sport, Robertson and Cornell's sports promotions company, at a cost of more than $2.6 million. Most agreed to terms of two or three years. Some, like steely Englishman John Snow, then 35, committed for only one.

Each player approached kept the details confidential. 'But there were no secrecy clauses or anything like that,' said Robertson. 'They were just asked to keep it to themselves. Their word was good enough for me.'

Nothing was leaked in the press – though in April there was a single-column item in a South African Sunday paper with an indirect reference to a privately promoted international cricket series likely to involve four of the leading Springbok players.

On the last day of the Centenary Test, with Australia in sight of its 45-run win, Rod Marsh, having just agreed to sign, took up his usual position behind the stumps after the lunch break and said to Greg Chappell at slip, 'Well, pal, looks like this is about the last time we're going to be standing out here for a while.'

With his best poker face, Chappell said, 'What do you mean?'

'You bloody well know what I mean,' said Marsh, smiling.

THREE OF THE few big-name players World Series missed in their worldwide raids on the game's elite were England's Geoff Boycott, South African master Graeme Pollock and India's Sunil Gavaskar.

Gavaskar was committed to come to Australia anyway with the 1977–78 Indians, while Pollock and fellow South African signee Denys Hobson were late exclusions after members of the West Indian team, particularly Jamaican fast bowler Michael Holding, said they were not prepared to play alongside anyone with direct links to apartheid cricket. Neither Pollock nor Hobson had played professionally outside South Africa. Packer met with Jamaican Prime Minister Michael Manley and a compromise was achieved. WSC agreed to contract only those South Africans who had played at English county level.

Soon afterwards, Packer expanded his operation to include an entire West Indies squad, 11 of whom had toured England in 1976. He hosted a party for the West Indian players, wives and partners at the luxurious Sandy Lane Hotel in Barbados, using his private jet to help pick up the guests from each of the islands.

Packer had earlier won an injunction and claimed damages in the London High Court in an action against the ICC and the English Test and County Cricket Board, which had decided from 1 October 1977 that any WSC-contracted players would face Test bans. In a marathon hearing which went into a seventh week, Justice Slade said such a ban was an unnecessary restraint of trade. He was surprised that a private promoter had not challenged establishment cricket earlier.

The 66 players contracted to World Series Cricket were:

AUSTRALIA (28): Ian Chappell (captain), Ray Bright, Greg Chappell, Trevor Chappell, Ian Davis, Ross Edwards, Gary Gilmour, David Hookes, Martin Kent, Bruce Laird, Rob Langer, Dennis Lillee, Ashley Mallett, Mick Malone, Rod Marsh, Rick McCosker, Graham McKenzie, Kerry O'Keeffe, Len Pascoe, Wayne Prior, Ian Redpath, Richie Robinson, Jeff Thomson, Max Walker, Doug Walters, Graeme Watson, Kepler Wessels, Denis Yagmich.

WEST INDIES (18): Clive Lloyd (captain), Jim Allen, Richard Austin, Colin Croft, Wayne Daniel, Roy Fredericks, Joel Garner, Gordon Greenidge, Desmond Haynes, Michael Holding, David Holford, Bernard Julien, Collis King, Deryck Murray, Albert Padmore, Vivian Richards, Andy Roberts, Lawrence Rowe.

REST OF THE WORLD (20): Tony Greig (captain), Dennis Amiss, Alan Knott, John Snow, Derek Underwood, Bob Woolmer (England); Eddie Barlow, Garth Le Roux, Mike Procter, Clive Rice, Barry Richards (South Africa); Asif Iqbal, Haroon Rashid, Imran Khan, Javed Miandad, Majid Khan, Mushtaq Mohammad, Sarfraz Nawaz, Zaheer Abbas (Pakistan); Richard Hadlee (New Zealand).

Alvin Kallicharran (West Indies) withdrew; Intikhab Alam (Pakistan) originally signed but wasn't required.

PETER MCFARLINE, CRICKET writer with the Melbourne *Age*, had known since March that something big was about to break. A contact high up in cricket administration had asked him to try and find out if there was any substance to the story said to involve some leading players and a series of exhibition games. In association with Alan Shiell, an Adelaide-based journalist with the Murdoch group, McFarline went delving. A colleague, Mike Sheahan, who was in New Zealand for the short tour which preceded the Centenary Test, had reported back that the television personality John Cornell was spending a lot of time with the team, especially Dennis Lillee. When quizzed, he had said it was all about arranging some TV work for Australia's No. 1 fast bowler to help supplement his cricket income.

McFarline went to England none the wiser, but keen to do some more exploration of his own. The Australians were at Hove, playing an inconsequential county game against Sussex, when the story finally came together. Shiell learned about it over lunch with the manager of Barry Richards, the great South African whose Test career had tragically finished so early. McFarline, too, found out much in conversation with the legendary John Arlott, the doyen of English broadcasters.

At last some of the throwaway lines from cricketing acquaintances and friends that they would be seeing him for Christmas started to make sense. 'Sheff [Shiell] and I went for a walk,' said McFarline in the *Age*, 'and pooled our information . . . Together we went to the Australian dressing room and asked to see Greg Chappell, the captain. After explaining what we knew, Chappell uttered one of sport's great untruths. Leaning against the door, he said, "It sounds like a good idea. I would like to know more about it." With that, he retired to the sanctuary of the dressing room. But Shiell and I had our story. With a lot of guessing we came up with 44 names we believed had signed with Packer. Forty-four out of 52 [who initially signed] wasn't bad.'

When news of the scoop circulated that night at a party at Tony Greig's house in Hove, beginning a wave of headlines which made the Ashes series seem inconsequential, Chappell wrote to Parish and Sir Donald Bradman outlining his reasons for signing with World Series Cricket and saying that the players hoped they could play in the private matches with Board permission. Deep down he knew that was an impossibility and resigned himself to never playing for Australia again after the tour's end. Chappell had committed to Packer for five years. Twelve of the other 16 tourists to England in 1977 had also agreed to join.

Had the ACB had their time again they might have withdrawn the rebels then and there and picked an entirely new squad. It was still almost six weeks before the first of the five Ashes Tests. Maybe they were still basking in the euphoria of the Centenary Test. The team battled on but was ultimately thrashed 3–0 and in fact won only eight of their 31 matches on tour. There was little camaraderie or focus. Their hearts may have been in it, but their minds were elsewhere.

Chappell's biographer Adrian McGregor said that on Parish's arrival in London in June for an ICC meeting, Chappell saw him in the foyer of the team's hotel, the Waldorf. Chappell said, 'Excuse me, Bob. I'd like to have a chat with you at some stage.' Parish replied, 'I don't think we have anything to discuss.'

Given the enormity of their decision to leave the cricket fold, the failure of the 1977 team was understandable. They were facing lengthy bans, which for the younger players, in particular, left them alone and uncertain. The youngest, David Hookes, who had only just turned 22, had joined initially believing he could play both World Series and traditional cricket.

Even a convivial meeting with Packer and Cornell in Packer's swank private suite at the Dorchester had left questions unanswered. The itinerary was open-ended and dependent entirely on venues, which were still to be negotiated. It was debatable whether any of the usual mainstream grounds would be available. There was talk of bans and restraint-of-trade actions. Also weighing heavily was the public backlash against the players, who were perceived as mercenaries unconcerned with centuries of tradition. One newspaper dubbed the players 'The Dogs of Cricket'.

As team captain, Chappell was accused of betraying trust and

deceiving the Board. He was part of the player subcommittee established just a year previously to give players a stronger say in the running
of the game, including increased pay and improved conditions.

It was a troubled time and merely the prelude to almost two years
of accusations and division in a full-on, old-fashioned feud which cost
jobs and sponsorships, affected friendships, slashed dividends and
triggered heavy financial losses to both the states and the national
body.

MANY PEOPLE BELIEVE that Dennis Lillee's then-record haul of 355 wickets at Test
level would have extended well beyond the magical 400-wicket mark but for
his entry into WSC ranks, which cost him 24 traditional Tests. In reality, it is
doubtful if Lillee would have played much past 1977 in establishment cricket
unless payments and conditions had dramatically improved.

While he loved cricket and, in particular, bowling as fast as was
humanly possible, had World Series not evolved there would have come a
point well before his 30th birthday where Lillee might easily have quit big
cricket. For years, even the top-liners received only minimal rewards and as
Test selection was by invitation only, if a player preferred not to play there
were hundreds of others who would take his place.

Lillee's enthusiasm and motivation for the game were rekindled by
Packer's dollars and the challenge of the Supertests, which were played
with an unmatched intensity and hostility. When the plan was being
hatched and fine-tuned in New Zealand in early 1977, WSC recruiters
Austin Robertson and John Cornell conducted an experiment during the
Auckland Test. Having gleaned from Lillee how keenly the players would
compete for winner-take-all prize money, they offered him $50 for every
run he made over 20 and $200 for every wicket he took before their late-
afternoon connection back to Sydney. He made 23 not out and was savage
when Australian No. 11 Max Walker holed out. In the first 40 minutes
before Cornell and Robertson left, he took four wickets for a $950 bonus.

They seem to think we're only interested in bleeding the game dry, without worrying about the consequences it would have on future cricketers.

IAN CHAPPELL

There are five hundred thousand cricketers who would love to play for Australia for nothing.   **Australian Cricket Board of Control secretary ALAN BARNES**

We've been accused of betraying the game because we decided to play for the money we think we're worth.   **TONY GREIG**

People think I'm crook on cricket circuses. I'm not. I think there's a place for that kind of cricket – some place like Siberia.

Australian Cricket Board of Control treasurer RAY STEELE

He [Ian Chappell] pointed out that if I did not join WSC cricket, there would be something missing from my life.   **SUNIL GAVASKAR**

I feel privileged to have been personally involved in something which shook the cobwebs out of our game, breathed new life into it and elevated the professional cricketer to a financial status he had never before enjoyed.

VIV RICHARDS

World Series Cricket, or some such revolutionary institution, was always going to happen. You cannot suppress highly talented, intelligent men.

English cricket writer IAN WOOLDRIDGE

If you want to look at circuses, you'd better look at Australia fielding its third XI.

KERRY PACKER

The use of private promotional money to establish top-class cricket outside the existing international framework is undesirable.

English cricket writer ROBIN MARLAR

He [Kerry Packer] had no intention of screwing the [traditional] game, but the ACB forced his hand.   **DAVID HOOKES**

So who faced the first ball and scored the first runs in World Series Cricket? If you answered Rick McCosker, you're correct on both counts. 'It was the first ball of something completely new,' McCosker told Jim Tucker in *Inside Edge* magazine. 'We all knew we were involved in something taking a whole new direction. It was unsettling, tense and very exciting.'

FIVE WORLD SERIES HIGHLIGHTS

- Greg Chappell's Caribbean batting brilliance in 1979: he hit three 100s in consecutive Supertests, none better than his 150 in Port-of-Spain when he came to the wicket at 2/0 and left at 9/256, a match-winning contribution in a low-scoring game won by the WSC Australians by just 24 runs.
- Dennis Lillee's 7/23 to rout the WSC West Indies for 89 in the fourth Supertest at the SCG in 1978–79. He dismissed six of the top seven batsmen in one of his finest yet least-recognised moments.
- Barry Richards' masterly double-century for the WSC World XI in the Supertest at Gloucester Park in Perth in 1977–78. He added a WSC-record 369 for the first wicket with Gordon Greenidge (140). In came Viv Richards, who made 177!
- David Hookes' amazing 81 from as many balls at the Sydney Showgrounds in 1977–78. He struck Joel Garner for 17 and Michael Holding for 22 from an over in an exhilarating display on the fastest, bounciest strip any of the players had ever encountered. Shortly after the tea break he was in a car being driven by Kerry Packer to hospital, his jaw broken courtesy of Andy Roberts' change-up bouncer.
- Wayne Daniel's huge six off Mick Malone at VFL Park, Waverley, to give the West Indies victory in one of the first International Cup finals with just a ball to spare, in January 1978. According to author Gideon Haigh, WSC Australia captain Ian Chappell's parting comment to Malone just before the delivery was 'Just don't give him any room.'

9. Thrown out: Ian Meckiff

Until the rise of match-fixing in the 90s, throwing was cricket's most heinous crime. The most high-profiled victim was left-arm express bowler Ian Meckiff, a slim Victorian billed as an ogre by the English, who was to be brutally no-balled out of the game in an undignified public humiliation of the highest order.

SATURDAY 7 DECEMBER 1963 is an unforgettable date in Ian Meckiff's life. His joy and jubilation at his shock recall to the Australian team was short-lived. Outlawed for almost three years for a suspect action caused by his permanently bent left arm, Meckiff was no-balled four times for throwing in his return Test. Stunned by the renewed taints and wondering if he'd fallen victim to a conspiracy, he retired immediately from all grades of the game, even refusing to play social matches in case someone yelled out 'Chucker'.

In just one gut-wrenching over from the Vulture Street end of Brisbane's rustic Woolloongabba ground, Meckiff's world crumbled. His second, third, fifth and ninth deliveries of the opening Test against Trevor Goddard's 1963–64 South Africans were no-balled by South

Australian Colin Egar, standing at square leg. As he repeatedly thrust out his right arm, Egar knew the ramifications. As Australia's senior umpire, he believed he had a responsibility to make a stand. 'Let's face it, somebody had to do something,' he said.

He said he could have called more, but the over would never have finished. Only one other Australian had ever been called for throwing in a Test match – Ernie Jones, almost 70 years previously.

For years, illegal bowling had been an enormously emotional issue. Australian captain-to-be Bobby Simpson called it 'an insidious evil' and recommended all throwers be run out of the game. India's Nari Contractor almost died from a skull fracture after ducking into an express delivery from the highly suspect West Indian Charlie Griffith in Bridgetown. South Australia's new-ball pair Alan Hitchcox and Peter Trethewey possessed actions so questionable they were dubbed 'Pitch-cox' and 'Treth-throwy'. In England, the actions of several were also under question but umpires, loath to damage their own careers and those of rising young professionals, rarely created ripples.

Many thought Meckiff a scapegoat of a purge and even today, almost 40 years on, an uneasy and intriguing silence surrounds the politics of the affair.

'I'd never say that "Meck" was a chucker,' said team-mate Ian Redpath, one of three South Melbourne players along with Meckiff and debutant Alan Connolly in Australia's team on that fateful day. 'He was stiff.'

Even a captain as scrupulously honest and highly regarded as Richie Benaud has been targeted, the inference being that he was 'in' with the dramatic events and that he had deliberately batted higher than usual, at No. 6, so the selectors, chairman Sir Donald Bradman, Jack Ryder and Dudley Seddon, could choose a fifth specialist bowler as 'insurance'. The truth was that Benaud had no say in selection and like everyone else read about it in the newspapers. And when Meckiff was no-balled, Benaud was as upset as anybody. 'His eyes were fairly popping,' said wicketkeeper Wally Grout in *My Country's Keeper*.

Ryder, 74, who had given a lifetime of service to the game on and off the field, was staunchly pro-Meckiff and even after his no-balling in Brisbane, told Meckiff he'd be picking him again for Victoria if he so desired. He'd refused to study slow-motion film, saying that umpires had to judge on eyesight and so would he.

Redpath said Meckiff was a genuine in-swing bowler who, especially earlier in his career, hit the pitch as hard as anybody he opposed, including all the much-vaunted West Indians. 'It's a very difficult thing to do: throw a ball and swing it at the same time,' said Redpath. 'We were all very surprised.'

Despite his wickets blitz, guaranteed to embarrass even the thickest-skinned selector, Meckiff's against-the-odds recall was the bombshell of the long-awaited Springbok season which also introduced the hottest teenage talent in the world, 19-year-old left-hander Graeme Pollock from Port Elizabeth.

Meckiff's re-emergence as the most devastating strike bowler in the country had seen him amass 75 wickets in two full seasons – two-thirds being top-order wickets including 20 opening batsmen. In the first matches of the new season, he was again irresistible, with 11 wickets in Victoria's first two games. From the time Meckiff had dismissed Western Australia's star West Indian import Rohan Kanhai for 0 and 5 in Victoria's opening game of the 1961–62 domestic season in Melbourne, loyal Victorians had been advocating his return. Not only was he genuinely sharp, he could swerve the ball back into the right-handers and jag it away.

Eventually the support for him reached a crescendo. At the MCG, Melbourne's sporting shrine, he was almost as popular as wintertime folk hero, Ron Barassi. He'd hold the new ball up to them at the start of a game and they'd roar like they were at a football match. His team-mates called him 'The Lord Mayor' or 'The Count' and said if he ever stopped cricket, he could take a pick of any job in politics.

Among his backers were many media men with influence. They

became particularly vocal, especially when selectors looked to bolster an ageing pace attack with other, not-as-well-performed alternatives. Tall Victorian Colin Guest played in the third Ashes Test against Ted Dexter's tourists, and the much-admired South Australian star all-sportsman Neil Hawke in the fifth.

Few could argue with Guest's inclusion, even if it was to be a one-off. He'd taken 31 wickets in five matches and played for the Australian XI against the Englishmen. However, a month later when the athletic Hawke won his first cap, his figures of 17 wickets in eight matches paled against Meckiff's 41 in seven. He was strictly medium pace and relied mainly on seam rather than intimidating speed for his wickets.

When visiting South African captain Trevor Goddard casually mentioned his hunch that Meckiff would make Australia's first Test XI, an Australian Board of Control member immediately offered him 33/1. According to Ray Robinson, one of Australia's most noted cricket writers, at least two Board delegates, including Queensland's Clem Jones, had objected to Meckiff's recall. Even with his so-called 'new' action, they reckoned he was a thrower and should never again be promoted. Wasn't it the International Cricket Conference's desire to eliminate bowlers with suspect actions? The makers of the *ABC Cricket Book* penned a list of 25 potential Australian players likely to play in the 1963–64 Test series and Meckiff wasn't included.

Bradman and Ryder had watched Meckiff bowl in Victoria's Sheffield Shield game against Western Australia in Melbourne, a game in which he took the first five WA wickets to fall during an inspired opening spell of 5/34 in eight overs. At one point he was into his third over and had 3/0. When John Inverarity took a single to momentarily thwart Meckiff, the crowd booed.

In an extraordinary high-scoring start to the summer – in which Bobby Simpson's first four knocks were 359, 4, 246 and 247 not out – few fast bowlers had any form at all. The great Alan Davidson had retired. So had potential first change, Queensland all-rounder Ken

Mackay. Western Australia's strapping young paceman Graham McKenzie was a stand-alone No. 1 replacement despite having taken just five Shield wickets at an average of more than 90 apiece in the lead-ups.

But the depth in the back-up ranks fell away dramatically. In the absence of the left-armer Hugh Bevan, chosen for the Australian XI after snaring 13 wickets mainly with angle in two games against the visitors, McKenzie's new-ball partner for WA was an Englishman, Peter Loader. In South Australia, the new ball was shared by another player ineligible for the Test team, visiting West Indian Gary Sobers. New South Welshman Frank Misson hadn't figured in any of Australia's previous eight Test matches, controversial team-mate Gordon Rorke with the big drag had played his last interstate match, SA's Hawke was out of form and experimenting with his action, while Meckiff's club and Victorian team-mate Connolly was then an uncapped tearaway.

When Bevan failed to take a wicket against the Springboks for the Australian XI in the Melbourne 'Test trial' and Misson was only marginally more successful against the tourists in the following match – the same weekend in which Meckiff devastated the WA top-order – Bradman and Co. decided they had no choice but to pick the much-loved Victorian. Retirements of key players had left Australia vulnerable. The Springboks were shaping as a very powerful unit, Brisbane was a batting paradise and young Pollock a threat, as shown by his century-in-a-session against formidable New South Wales.

Despite the selectors' change-of-heart to recall Meckiff, it seemed it must have been a split vote. Or maybe they sought a once-and-for-all answer into the legality of Meckiff's action, with two neutral umpires making judgement away from Meckiff's home town. Egar's umpiring partner was Brisbane detective Lou Rowan, who said he was shocked when he heard of Meckiff's recall.

Meckiff himself said you could have knocked him down with a

feather. 'I still can't believe it has happened,' he told reporters. Three long, frustrating years in the wilderness were over. But more agony was ahead.

As a fourth-form student at Mordialloc–Chelsea high school in Melbourne, Ian Meckiff (who batted right-handed) once hit a ball over fully-grown pine trees bordering the school and onto the opposite side of the local creek, a huge hit, especially for a schoolboy.

As shown below, in his first four seasons of competitive cricket with the Mentone under 16s in the Frankston–Glenhuntly (later Federal) Cricket Association, Meckiff was a sensation, taking almost 200 wickets. Mentone Oval where he began his career on matting-covered concrete is now known as the Hogben-Meckiff Oval.

Season	Wkts	Ave
1947–48	26	11.31
1948–49	51	4.03
1949–50	62	3.20
1950–51	58	3.48

In his final year, aged 15, he played in the under 16s in the mornings and with South Melbourne in the afternoons. In 1951–52, having just turned 17, he opened the bowling in South's first-ever senior premiership. One of his team-mates, Jeff Hallebone, was to be stand-by player for Australia's 1956 touring team to England.

After seeing his cricket career end prematurely, Meckiff became a single figures golfer and reduced his handicap to three. He also rose to the rank of captain at the prestigious Victoria Golf Club, in tree-filled Cheltenham, south of Melbourne.

THE INTERNATIONAL OUTCRY against the legality of Meckiff's action had begun in the New Year of 1959 when Peter May's Englishmen were humbled for 87 with Meckiff, in only his sixth Test, taking 3/69 and 6/38. That night in the Melbourne *Herald*, Meckiff, the local hero, was accused of 'throwing England out' by just-retired Test player Johnny Wardle, his rapid-fire demolition sharing front page billing with a Soviet attempt to fire a rocket at the moon. Many in Fleet Street shared Wardle's indignation, one dubbing Meckiff a ferocious cheat who was bringing the game into disrepute.

In the *Age*, cricket writer Percy Beames had a more measured response: 'It is a great pity English pressmen had to wait until Meckiff's success on Saturday to launch their accusations against the fairness of his delivery,' he wrote. 'But it is not surprising. It has its precedent in the first match of the tour with West Australian Keith Slater. No exception was taken to Slater's bowling action until he burst into prominence by taking 4/17 in a devastating burst in the second innings. Immediately he was dubbed a chucker.'

For Meckiff, a softly-spoken father of two, who had never been called at any level, it was impossible to ignore the criticism, especially with the throwing controversy ballooning. In the 1960 English season, five county players were called and the South African Geoff Griffin reduced to bowling underarm after being repeatedly no-balled by England's No. 1 umpire, Sid Buller.

Australian administrators were so concerned that its potential 1961 Ashes attack could be decimated by similar calls that six months before the tour's scheduled start, it negotiated a truce where throwing *would* be allowed without penalty, at least for the first six weeks of the tour leading into the first Test. Only from 7 June would English umpires be permitted to call any suspect bowlers. Previously, if they had suspicions, they could object only in writing. It seemed an extraordinary compromise. As it eventuated, none of Australia's most suspect bowling specialists, Meckiff, Rorke or Slater, were chosen.

Meckiff's omission was particularly controversial, Victorians believing he'd been made a martyr. Other than the country's premier paceman, Alan Davidson from NSW, Meckiff was the most experienced fast bowler in the nation. He was also the fastest, despite being hamstrung in the only two Tests he did play in 1960–61, an Achilles injury re-flaring in the tied Test in Brisbane and a back problem ending his summer in mid-Test in Sydney.

Four fast bowlers were chosen: Davidson, who had played 34 Tests, Frank Misson three, Ron Gaunt one and Graham McKenzie none.

With the Australian Board of Control's 'no comment' contracts applying only to the 17-man squad, Meckiff released a book, *Thrown Out*, proclaiming his innocence. He'd been passed in five major cricket playing countries, Australia, New Zealand, South Africa, Pakistan and India, and was sick of being branded. Ever since the salvo from the English press, he'd been harassed, at practice, in his office, even on the golf course. If he happened to land in a bunker, wise-cracking partners told him to chuck it out.

Meckiff admitted his wristy, front-on action may not have been as pure as some, but any jerkiness was only an optical illusion. He'd been born with a permanently bent elbow, was unable to fully extend his arm and believed he remained within the laws and spirit of the game. Despite only a languid, 16-pace run-up and shortish follow-through, he could bowl at express pace thanks to being double-jointed in the shoulders, which allowed him extra flexibility.

A first-XI-standard cricketer with the famous South Melbourne club at 16, Meckiff had enjoyed a meteoric rise, making his first Australian touring team, to New Zealand in 1957, after just seven first-class matches. His demolition of England in his home-town debut in 1958–59 was to be his highpoint. And for two years he was the headline cricketer in the country, before suffering the ligament damage to his back in the 1960–61 Sydney Test which sidelined him for the rest of the summer.

Casting aside his immediate thoughts to retire after his non-selection for England, Meckiff began training with the South Melbourne footballers, looking to increase his endurance. He also modified his action leading into the popping crease, trying to keep his left arm as straight as possible.

Several at Board level, however, believed his action still regularly contravened. By not calling Meckiff and others with suspect actions, administrators believed they were inadvertently encouraging a legion of fresh chuckers.

At the centre of the issue was Sir Donald Bradman, Australia's selection chairman and prominent member of the Australian Cricket Board of Control. He and the chairman Bill Dowling had been to London where the issue was keenly debated by the International Cricket Conference, the game's ruling body. As part of a clean-up campaign, it was decided that umpires would have full official backing to enforce Law 26 against those they felt were throwers or draggers (bowlers who flouted the no-ball rule by dragging their back foot across the crease). Each State held a forum involving captains, senior players and umpires. In Adelaide, at the old members' dining room, Bradman made an address, reinforcing the need for bowlers with suspect actions to be discouraged.

In the opening months of 1963, Meckiff was twice no-balled for throwing, by Jack Kierse in Adelaide and second-game umpire Bill Priem in Brisbane. And in 1963–64, 11 players in club ranks around Australia were called. Egar, who had stood in nine of the previous 10 Australian Test matches, led by example, targeting two Adelaide club players, West Torrens' Fred Bills and a long-time offender, Prospect's Tom Watt. Two years earlier, at Sheffield Shield level, he'd caused a stir by standing back from the bowler's end stumps and twice calling South Australian Brian Quigley at the Adelaide Oval. Quigley never represented his State again.

Until January that year, one of Meckiff's biggest allies had been his Victorian captain Bill Lawry. During the Adelaide Test, Bradman held a dinner for the visiting Sheffield Shield captains at his home in suburban Kensington. Lawry, Richie Benaud (NSW), Barry Shepherd (WA) and Ken Mackay (Queensland) were present. He showed frame-by-frame film of Meckiff and others with suspect actions. The case against Meckiff was damning, even with his so-called 'new' action.

Previously Lawry had sided with Jack Ryder. He didn't believe Meckiff was a thrower. 'But that evening . . . a camera showed that Ian Meckiff bent his left arm at the point of delivery,' he said.

In what amounted to the first emphatic use of video film technology in Australian cricket, it was clear that when slowed down, Meckiff's action contravened the laws and spirit of the game. Benaud's reaction was immediate. He said he wouldn't continue to bowl anyone who had been called for throwing. Furthermore, he'd not bowl anyone in his team he considered suspect. Yet, just 10 months later, here he was being asked to captain a player whose action had been damned and by one of the people who selected him, Bradman.

As Lou Rowan and Col Egar walked onto the 'Gabba for the start of the Test, they already knew their ends. Rowan, being from Brisbane, would take the northern end and Egar, from Adelaide, the south. It was a habit they were to have through all 19 of their Tests together.

WILL HE, OR WON'T HE?, the *Courier-Mail* had asked on the morning of the match, pondering Meckiff's fate.

Local umpire Bill Priem was so convinced that something was about to erupt that he'd taken his camera to the game and fully focused on Egar. Standing outside the square leg boundary filming Meckiff from in front of the scoreboard was South Africa's team manager Ken Viljoen.

After Australia had started with 400-plus and South Africa began its reply right on 2 p.m. on day two, Richie Benaud opened with Graham McKenzie down-breeze and Meckiff, the quicker of the two, coming back up the slope. Normally at the 'Gabba, the fastest bowler came down the hill from the Stanley Street end.

Egar, at square leg, was suddenly in the position of being the chief executioner. He allowed the first ball, to Springbok captain Trevor Goddard, to pass before making the first of four calls which created worldwide headlines and closed down a career.

'It was the biggest decision I had to make in cricket,' he said years later in the Melbourne *Sun*. 'I thought the first ball Meckiff bowled was suspect. On the next I took the plunge and called him. I think I heard a pin drop in the outer. It was that electric. Then I called him again . . . and again – four times in all. Meckiff bowled 12 balls and I would rate eight of them as illegal. But if I had kept calling him, when would he have finished his [8-ball] over?'

At the first call, Meckiff stood in mid-pitch bewildered. 'My God,' he thought to himself, 'He's called me.' Watching on from the pavilion, South African fast bowler Peter Pollock said it was as if 'an atomic bomb had hit the place'.

Benaud approached Meckiff in mid-over and said, 'I think we've got a problem here, Dad.' Meckiff replied, 'I think you're right.'

Others too had been no-balled for throwing, but not after being recalled from years in exile, like Meckiff. No cricketer had ever been so publicly humiliated.

CALLED FOR THROWING IN A TEST MATCH

1. Ernie Jones (Australia)	v England (Melbourne), 1897–98
	(by umpire James Phillips)
2. Tony Lock (England)	v West Indies (Kingston, Jamaica), 1953–54 (Perry Burke)
3. Geoff Griffin (South Africa)	v England (Lord's), 1960 (Sid Buller)
4. Haseeb Ahsan (Pakistan)	v India (Bombay), 1960–61 (S. K. Ganguli and A.R. Joshi)
5. Ian Meckiff (Australia)	v South Africa (Brisbane), 1963–64 (Col Egar)
6. Syed Abid Ali (India)	v New Zealand (Christchurch) 1967–68 (Fred Goodall)
7. David Gower (England)	v New Zealand (Nottingham), 1986 (Ken Palmer)
8. Henry Olonga (Zimbabwe)	v Pakistan (Harare), 1994–95 (Ian Robinson)
9. Muttiah Muralitharan (Sri Lanka)	v Australia (Melbourne), 1995–96 (Darrell Hair)
10. Grant Flower (Zimbabwe)	v New Zealand (Bulawayo), 2000–01 (Darrell Hair)

COL EGAR SAID the no-balling of Meckiff was the biggest decision he made in cricket. 'But if I had not made it, I would have been less than fair and honest to myself, Ian Meckiff and to the game of cricket,' he said.

He'd umpired Meckiff five times previously without calling him. 'The season before he'd stood in a [Sheffield] Shield game in Adelaide and I bowled something like 30 [eight-ball] overs for the game without him calling me,' said Meckiff. 'He was at the bowler's end all the way through.'

Asked if he believed he'd been victim of worldwide action to suppress throwing, Meckiff said: 'It's difficult to know if or not if it was pre-arranged . . . but the more I hear, the more I believe it was got up to put me out of business.'

Umpire Lou Rowan said if there had been a conspiracy to no-ball Meckiff out of cricket, he hadn't been told. 'I simply refuse to believe that such was the case,' he said in his autobiography, *The Umpire's Story*.

Asked how he felt at the start of the fateful over, he told *Cricketer* magazine: 'I remember thinking to myself, "well, it's on now". I looked across at Col a couple of times during that over. We didn't say anything then, but I gave him a little signal. I remember saying to him, "Whatever happens, pal, I'm with you."'

Egar said suggestions were incorrect that his calling of Meckiff was pre-meditated. 'My only judgement was what I saw at the time,' he said.

Asked why he hadn't no-balled Meckiff on previous occasions, Egar said he was either at the bowler's end or hadn't believed, then, that Meckiff was operating illegally. 'Never did I have pre-meditated thoughts about any of the bowlers I called,' he said. 'At times there were bowlers I believed suspect and I did speak to their captain. Invariably they'd oblige and say, "Let him finish the over" and then take him off. This happened at club and Shield level.

'With Mecko the press kept writing things up. You tended then to occasionally have a look. It had been an unwritten law though that only the fella at square leg would call. When I broke it and called a guy for throwing from the bowler's end, the crowd gave me a real shellacking.'

In 1965, Egar was invited to South Africa and stood in three games. He also privately offered his opinion about several bowlers Springbok officials thought may be suspect.

Richie Benaud denies that a deliberate example was made of Meckiff. He says throwing had been cricket's hottest topic in the late 50s and early 60s. He regards Colin Egar as one of the finest umpires he has ever seen in more than 50 years in the game. 'His work in the tied Test series with Col Hoy (1960–61) was outstanding and if I had the choice of two umpires to stand in a cricket match it would be Egar and England's Sid Buller,' he said.

Having also umpired Australian Rules football from 1950, Egar said he was used to the abuse. 'I've never regretted anything I've done,' said Egar, 'or things like the criticism, the brick through the window [at work] or the filthy letters which my wife refused to show me.'

MECKIFF WAS JUST 28 and in his prime. Having bowled the final deliveries at half pace, he trudged in a daze into the off-side ring. While the 'Gabba crowd sheltering from the heat on the old mounds under the ground's huge weeping fig trees clapped and roared encouragement, not a word was said on the field. Everyone was too stunned.

'I still don't know to this day whether it was set-up,' said Meckiff. 'It has always been a contentious point.'

The 'Gabba crowd was so boisterous and Alan McGilvray's ABC description so loud and invasive in the middle that Goddard complained and umpire Rowan approached the pavilion, asking for a message to be relayed to the crowd to turn down their transistors, or at least use their ear-pieces.

During the delay, Benaud consulted with Meckiff. 'I'm afraid this is the finish, Dad.'

Meckiff: 'Well, if that's it, OK.'

Minutes later, at the start of the fourth over, Benaud introduced Connolly for his first over in Test cricket. Meckiff, capless and standing at the stumps, was a forlorn figure. There were prolonged jeers all around the ground, even from the members, for Benaud for withdrawing Meckiff, and later too, when it was obvious he didn't intend to switch him around to the Stanley Street end.

'I wasn't just the brunt of the booing, I was almost the total booing!' Benaud said. 'There was just over 10 000 in, but they sounded more than that. They wanted to see Ian bowl from CJ's [Egar's] end so that Lou Rowan would have to give a second opinion. I stuck to what I'd said for some years, that I would accept whatever an umpire said and did about any of my bowlers. I can't remember being surprised [at the hostile reception], but Alan Connolly and Tom Veivers were, as they were also booed when I brought them on to bowl. And, they were making their Test debuts, Tom on his home ground!'

The eight-minute over and resultant uproar was the most dramatic scandal in Australian cricket since Sid Barnes took the Board to the Supreme Court over his non-selection for reasons other than cricket in 1951–52.

Pro-Meckiff supporters condemned umpire Egar and the timing of his calls. Benaud was also grilled, many feeling a switch of ends should at least have been tried. Chants of 'We want Meckiff' and 'Give 'im a go!' continued all afternoon. At the close, a number of the crowd rushed the field and hoisted an embarrassed Meckiff shoulder-high and carried him to the players' race.

'It was just not possible to bowl him again,' Benaud said at his Saturday night media conference. Explaining he wanted to avoid any more acrimony, Benaud said to have continued with Meckiff would have only added to the fallout. 'I bowled Meckiff for hundreds of overs before umpires who approved his delivery and I have accepted their decision. Now that an umpire does not accept Meckiff's delivery, I accept that decision, too. I will not bowl him again.'

Former Australian captain Lindsay Hassett was among several high-profile critics who believed Benaud had taken the easy way out.

Others to support Meckiff included another ex-Test captain Ian Johnson and Invincible tourist Doug Ring.

Benaud said there had been widespread suggestions pre-match that Meckiff's action would be subject to the closest scrutiny. But the no-ball calls had still come as a tremendous shock. Writing in his Sydney newspaper column several days later, Benaud wrote: 'It defies description – the feeling that hits players when there is a no-ball called for throwing . . . one can only assume that the game was carried on by instinct for a while, for the Australian players were not, as one might say in the modern idiom, "with it". You could count the number of words spoken on the field on the fingers of both hands . . . it was an experience no one would wish to go through again.'

Yet no one went through as much as Meckiff, and it seems amazing that he had to be publicly humiliated in a game as important as a Test match. Later on that night, at Lennon's Hotel, Egar was invited to join several of the players, Meckiff included, for dinner. 'I'm sorry this had to happen,' he told Meckiff. 'The second most upset person in the world is me.'

SHORTLY AFTER HIS explosive finale in big cricket, Meckiff agreed to a series of ghosted articles, written by Bob Gray in Sydney's *Daily Mirror*. 'In the cold hard light of everything,' he said, 'when it is looked at realistically, I must now concede I was a chucker.'

One night at a cocktail party at the Melbourne Cricket Ground, Meckiff was abused by a cricket official who'd heard Meckiff was considering legal action to clear his name. 'He threatened that if I went ahead with a court action, I'd be very sorry,' Meckiff said in *Cricketer* magazine.

THE REACTION
When you get your feet chopped from underneath you, it's pretty hard to feel any other way than bitter.   **IAN MECKIFF**

A very decent Australian has been sacrificed from the altar of stupid officialdom and I don't mean by that umpire Egar. I have never liked Meckiff's action but it should never have come to this.   **JACK FINGLETON in the Brisbane *Telegraph***

I feel sorry for the wretched Meckiff. There is something pathetic about watching a man's life crumble, especially a man who is a charming character off the field, without a shred of conceit or malice in his make-up.

South Africa's GRAEME POLLOCK

No dog's hind leg could have been straighter than Meckiff's arm as he delivered most balls of the fateful over.   **RAY ROBINSON**

The selection misfired and it must now be recognised as the greatest mistake in cricket administration wished on a nation for many years.

PERCY BEAMES in the *Age*

When 'Meck' was younger, jeez he was sharp. You'd stand in the slips to him and any edges would really fly. He was one of the quickest blokes into the pitch you'd ever see, easily as quick as the West Indian fellas. I have no hesitation in saying he was forced out of the game.   **IAN REDPATH**

'Meckie' was one of the nicest guys you could possibly play with. It's a great credit to him that he hasn't been soured by the whole incident. It was a tragic thing to happen.   **ALAN CONNOLLY**

TWENTY YEARS AFTER the Brisbane drama, Ian Meckiff bowled again, with Col Egar umpiring. Both were at a gathering of former cricketers and media men at Ayers Rock for a friendly match between celebrity teams captained by Colin Cowdrey and Rod Marsh. Egar was one of the umpires. And he was at the bowler's end for Meckiff's first delivery. 'No-ball,' he yelled, just for old time's sake. Everyone knew it was a set-up.

10. Banned by his own Board: Sid Barnes

Had Sid Barnes been at his buccaneering best today, he may not have played even one Test, let alone the 13 which statistically see him rated behind only Don Bradman as Australia's finest batsman. No one coloured opinion or bucked the system quite like Barnes. He was a showman, a firebrand and an opportunist, who saw selection for the most famous tour of all, in 1948, not only as an honour, but a chance to swell his tour fee through his wheeling and dealing.

He was also the biggest name ever excluded from selection 'for reasons other than cricket' by a dictatorial, aloof and vindictive Australian Board of Control which was plunged into Supreme Court action in 1952 after Barnes was sensationally omitted from a Test team.

Not only was Sid Barnes a champion in the most legendary team of all, Don Bradman's 1948 Invincibles, he was also the most outspoken cricketer of his generation, a fiercely ambitious player so dismissive of authority that a 40-year-old clause was used to terminate his international career.

NOT SINCE 1912, when Australia's six elite cricketers withdrew from the triangular Test tour to England, had there been a more publicised dispute or as stark a gulf between player and administration.

The headline-chasing, argumentative Sid Barnes had a spec-
tacularly high Test average but collected some powerful enemies along
the way. Denied seven of his best run-scoring years by the war, Barnes
withdrew from the 1949–50 tour of South Africa complaining of what
he considered to be a miserly tour fee.

When Freddie Brown's Englishmen arrived in 1950–51, he again
sat out, preferring to pocket a more lucrative wage as a newspaper
columnist rather than taking his chances at the selection table. His
hard-hitting column in Sydney's *Daily Telegraph* was called 'Like It or
Lump It' and he regularly took contemptuous aim at administrators,
the majority of whom he reckoned had never played anything but
park cricket and were totally out of touch.

Had Australia not been as powerful and Barnes less brash and
provocative, there may have been a greater urgency and well of
support for his return in an Ashes year. Fast bowler Ray Lindwall
claimed Barnes at the time to be the premier batsman in world cricket,
superior even to the record-breaking Englishman, Len Hutton.

After three years of virtual inactivity, Barnes, then 35, committed
himself to a comeback for the arrival of John Goddard's 1951–52 West
Indians. He'd rise at dawn on the frostiest of Sydney winter mornings
and jog around nearby Lindfield Oval. At lunch times, he'd practise his
batting skills and hand presents to those who acted as net bowlers.
Such was his reputation that after only mediocre grade form with
Gordon, he was immediately lifted into the New South Wales team for
the traditional season opener against Queensland in Brisbane. He also
acted as NSW's stand-in captain when Arthur Morris was absent on
Test duty.

Australia's new opening pair Morris and Queensland's Ken Archer
had been only partially successful and when the old firm Barnes (107)
and Morris (210) amassed an enterprising double-century stand for
NSW against Victoria in Melbourne, there was a clamour for his
reselection. Among those present were Test selectors NSW's Edmund

'Chappie' Dwyer and Victoria's Jack 'The King' Ryder, who warmly congratulated Barnes in the rooms afterwards.

Barnes was confident ex-team-mate Sir Donald Bradman, now a selector, would support him. He was also encouraged by a conversation earlier in the summer with Aubrey Oxlade, chairman of the Board of Control, who scoffed at speculation that Board officials were disapproving of Barnes and said the sheer weight of runs remained the most important factor in Barnes' bid to regain his Test place. In his book *It Isn't Cricket*, Barnes says Oxlade told him: 'You know what I think of you as a cricketer and as a man. It's just a matter for your own cricket bat. Good luck.'

While he'd averaged only 35 for the season, Barnes was included in a squad of 13 for the third Test, an extra player having been named because of doubts over the fitness of Australian captain and No. 3 batsman Lindsay Hassett.

But the Board referred the list back to the selectors, saying they objected to one of the 13. While they didn't name Barnes, it was clear who they were targeting. A newspaper poster proclaiming BARNES IN, BARNES OUT was the opened salvo in the controversy which was to grip even leading politicians and end in the Supreme Court of Australia.

'I felt bitterly resentful,' said Barnes. 'It would not have worried me had the selectors not chosen me, had they considered me not good enough. That would have been their judgement, a judgement deserving every respect because of their deep knowledge of the game, but to have been chosen by the selectors and then tossed aside by the Board was the supreme insult. It made me feel like an unwanted cur.'

Provocative Sydney columnist Jim Mathers said the Board had treated the selectors 'like flippant schoolboys'. He believed the NSW Cricket Association had also been insulted as it had made Barnes captain earlier in the season.

An editorial in the *Sydney Morning Herald* said: 'If the Board thinks that its decisions are beyond question, it is due for disillusionment.

This secretive and even furtive method of damning a player deserves strong censure.'

Most former Test players backed Barnes unequivocally. Arthur Mailey said if he was a selector he'd resign, Jack Fingleton claimed Board delegates were thin-skinned and snooty, Bill O'Reilly believed the Board deserved nationwide condemnation and Stan McCabe, best man at Barnes' wedding, called the affair 'scandalous'.

Days earlier in Melbourne, Hec de Lacy of the *Sporting Globe* had telegraphed Barnes' omission when he wrote: 'If Barnes doesn't make the third or fourth Test teams, don't blame lack of ability or the selectors. If the selectors were unanimous in wanting Barnes, I doubt whether their wishes would be granted. When the selectors choose the side they must send it to the Board [for approval]. That might be Barnes' biggest hurdle. Usually approval is automatic. But I know for certain that if Barnes were named by the selectors, opposition by Board members would be strong enough to keep him out.'

The Board had never before exercised its option to veto. Chairman Oxlade, Frank Cush (also from Sydney) and Bradman opposed the motion, but nine other delegates voted against Barnes' inclusion. Recognising the likely backlash, given Barnes' overall popularity, they successfully moved that matters of selection remain confidential, and not even be recorded in the minutes.

By chance, Barnes met Oxlade at McCabe's Sydney sports store, Oxlade congratulating him on his Melbourne century and in the hearing of others claimed he had 'nothing to do with this nasty business'. Oxlade said what happened was scandalous and vowed at the next meeting to ask questions.

Instead, Barnes had to endure a massive wall of silence. Frustrated by the inactivity, he eventually issued a press release, via prominent QC Jack Shand, saying that the secrecy surrounding the Board action had led to disturbing speculation 'injurious' to the well-being of both himself and his family.

He was also angered that the NSW Cricket Association continued to appoint him state captain, yet not demand an explanation from the Board as to his banishment from international cricket. It was clear that there were divisions at state headquarters in George Street as well, the third NSW delegate to the Board, Keith Johnson, manager of the '48 tour, inadvertently having been embroiled in affairs of protocol when Barnes took film of the royal family.

As the controversy raged, it was learnt that hard-nosed Brisbane lawyer Jack Hutcheon, soon to be honoured with a CBE for his services to cricket, had led the pre-Christmas confidentiality motion. A domineering, stubborn and authoritarian figure, Hutcheon was Barnes' most powerful adversary, the two having fallen out years before when Barnes threatened to withhold his NSW team from the field in response to the Brisbane outfield being cut on the second morning of a Shield game against Queensland. Hutcheon told him to mind his own business but backed off when Barnes said: 'Call off your panzer unit [curating staff] or I'll take my team off.'

Barnes further fuelled the controversy with a century against the Queenslanders in Sydney, days after the Australians had been beaten by the West Indies in just three days in Adelaide. In that Test, Hassett's eleventh-hour withdrawal and Barnes' non-selection created an imbalance, with fast bowler Lindwall batting at No. 6.

At the advice of Shand, Barnes wrote letters to each of the Board delegates but received only guarded replies, each word-for-word:

'Dear Sir, – I have your letter of the 11th inst., and I have noted the contents. I am unwilling to enter into any correspondence with you on the subject matter set forth in your letter.'

A dispirited Barnes felt defeated and that he had no further option, other than to appear in front of the Board at their next meeting, in spring. 'They were too strong and too silent for me,' he said.

But the issue was unexpectedly re-ignited in April when a letter from a Mr Jacob Raith, a master baker and former president of

Petersham Cricket Club, appeared in the Sydney *Daily Mirror*: 'It must be abundantly clear to all that they [the Board] would not have excluded Mr Barnes from the Australian XI capriciously and only for some matter of a sufficiently serious nature.'

At last Barnes and his supporters, who now included Dr Herbert V. Evatt, Leader of the Opposition and a vice-president of the NSW Cricket Association, had the ammunition they needed. Barnes claimed he had been slurred and went to court, seeking damages from Raith for libel – but more particularly to clear his name.

In essence, the Board of Control was on trial and Shand portrayed the delegates as elitist, cloistered, unaccountable and vindictive. To defend himself, Raith was forced to subpoena Sir Donald Bradman, Oxlade and other key members of the board.

Sir Donald was unable to attend as his son, John, had polio. But over two days, fellow Board men from secretary Bill Jeanes to Johnson and chairman Oxlade were grilled. Jeanes' initial objection to Board documents being made public was overruled by Mr Justice Lloyd.

Oxlade said in his evidence that Barnes was 'a bit childish' but did not consider overly serious any of his so-called misdemeanours which included:

- hurdling a member's turnstile after failing to produce his player's admission ticket during a Test in Melbourne;
- bowing to the crowd;
- filming the Royals; and
- playing tennis while a county match was in progress during the 1948 tour.

JOHNSON WAS FORCED to expand on his written report after the '48 tour in which he said that the behaviour of the team, both on and off the field, had been exemplary. Indeed, Barnes had received a £150 good conduct bonus. As Mr Shand asked, why should he now, three years later, be making an issue of Barnes' behaviour?

Shand inferred that Johnson as a friend was treacherous. In fact, he was popular with most players it seemed, except Barnes.

Asked in detail about the incidents which made Barnes unworthy of selection, Johnson agreed the turnstile incident was prior to the 1948 tour and certainly had not made him unworthy of representing Australia on that tour.

Ernie Toshack and Barnes had played tennis at the back of the pavilion at Northampton in 1948, but it was Barnes' game off and Toshack, as 12th man and over the age of 21, was responsible for his own actions.

Barnes had also obtained permission from Lord Gowrie, the aide-de-camp to the King, to take film of the Australians being presented to the Royals at Lord's. Permission had also been granted for him to film the Queen Mother at Windsor Castle and he had continued to be selected afterwards.

Johnson was forced to admit at best he was a fourth grade cricketer who had never played at senior level. He conceded the worst thing that could happen to a cricketer was to be dismissed from a team on grounds other than cricket ability and agreed the public could think the discarded player was guilty of dishonourable conduct. Quizzed further about the significance of the incidents, Johnson said that none of them, treated in an isolated fashion, justified exclusion from the Australian side; nor did two of the incidents. But he considered all three did. He also believed Barnes temperamentally unsuitable to be NSW captain, but had been outvoted.

Asked if he would select Barnes if he became a world beater who could bowl slow and fast, never missed a catch and averaged 200, Johnson initially refused to answer. When pressed by the judge, he said: 'No, I wouldn't.'

SHAND: And you say you have a wide national outlook for the best of the game?

JOHNSON: Yes.

SHAND: Do you still think you are qualified to be a member of the Board?

JOHNSON: Yes.

The Board lost at almost every turn, emerging as an elitist band of autocrats, who had acted in a high-handed and unjustified manner. Raith told Barnes he would have never written his letter, had he known all the facts. Raith agreed to pay Barnes' costs, Barnes waiving his damages claim of £1000, happy to settle for the crushing moral victory over the Board.

Newspapers proclaiming Barnes' victory sold out all over Sydney and beyond. It was as big as a St George premiership. VINDICATED trumpeted the *Daily Mirror*'s banner.

'I have fought my fight and won,' said Barnes, ever the crusader. 'Another fight yet to be won is the saving of cricket from the hands of the autocratic few, drunk with power and self-importance. They have reigned too long.'

DESPITE HIS FAMOUS court victory, Sid Barnes never played for Australia again, nor recovered from his slighting by the Board. He became bitter and vitriolic, squandering friendships and targeting even loyal mates like Keith Miller – the pair lashing out at each other in a front-page war which sent newspaper sales soaring.

Barnes blamed the loss of the Coronation year series in England to the excesses of the team, especially vice-captain Miller who he believed had acted imprudently, quarrelling openly with umpires, being absent from the team when English race meetings were on and 'conveniently' developing a sore back at the same time as the running of the Epsom Derby.

In an extraordinary tirade, Barnes wrote: 'Miller repeatedly transgressed in a way which affected adversely Australia's cricket prestige and repeatedly offended against the code of sportsmanship and ethics.'

Barnes further claimed the Australians lost the second Test at Lord's because players were in a London night club until early morning before the last day of play. They were more anxious to get to Wimbledon for the tennis than they were in the outcome of the match. Barnes further accused them of neglecting practice for personal gain and of rudeness to the Nottinghamshire County Cricket Club which made arrangements and paid for the tourists to go to the Coronation.

Australia's popular captain Lindsay Hassett was also targeted, Barnes alleging Hassett wielded a 'fatal lack of control on the team'. Furthermore, social junkets and slovenly demeanour on the field characterised the team's five months in England.

Miller said Barnes was bitter and jealous, a former great cricketer and clown who missed the crowd's applause. He defended his attendance at horse racing meetings by saying players took it in turns to miss a game. How they relaxed was their own business. He denied ever arguing with umpires and added dryly, 'And when it comes to sportsmanship I know as much about it as Sid Barnes.'

His defence filled the front pages of newspapers in Australia and England. 'Barnes is known as the Master Gimme man of Australian cricket. Gimme this – gimme that!' said Miller.

'Sid is a shrewd man,' said Miller. 'He has made sure his book will be a best-seller by attacking me and the Australian XI. But he will be remembered as the only Australian squealer after we lost the 1953 Ashes tour. Actually, this was the quietest tour I've been on,' he added. 'The youngsters looked up to Lindsay Hassett as an idol, much the same way as members looked up to Don Bradman in 1948. Lindsay was the ideal touring captain.'

Barnes was ever shrewd. His 1948 room-mate Arthur Morris had become so tired of goods being bought and sold via their hotel room that he moved in with someone else. After his broadsides against the 1953 tourists, Barnes' book *Eyes On the Ashes* went into reprint within a month – but the rifts with many old mates were irreparable.

He played his last game of both state and club cricket, at 36, before pursuing his business interests. He believed there was no point to playing if he was considered too old for his country. Even an opportunist recognises when he's beaten.

Barnes struggled with his increasing anonymity and even his beloved business deals suffered. He hated growing old and in his later years suffered badly from depression. In 1973 he was found dead, with a bottle of sleeping tablets next to him. He was just 57.

Barnes was a lovely, warm-hearted bloke who did a lot of charity and cricketers down on their luck always found him a soft touch, but somehow the warm, human side of him never got through to the newspapers.

Fellow Invincible ERNIE TOSHACK

THE AMAZING WORLD OF SID BARNES

- A teenage Sid Barnes once took 40 runs from a 9-ball over from North Sydney's 'Ginty' Lush (four 6s and four 4s) in a Sydney grade match in 1936–37.

- World War II robbed Barnes and other emerging youngsters like Keith Miller and Arthur Morris of six of their very best years. In the final full season of Sheffield Shield in 1940–41, Barnes, 22, made six centuries in consecutive first-class matches, passing 1000 runs and averaging 75. All six were first-innings centuries.

- There were almost eight years between Barnes' first and second Test appearances. His debut game against the Englishmen at The Oval was memorable for Len Hutton making 364, Test cricket's new all-time batting record.

- Barnes loved to monopolise the strike, even if his batting partner was Don Bradman. In the 1946–47 Sydney Test, Barnes became the first man to bat for 10 hours, he and Bradman adding 405 for the fifth wicket, a Test record which stood until 1990–91. Both were out for 234, Barnes later claiming he had deliberately tossed his innings away so he could be bracketed with The Don, rather than ahead of him!

- Playing a season of English League cricket with Burnley in 1947, Barnes was disappointed at the size of the first 'collection' – bonus monies donated by appreciative spectators to players who'd made a 50 or taken five wickets. On being told that some patrons, seeing his flash Sunbeam Talbot and fine dress, may have felt he didn't need their donations, Barnes parked his motor car a mile from the ground and appeared in an old suit, cloth cap and raincoat. According to historian Rick Smith, his proceeds immediately doubled!

- Some benefits arose from Barnes brooking authority. His move, in 1948, to question an antiquated Australian Board of Control rule and have wives at least within visiting distance on tours of England has been welcomed by tourists ever since.

- Tired of the demands of having to sign dozens of autograph sheets on board the *Strathaird* on the voyage to England in 1948, Barnes had a rubber stamp made of his signature and paid a youngster to stamp the sheets. The original sheet is now one of the most eagerly-sought by collectors of Bradman team memorabilia.

- Ever mischievous, Barnes thrust a mongrel dog under the nose of English umpire Alex Skelding one day, saying the dog could go with his white stick.

- After backing himself to make 100 in the 1948 Lord's Test, Barnes celebrated his money-making feat by smashing Jim Laker for 20 runs from five balls. Noted cricket writer Ray Robinson said when Barnes was in such a mood 'the ball beat against his bat as helplessly as a dog's paw against a barn door'.

- Barnes and Arthur Morris were one of the greatest of all opening pairs, averaging more than 50, including back-to-back century stands in their last two Tests as team-mates in 1948. 'I'm sorry he didn't stop in cricket longer,' said Morris.

- In Don Bradman's testimonial game in Melbourne in 1948–49, Barnes took guard with a mini bat.

- In his final season, Barnes dropped himself to 12th man in a Sheffield Shield game in Adelaide. Appearing at a drinks break in an expensive double-breasted suit, he brushed players' flannels, gave bowlers iced towels, combed players' hair, sprayed deodorant under their armpits, played a portable radio and even offered around cigars.

- On the day the 1953 Australian touring team to England was announced, the just-selected Alan Davidson answered his door. It was Barnes with his cricket bag. 'Here, son,' he said. 'I won't be needing this any more.'

- In 1956, when Barnes wrote off the touring Australians as 'a bunch of pie-eaters', the Aussies won at Lord's and Barnes posed for photographs beside a huge tray of pies, pretending he'd eat the lot.

HOW SID BARNES COMPARES WITH THE BEST

ALL-TIME BEST TEST BATTING AVERAGES

Ave	Name (country)	Tests	Runs	HS	100s
99.95	Don Bradman (Australia)	52	6996	334	29
63.05	Sid Barnes (Australia)	13	1072	234	3
60.97	Graeme Pollock (South Africa)	23	2256	274	7
60.83	George Headley (West Indies)	22	2190	270*	10
60.73	Herbert Sutcliffe (England)	54	4555	194	16

THE BEST-EVER AUSTRALIAN OPENERS

Ave	Pair	Runs	100s
63.75	Bill Brown & Jack Fingleton	1020	3
63.27	Arthur Morris & Colin McDonald	949	3
59.83	Bill Lawry & Bob Simpson	3596	9
53.85	Sid Barnes & Arthur Morris	754	3
51.28	Mark Taylor & Michael Slater	3898	10

11. Evil, insidious, brutal Bodyline

Bodyline bowling not only exposed its general Douglas Jardine as a cricketing fanatic obsessed with winning, it threatened the very fibre of the game and the friendly sporting relations between England and Australia.

Designed to stifle the batting genius of young batting virtuoso Don Bradman, who had been unstoppable in England in 1930, it triggered extraordinary feeling. Australian batsmen were hit 25 times in five ill-tempered Tests by the Nottinghamshire Express, Harold Larwood, in the most violent and volatile summer of all.

ONLY FIVE MEN were present in the Australian dressing rooms at the Adelaide Oval when Bill Woodfull, still ashen grey after been struck a tremendous blow under the heart by Harold Larwood, delivered the most stinging rebuke in Anglo–Australian cricket history: 'Mr Warner, there are two sides out there. One is playing cricket. The other is not. The game is too good to be spoilt. It is time some people got out of it.'

P. F. 'Plum' Warner, England's genteel 'Mr Cricket' and his assistant manager, Richard Palairet, had come to extend their sympathies. Instead they'd been hit with a sledgehammer.

Within 24 hours, Woodfull's reprimand was headline news, both around Australia and in London. The Australian captain was the gentleman's gentleman, scholarly, erudite and caring. For him to be so provoked and accuse the English of playing outside the spirit of the game showed just how raw the emotions were in the face of Bodyline.

As well as the Australian team masseur, who was deaf, Australian 12th man Leo O'Brien was present. Just before Warner and Palairet's arrival, Woodfull emerged from a shower and told O'Brien: 'There are some terrible things happening out there, Mo [O'Brien].' O'Brien rejoined his team-mates and said: 'Woody's in a bad way', before relating his captain's steamy tirade.

As the only professional journalist present, Jack Fingleton was blamed as the one who went public with the story. However, he always denied his involvement and said there were others, too, who had media links – Alan Kippax, for example, who wasn't playing, and Vic Richardson, Stan McCabe and Don Bradman, who were.

The furore became an international incident when popular wicketkeeper Bert Oldfield reeled from the wicket, his skull fractured, after edging an attempted hook shot onto his temple on the third day. While Oldfield was to tell a concerned Larwood that it wasn't his fault, the view from around the boundary was stark. Oldfield had slumped to the ground, motionless. Seeing their hero seriously hurt, there was an immediate hush, before an angry swell of shouting. Had one person jumped the fence, there could easily have been a riot.

To the mob, it mattered little that Larwood wasn't bowling Bodyline either when Oldfield was sconed or when Woodfull had been struck under the heart late the previous afternoon. The Australians had been intimidated all summer, the pitches had become battlefields and the ballooning resentment had reached a fever pitch.

As Oldfield was being treated, the noisiest elements on the northern banks of the 30 000 strong crowd began to count Larwood out. The Englishmen gathered in the centre, looking anxiously back over their shoulders. Umpires George Hele and George Borwick were so sure of an invasion that they'd resolved to arm themselves with a stump each for protection.

Oldfield said later that he had 'lost' the ball in the background, Larwood's arm at the point of delivery being higher than the oval's sightscreen. Seeing Oldfield crumpled on the ground seriously hurt, Larwood had raced up to him saying 'I'm sorry, Bertie.'

'It's not your fault, Harold.'

As 'Gubby' Allen tended to Oldfield's cut with a towel and a jug of water, Woodfull, dressed in civilian clothes, came onto the field, helped Oldfield up and supported him as they walked off.

Next-man-in Bill O'Reilly said it was a task in itself even getting down the steps from the George Giffen Stand onto the Adelaide Oval amidst the pandemonium, members standing on their seats and in the aisles remonstrating against Larwood. A platoon of mounted horse troopers stood at the ready.

'It was a toss-up for several minutes whether someone would jump the fence,' said Richardson. 'If one man had, it is almost certain that thousands would have followed him. What could a few policemen have done had the field been invaded by angry spectators?'

Larwood was booed and hooted and sat down waiting for the noise to subside. Play restarted to the extraordinary spectacle of police ringing the boundary. Throughout it all, English captain Douglas Jardine remained composed, his face set. He even went down to deep fine leg, contemptuous and defiant in the face of danger. Later, when England batted again, he wore his elitist, multi-coloured Harlequin cap.

After unsuccessfully asking managers Warner and Palairet to intervene and stop leg-theory bowling, within days the Australian Board of Control, through its chairman Dr Allen Robertson in Melbourne, had penned the first of the famous set of telegrams which almost ended the tour and endangered the good relations between the two countries:

> Bodyline bowling has assumed such proportions as to menace the best interests of the game, making protection of the body by batsmen the main consideration, causing intensely bitter feelings between players as well as injury. In our opinion it is unsportsmanlike. Unless stopped at once it is likely to upset friendly relations existing between Australia and England.

Marylebone Cricket Club, responsible for the English team, sent a dignified, strongly worded reply :

> We, the Marylebone club, deplore your cable and depreciate the opinion that there has been unsportsmanlike play. We have the fullest confidence in the captain and team managers. We are convinced that they would do nothing that would infringe the laws of cricket or the spirit of the game and we have no evidence that our confidence is misplaced. Much as we regret the injuries to Woodfull and Oldfield, we understand that in neither case was the bowler [Larwood] to blame. If the Board wishes to propose a new law, or rule, it should receive our careful consideration in due course. We hope the situation is not now as serious as your cable appears to indicate, but if it is such to jeopardise the good relations between England and Australian cricketers, and you consider it desirable to cancel the remainder of the program, we would consent with great reluctance.

Jardine, too, felt suitably insulted by the Australian cable and vowed not to lead England into the fourth Test unless the charge of unsportsmanlike conduct was withdrawn. In his book *In Quest of the Ashes*, he said: 'I had long since ceased to care what the Australian press said about me, nor did I pay any heed to what individuals frequently said behind my back. I had, however, made up my mind that no Australian body, however august, should, as far as I was concerned, be at liberty to stigmatize the MCC team as "unsportsmanlike" and be allowed to escape from retracting that amazing charge.'

Iron-willed, exacting and determined to win at all costs, Jardine would brook no interference from Warner, a former English captain, who had pleaded with him to reduce his number of leg-side fieldsmen. Often Jardine would have eight on the on-side, except when Larwood was operating against the fleet-of-foot Bradman, whose cross-bat swishes demanded a third man, as well as a cover point.

Warner told Richardson, Australia's vice-captain, that he was powerless to act: 'The skipper is adamant,' he said. 'I can do nothing with him on this subject.' They had argued on the *Orontes* on the voyage out and Jardine showed him scant courtesy for the rest of the campaign.

Even before the Tests started, Richardson had known this would be a tour with a twist. 'If we don't beat you,' old foe Bill Voce told him soon after arrival, 'We'll knock your bloody heads off.'

THE TERM 'BODYLINE' was first used by famous Melbourne sporting identity and ex-Australian Test cricketer Jack Worrall of the *Australasian*, who talked about 'half-pitched slingers on the body line'. A far-sighted sub-editor used it in a headline, giving birth to cricket's most infamous term.

EVER SINCE THE opening weeks of the tour Larwood and his burly sidekicks, Voce and young giant Bill Bowes, directly attacked the batsmen, with the leg-side stacked with fieldsmen – as many as five and six in the inner ring and two protecting the fine leg boundary. Puzzled by the gathering of English fielders on the leg side, Leo O'Brien, playing for the first time in the Australian XI side, motioned, 'But I'm a left-hander!'

By mid-series Vic Richardson was taking block 18 inches outside his leg stump and the ball was still coming directly at him. The Australian batsmen expected to be hit. There were 34 instances in the Tests, Larwood responsible for 25.

On the slower English wickets, the 1930 Australians had mainly been untroubled, but on the harder, faster wickets of Australia, even the most agile and quick-footed players like Bradman were pinged, Larwood being at least two yards faster than previously. Captain Bill Woodfull was struck seven times in four Tests and his opening partner Bill Ponsford, six in three.

By the tour end even the English fielders had stopped trying to sympathise. There was little or no camaraderie between the sides, the Australians reciprocating Jardine's cold disdain. When he wanted to see Woodfull, he was made to wait in the corridor, with the door shut.

When Jardine was struck on the thigh in the fifth Test by the thickset Victorian Harry 'Bull' Alexander, thousands stood and cheered. No English cricketer had ever been more detested – or had so openly shown his contempt for the colonials. He genuinely considered himself superior, especially to the Australian public.

Indian-born and English-educated, Jardine was a zealot, a complex and aloof man with a liking for Chaucer, Asian philosophy and mysticism. Even a few of his team-mates had reservations, Herbert Sutcliffe referring to him as 'a queer devil' during their first trip together in 1928–29, before making a complete about-face in 1932–33 when he described him as one of the greatest men he'd met!

How Jardine could lead a plan so abhorrent to the very spirit of the game showed just how paranoid all England was about another humiliation at the hands of Australia's batting maestro, Don Bradman. The thrashings Bradman had handed Percy Chapman's conventional attacks had forced Jardine to formulate something different. He believed the Ashes could not possibly be retrieved unless the maulings were stopped. He adopted a policy of hate, maybe as a payback for some of the abuse he'd received during his maiden tour.

Jardine's plans hinged almost entirely around his fastest bowler, the 173 cm (5'8") Larwood, who had been in Test cricket since 1926. A strong and willing man who could bowl at thunderous pace, Larwood was, with Bowes and his county new-ball partner Voce, the outstanding strike bowler in England. His 141 county wickets (and 106 from the left-armed Voce) had lifted Notts into fourth place in the 1932 English championship. While he'd previously been expensive at Test level (31 wickets at 41.06), Larwood's skidding speed had been estimated at around 90 mph (144 km/h) and his accuracy and stamina had improved too. With the opening overs with the new ball he could take the ball 'away', but like Voce, his natural swerve was 'in' to the right-handers.

Two English summers previously, in 1930, 25-year-old Larwood had unsettled Bradman, albeit momentarily, in the final Test at The Oval. On a wettened wicket, Larwood struck his arch foe under the heart. Play was held up for five minutes while the champion regained his composure. He was 175 at the time and went on to make 232.

At a meeting with Larwood, Voce and their county captain Arthur Carr at a hotel in Piccadilly after the touring team had been announced, Jardine spoke of leg-theory and his desire to curb Bradman. He talked of The Oval Test, in which Larwood had been threatening, albeit for a short time.

'I told Jardine I thought Bradman had flinched and he said he knew that,' said Larwood in his book *The Larwood Story*.

Bowled accurately and with enough speed, Jardine felt even Bradman may be vulnerable to a sustained leg stump attack. Others such as feted openers Bill Woodfull and Bill Ponsford and the veteran Alan Kippax could also be discomforted.

Larwood had bowled leg-theory against Bradman and Archie Jackson out of desperation on his maiden trip to Australia in Adelaide in 1928–29. But with only five and six fieldsmen on the leg side and on the flattest of wickets he'd been heavily punished and returned match figures of 1/152. 'They both seemed to play it well enough,' said Larwood, who didn't try it again.

Jardine's brutal intentions were well and truly telegraphed with the 11th-hour inclusion of 193 cm (6'4") Yorkshire giant Bowes, the 17th man and a fifth fast bowler to the squad. Touring sides of the era generally included only three pacemen, plus three specialist spinners. In one game late in the 1932 English summer at The Oval, Bowes had bowled persistently short at Jack Hobbs. The old master was so angered he walked down the wicket and remonstrated with Bowes saying he was ignoring the spirit of the game.

Having experimented with his leg-theory tactics during the lead-up games, Jardine was still far from sure that the tactic would work in the Tests. He'd discussed field placings with Frank Foster, the great Warwickshire left-arm bowler and part-destroyer of the 1911–12 Australians, and was hopeful, rather than being convinced, that leg-theory bowling with a clustered field, similar to Foster's 'death trap' (where he employed four short legs), may at least halt the run avalanche called Bradman.

For the opening Test in Sydney, Jardine played his frontline spinner, Hedley Verity, as his fourth specialist bowler. He used the medium pace of Wally Hammond as a back-up to the pace of Larwood, Voce and the amateur Gubby Allen, the only paceman in the Tests who refused to bowl Bodyline. Stan McCabe's great 187 almost ended Bodyline there and then. Had Bradman played and also succeeded against the bouncer barrage, Jardine may have withdrawn, or at least modified the attack. Along with Richardson, McCabe was one of the strongest of the Australians on the leg stump. It was no coincidence that Bodyline tactics were to be used only sparingly against those two.

Despite the shock effect and immediate success of his tactics against all bar McCabe, Jardine was so nervous about the outcome of the opening game that, for long periods when England batted, he sat behind a pillar, able to bear to watch only the occasional delivery.

Bradman's return for Melbourne, his health improved and a Board stand-off resolved, saw Jardine intensify his attack, with Bowes coming into the XI at the exclusion of Verity. His vice-captain Bob Wyatt thought it a major error in judgement. Amidst a protracted argument at the selection table, he told Jardine if he couldn't bowl Australia out twice with three fast bowlers, he wouldn't do it with four.

But Bowes played, and in an extraordinary moment, dismissed the great Bradman first ball with a quick long hop that the Don tried to pull but only succeeded in bottom-edging onto his stumps.

'The crowd was stupefied,' said Bowes in *Express Deliveries*. 'Bradman walked off the field amid a silence that would have been a theatrical producer's triumph. The spell was broken by a solitary woman's clapping. The feeble sound rippled above the hushed throng and then an excited chatter broke out from all parts of the ground. And it was then that I noticed Jardine. Jardine, the sphinx, had forgotten himself for the one and only time in his cricket life. In his sheer delight at this unexpected stroke of luck, he had clasped both his hands above his head and was jigging around like an Indian doing a war dance.'

Wyatt, fielding on the fence at fine leg, said Bradman had simply got too far over and hooked the ball down onto his leg stump. Later he impishly baited the fans, asking when Don Bradman was going to come out.

The Australians had included three spinners in their XI against England's none and were to win on an unusually sluggish wicket by 111 runs, Bradman's second innings century all-important.

However, the quality of Larwood's bowling had delighted Jardine and, despite the loss, justified in his own mind his leg-theory tactics. He told journalists in Launceston: 'I can assure you there is nothing new in the leg-theory attack and nothing dangerous in it. The only difference we have made is in evolving a new field. We hope it will go on being successful.'

Larwood had taken 10 wickets in Sydney and four on a wicket affected by lead-up rain in Melbourne. He'd bowled lengthy spells at hostile pace and was revelling in his work. So accurate was he, that his battery of short legs were rarely endangered.

In Adelaide, the most sensational Test of the series, the one in which Woodfull and Oldfield were struck, the fury against Bodyline so intensified that every available police reinforcement was sent to the oval in case of a riot.

Jardine had relented and returned Verity to the XI, ahead of Bowes, who'd had his 15 minutes of fame in Melbourne. Curator Bert Wright's wicket, normally unsympathetic to the faster bowlers, had good pace and bounce, and according to Jardine was the equal of any wicket the tourists encountered all tour.

After England had made 341, Australia was immediately under fire with Jack Fingleton falling in Allen's first over and Bradman soon afterwards to Larwood. Larwood's very first delivery with the leg-side packed was so fast it knocked the bat out of Woodfull's hands, incensing the crowd. When Woodfull, on five, was struck a crushing blow by Larwood, bowling to an orthodox field, the crowd erupted.

In *R. E. S. Wyatt: Fighting Cricketer*, England's vice-captain described it as 'an instant and violent explosion of rage from all over the ground'. 'As the storm broke Jardine signalled for a change to leg-theory bowling. It was an incredibly tactless move and not surprisingly it produced absolute pandemonium. We were all more or less inured to uproar from Australian crowds but this was different from anything we had experienced. We heard that 200 armed police were massed behind the pavilion and ready to intervene if the crowd invaded the field.

'Douglas intensely resented the agitation. He argued that he was fully within his rights in attacking the leg side, adding, "These Australians are yellow."'

Walter Hammond, one of the team's senior professionals, argued Jardine was merely following his practice of allowing Larwood to bowl conventionally for his two opening overs before reverting to leg-theory while the ball still had its hardness. However, his 'Well bowled, Harold', in Bradman's hearing, while Woodfull was being attended to, defies explanation. The spirit and high ideals of cricket had never before been so flouted. Had the incident occurred in Melbourne at Woodfull's home ground, rather than in conservative, law-abiding Adelaide, there would have been hell to pay.

Shortly before stumps, Warner and Palairet made their way along the landing to the Australian dressing room to see Woodfull, who'd been dismissed for 22. They wanted to sympathise with him – but also, as is not widely known, to find out who had called Larwood a bastard out on the field. Richardson answered the door and on being told of Warner's charge said: 'Which one of you blokes mistook Larwood for that bastard Jardine?'

Warner insisted on seeing Woodfull and received his stern rebuff, the most remembered and reported in cricket history, confirming the irrevocable split between the teams.

Woodfull hadn't meant it to become public. Nor had O'Brien, the Australian 12th man. But within hours it was being reported around the world, Jardine and the Englishmen accused of bringing the game into disrepute.

Jardine locked the door to the English dressing room and spoke with the team, saying there had been 'an unfortunate' conversation between Woodfull and Warner. He offered to stand down, but according to author Gerald Pawle, the team pledged their total support. Most considered that the Australians were making an unnecessary fuss.

After the first exchange of telegrams, in which the MCC said they'd reluctantly agree to the remainder of the tour being cancelled, the Australian Board backed down. The cricket might have been controversial, but the crowds were unprecedented with record and near-record gate-takings at every match. In Sydney, the daily attendances were almost 40 000 per day, in Melbourne more than

50 000 and in Adelaide, where the ground record was broken twice in the opening two days, almost 30 000 for each of the six days. More than 50 000 were present on the Saturday, an extraordinarily large crowd given Adelaide's small population.

The Englishmen won the Ashes in the next Test, in Brisbane and the last Test as well, in Sydney again, to take the rubber 4–1, replicating the result of Chapman's side four years earlier.

Englishmen back home rejoiced. They had been served but portions of the true story. Few believed it was a victory without honour. They tended to believe the writings of such notables as ex-Australian captain Warwick Armstrong, who in London's *Evening News* had accused Bradman's back-away tactics as tantamount to being frightened. Armstrong called The Don 'a cricket cocktail', accusing him of playing for himself rather than the team. Even Jack Hobbs in the *Star* had said Bradman 'seemed to jib a bit'.

Interviewed immediately after the tour end, Larwood said Woodfull was too slow on his feet to counter his bowling and Bradman too frightened. 'I knew it, as everybody did. Time and time again, he drew away from the ball,' he said.

However, he later withdrew his allegation saying that Bradman was quick-footed and there'd never be another like him. At the Centenary Test in 1977, he told one interviewer: 'I still have no regrets about the tactic though. Bradman had given me a hammering two years earlier. Attacking the leg stump was the only way to combat him.'

Had Bodyline been allowed to survive, Bradman believed cricket would have died, as few batsmen would have been prepared to tolerate it.

Larwood was to be outlawed from the game and in a strange twist, migrate to Australia, where he died in 1995. Jardine's career was also all but over, although he did captain England in the 1933 home series and at Old Trafford made 127 against a form of Bodyline from high-speed West Indian pair Learie Constantine and E. A. 'Manny' Martindale.

The MCC, highly embarrassed as they learnt more of the

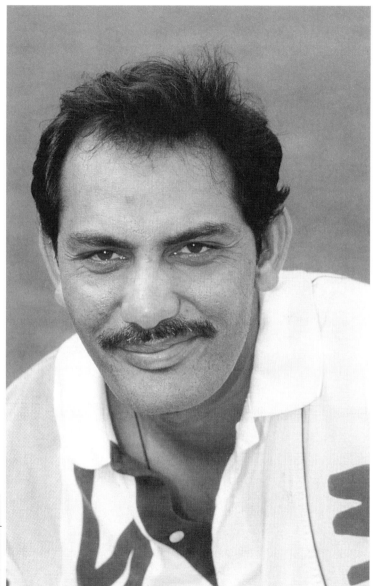

Mohammad Azharuddin: named by Hansie Cronje during the King inquiry in 2000 as having associated with illegal bookmakers. His house was later raided by Indian taxation officials looking for unaccounted monies.

Cricket's greatest villain, Saleem Malik: banned from cricket for life in 2000.

Shane Warne accepted a US$5000 gratuity from 'John' the book-maker, which the spin bowler promptly lost on the roulette table in Colombo in 1994.

Mark Waugh with Ricky 'Punter' Ponting at the races at Bridgetown in 1995. Waugh was another Australian under suspicion after it was learnt he'd taken money for providing weather reports and pitch information.

Hansie Cronje's confessions made banner headlines all over the world.

Shane Warne on his way to forfeiting his entire match fee of more than $4000 for abusing South African opener Andrew Hudson at the Bullring in Johannesburg in 1994.

Curtly Ambrose has to be restrained by captain Richie Richardson after a stinging exchange with Australian Steve Waugh at Port-of-Spain in 1995. For the only time in his career, Waugh genuinely feared for his safety.

The 500/1 mid-match odds against an England victory at Leeds in 1981 were simply too good to ignore, said Dennis Lillee.

An enraged Rashid Patel attacks North Zone batsman Raman Lamba with a stump during the ill-tempered Duleep Trophy final between North Zone and West Zone at Jamshedpurin, 1990–91. One writer called it 'the most inglorious act ever perpetrated in Indian cricket'. Both players were given lengthy suspensions.

Umpire Tony Crafter is caught in the middle of warring pair Dennis Lillee and Javed Miandad at the WACA Ground in 1981–82. 'He kept calling me dirty names,' said Javed, the subcontinent's all-time most provocative player.

Terry Alderman dislocates his shoulder after having tackled a spectator who invaded the ground and clipped Alderman on the head during the WACA Ashes Test in 1982–83. The Australian bowler was out of cricket for a year.

Australian captain Graham Yallop lectures fast bowler Rodney Hogg during the 1978–79 Ashes series. At one stage Hogg invited Yallop behind the stands at the Adelaide Oval to sort things out after he'd been challenged about his habit of temporarily leaving the oval, often in mid-spell.

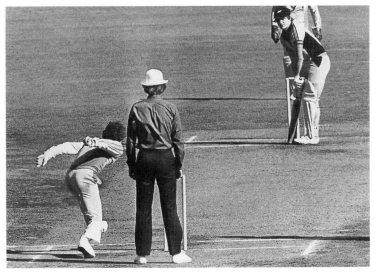

A new low for cricket: Trevor Chappell's infamous underarm, MCG, February 1981.

West Indian paceman Michael Holding kicks down the stumps in anger after having a caught-behind appeal against New Zealand's John Parker disallowed at Dunedin in 1980–81.

An Indian photographer falls to the ground at Eden Gardens in 1969–70 after a confrontation with Australian captain Bill Lawry. Hundreds of fans had spilled onto Eden Gardens when they were pelted by oranges and fruit from upstairs stands. After the match the Australian team bus was stoned as it made its way to the airport.

Clive Lloyd introduces Kerry Packer to members of his West Indian team during World Series Cricket in 1977–78.

THE SUN

MECKIFF QUITS!

'Magic-eye' shot

When Umpire Egar called 'NO-BALL!'

FROM RAY ROBINSON IN BRISBANE

CONTROVERSIAL fast bowler Ian Meckiff today expelled himself from international and Sheffield Shield cricket.

Meckiff ended his career by accepting a four-figure sum to write for a London newspaper in defiance of the Australian Board of Control's old ban on players commenting during a match.

Meckiff, no-balled out of action by umpire Egar in his first over on Saturday, made his decision to write after a series of hurried conferences with friends yesterday.

He told them, "If I mustn't play Test cricket I feel I should not play any — not even club games.

"It's beach cricket only for me from now on."

Meckiff made his retirement official today when he telephoned Victorian Cricket Association secretary, Mr Jack Ledward, with the news.

Meckiff said he would not play cricket, including district games, after the present Brisbane Test.

FULL STORY, PAGE 2.

Ian Meckiff retired immediately after being sensationally no-balled in the opening Test of 1963–64 at the 'Gabba.

South Australian Col Egar makes the biggest calls of his career, from square leg. He no-balled the second, third, fifth and ninth deliveries of Meckiff's opening over.

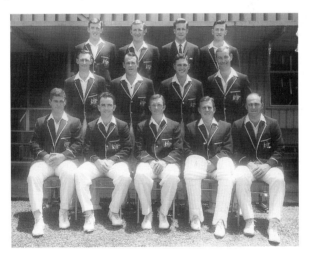

Ian Meckiff before his final Test, Brisbane, 1963–64. BACK ROW (left to right): Alan Connolly, Graham McKenzie, Barry Gibbs (team manager), Bill Lawry. MIDDLE: Brian Booth, Norman O'Neill, Tom Veivers, Ian Meckiff. FRONT ROW: Barry Shepherd (12th man), Bobby Simpson, Richie Benaud (captain), Wally Grout, Peter Burge.

Cricket buccaneer Sid Barnes treated the 1948 tour of England as a money-making venture, 24 hours a day, seven days a week, buying and selling commodities ranging from tinned food and quality shirts through to sporting gear. In between he formed one of the great opening combinations with his room-mate, Arthur Morris.

Barnes' name was cleared after an infamous court case.

Don Bradman almost withdrew from the 1932–33 Test series after being told by the Australian Cricket Board of Control he could not play, write or commentate.

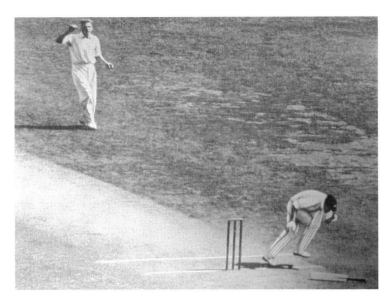

Harold Larwood struck 25 Australian batsmen, including Bert Oldfield in Adelaide, during the infamous Bodyline series in 1932–33. During this game the fury against Bodyline so intensified that every available police reinforcement was sent to the oval in case of a riot.

Right: Harold Larwood's wonderfully fluid and economic action allowed him to bowl at high speed and with incredible accuracy. In an ironic twist, he was later to migrate to Australia.

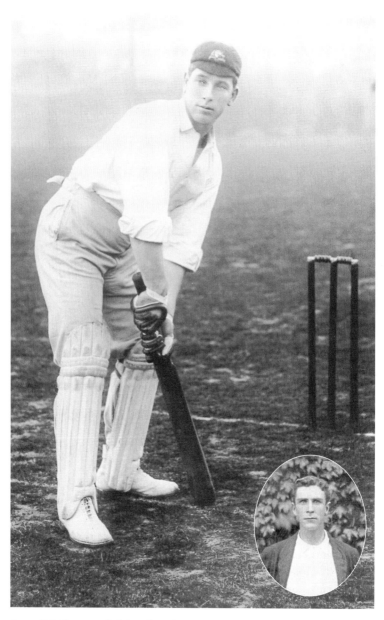

Australia's first great left-hander, Clem Hill, and the man he fought during the infamous boardroom brawl of 1912, Peter McAlister (inset).

tyrannical doings of Jardine, incorporated a new law forbidding more than two men to field behind square leg.

When Voce bumped the ball at the 1934 Australians, he was stood down in mid-match and county captain Arthur Carr sacked. Larwood didn't play and soon afterwards claimed politicians were trying to 'hound' him out of cricket. 'I was fit for the last Test,' he said, 'They feared I would burst the Empire.'

THE FALLOUT FROM Bodyline was all-embracing. After the first MCC–New South Wales game in Sydney, in which Bill Voce took six wickets bowling leg-theory and the Englishmen won by an innings, the Bodyline tactics were mimicked in park competitions around the country.

In *Anti Body-Line*, NSW captain Alan Kippax said that the Bodyline tactics caused injury, fist fights and resulted in games being abandoned: 'On Moore Park, Sydney, a batsman walked down the pitch and threatened to hit the bowler over the head with the bat. On the Domain, a match lasted 15 minutes, ending in a free-fight between the opposing teams. In Adelaide junior cricket, a match was abandoned for a similar brawl after 10 minutes of play.

'The ambulance officer on duty at Centennial Park, Sydney reported that his casualty list on that day was four times its usual length, the vast majority of the additions being head injuries.'

AT A DRINKS break during the final Test in Sydney, Douglas Jardine was handed a glass of cordial. 'Don't give him a drink,' said one barracker. 'Let the bastard die of thirst.'

On another occasion when he went to swish some flies away from his face, a barracker yelled: 'Don't swat the flies, Jardine. They're the only friends you've got!'

BODYLINE OPINION
We have seen sufficient of body-line bowling this season to realise that it does more to kill cricket than any other force ever brought into play . . . it's

premeditated brutality . . . With a speed merchant like Larwood, the element of physical danger is so great that in the interests of cricket he should not use it.

Former Australian captain M. A. 'MONTY' NOBLE

I doubt if England could have won the rubber without body-line bowling. If it had not been used, Bradman, for one, would have made 'buckets' of runs. He is a better batsman than ever . . . If this sort of attack is persisted in, somebody will be killed sooner or later. If I had to play this type of bowling, I would get out of cricket . . . The Australian batsmen had my sympathy.

Legendary England batsman JACK HOBBS

We call it body-line bowling but it is really bowling at the man. If the members of the MCC [Marylebone Cricket Club] had seen this attack in operation in Australia there would be no doubt about their [disapproving] attitude.

Former Australian captain CLEM HILL

The determination to win at any price was deplorable.

DR REG BETTINGTON, former NSW player and ex-captain of Oxford University

Bodyline is dangerous. I believe that only good luck is responsible for the fact that no one was killed by Bodyline.

England's champion batsman and former captain WALTER HAMMOND

If Jardine's team won the Ashes fairly and squarely by certain methods in Australia (and the M.C.C. maintained that the methods were fair and square) why were we not allowed to try and keep the Ashes by similar methods in this country [England, in 1934]?

ARTHUR CARR, former England and Nottinghamshire captain, sacked in 1934

It may be our last Test if the squealing goes on . . . It is about time that the Test cricket farce was ended. Throughout the world the Australians are branded as squealers and bad sportsmen.   **Queensland fast bowler HUGH 'PUD' THURLOW**

Jardine planned for us, he cared for us, he fought for us on that tour and he was so faithful in everything he did that we were prepared on our part to do anything we could for him.   **England opener HERBERT SUTCLIFFE**

There were occasions when any normal captain would have been ruffled by the unprecedented incidents, due solely to England's bowling methods, but to the credit of Woodfull it must be said that no captain could have led his side in a more restrained and exemplary manner.   **Australian wicketkeeper BERT OLDFIELD**

Jardine bore much harsh treatment and barracking in Australia with dignity and courage. He considered that this type of bowling was within the law, but I fancy that he would admit that it was a stern policy.

P. F. 'PLUM' WARNER, former England captain and manager of the 1932–33 team

BODYLINE WAS NOT dead and buried after the 1932–33 Australian season. It was used in the 1933 home series by the West Indies and again in England's wintertime tour of India, under Jardine's captaincy in 1933–34.

The bowler most responsible was the highly strung and volatile Northants speedster E. W. 'Nobby' Clark, who took 10 wickets in three Tests before further controversy in Ceylon when he was accused of deliberately scuffing up the wicket. Operating with three short legs at Chepauk, he caused Indian opener Naoomal Jeoomal to retire hurt after he snicked a bouncer onto his forehead dangerously close to his temple. He also bowled at a body line to The Yuvraj of Patiala, on his debut, the future Maharaja only just avoiding being struck.

'If the young Prince had been hit, I believe the crowd would have rushed the ground,' said Australian Frank Tarrant who umpired two of the three Tests. 'Jardine realised this and took Clark off. To me this was an admission that Clark was bowling with intent to intimidate the batsman.'

In the *Australian Cricketer*, Tarrant said if Clark killed a batsman and had to answer a manslaughter charge, he would give evidence against him.

12. The boardroom brawl which shook a nation: Clem Hill

Australia's first great left-hander, Clem Hill, was charming, popular and sunny-natured, his geniality matched only by his considerable acumen and cricketing ability. One of an exclusive club of just 40 to captain Australia, Hill was also among the most even-tempered . . . that is until his captaincy was questioned and he responded by punching a co-selector on the nose!

The resultant boardroom brawl highlighted the rising bitterness in the power-play between rebellious players and administrators for control of the game, which bubbled into open warfare on the eve of the 1912 tour of England.

AUSTRALIA'S MOST FAMOUS No. 3 before Charlie Macartney and Don Bradman, Clem Hill was a formidable, focused and influential South Australian, good enough as a teenager to make 360 in Adelaide's famous inter-collegiate between St Peter's and Prince Alfred College, and as a Test-man the first Australian to 3000 Test runs at an average superior even to the much-loved Victor Trumper.

As Australia's captain from 1910 to 1912, his record was mixed – five wins and five losses – but he led at a time when England possessed the great Syd Barnes and Frank Foster, the most famous and overwhelming of all Golden Age new-ball pairings.

One of the most ambitious of Hill's team-mates was the stern, fiery-eyed Victorian Peter McAlister who, once crossed, was a formidable enemy. For years their relationship was rarely anything but tepid. Hill was disdainful of McAlister's playing abilities and McAlister resentful of Hill's prominence and popularity. He felt Hill favoured others ahead of him, especially all-rounder Frank Laver, his long-time team-mate at East Melbourne.

Despite only mediocre lead-up seasons, McAlister's inner rage at his omission from the 1902 and especially the 1905 tours to England spilled publicly during Hill's tenure as Australia's captain. Enjoying fresh power as chairman of the very first selection panels established by the Australian Board of Control, McAlister, then 39, not only voted himself into the 1909 touring squad to England, he made himself vice-captain and team treasurer!

In a preview of the internal trouble which was to irrevocably split the game in Australia less than three years later, Hill immediately withdrew, his dislike of the power-hungry McAlister surpassed only by his objections to 'the high taxation' imposed by the Board.

According to Adelaide-based historian Bernard Whimpress, it was the first shot in a long-running battle for power between the Board and the leading players unused to having their healthy on-tour pickings under challenge.

Hill was also reluctant to spend another 10 months away from home. In 1905, he'd been accompanied throughout the tour by his wife, Florrie, who he'd married only weeks before the boat left for Britain.

Fellow players outside the clique were becoming increasingly frustrated, having recognised that their chances of touring overseas seemed dependent on the whims of the very best players, who, until then, had been responsible for selection. Some, like McAlister, saw a more active and powerful Board as their only means of breaking the monopoly.

It was said McAlister had talked himself into the Test team and stayed there for four matches of five in 1907–08, despite a set of undistinguished performances. His reappointment as Victoria's Australian selector ahead of Hugh Trumble in December 1908 was very unpopular among the leading players, confirming their opinion that he was a Board watchdog.

Hill and he had openly disagreed at an acrimonious selection meeting before the release of the 1909 side. McAlister felt he should be in the side; Hill claimed him to be past his best and his style unsuitable to English conditions. Hill also wanted fellow South Australian Alby Gehrs, who had toured in 1905, but was outvoted.

Financially, Hill and the elite players were also on the back foot. In January 1909, Laver was sent to Sydney to renegotiate the financial terms for the tour, but found the Board dictatorial and unbending. Under no circumstances were any players, even the best ones, to be given special consideration. While the Board agreed that Laver could manage, they insisted that a Board nominee, McAlister, also tour, as treasurer. Insulted, Hill immediately telegrammed his withdrawal.

If Hill was nettled enough by the off-field events to stay at home, he sorely missed the challenge and glamour of Test cricket, if not the team politics. However, the retirement of M. A. 'Monty' Noble, one of Australia's finest captains at the conclusion of the tour, was to provide fresh impetus for his career. Named Australia's new captain against Percy Sherwell's visiting South Africans, Hill, for the only time in his career, made two centuries in the same series. His average of 53 was his highest for eight years.

The Board of Control's thorny relationship with Hill and the other leading players was, however, becoming even pricklier. They wanted to be the ultimate policy makers and as the controllers of the game, have the ultimate say in team and tour selection, including the choice of captain and manager. Even more importantly they wanted a goodish share of the profits. Private clubs such as the Melbourne Cricket Club, which had previously backed the tours, were never again to wield as much influence.

While Hill and others could see merit in a central, controlling authority, they were angered by what they saw as Board greediness in the new financial arrangements – the Board having set the terms in 1909 at six per cent of profits up to the first £6000 and 12.5 per cent thereafter. Previously profits had been divided basically on equal terms, and purely among the players.

Open warfare developed with a sudden change in rules denying the players their long-standing privilege of selecting their own manager. The Board's decision, in a split-vote, saw six elite players threaten to withdraw their services from the soon-to-start triangular Test tour to England. The rebels were Hill, his vice-captain Victor Trumper, Vernon Ransford, Warwick Armstrong, A. 'Tibby' Cotter and H. 'Sammy' Carter. 'The Big Six' wanted Laver as manager, but he had been outlawed by senior Boardmen after initially withholding his accounts from the 1909 tour – saying that by rights, it was part of McAlister's touring duties to keep official accounts.

There was a tremendously emotional and very public reaction, lifelong friendships stalling amidst a series of swipes and allegations which sent newspaper circulations soaring.

'What are we to do?' asked one of the key dissenters Trumper, normally the most kindly and generous of men. 'Go down on our knees and ask the Board to let us go to England on any terms they like?'

It was in this angry, unsettled climate that P. F. 'Plum' Warner's 1911–12 Englishmen arrived and the early Ashes battles were played, England taking a 2–1 lead thanks to new-ball pair, the legendary Syd Barnes and Frank Foster, who claimed 40 wickets in the first three Tests.

On the eve of the third Test in his home town of Adelaide, Hill sent a telegram to McAlister in Melbourne saying:

> Macartney all right. Think must have a left-arm bowler. Suggest Macartney and Matthews in place of Whitty and Minnett. Minnett 12th.

McAlister's response was extraordinary:

> My team as forwarded yesterday. Still opposed Macartney's selection. If [co-selector Frank] Iredale agrees with you, favour yourself standing down and not Minnett.

It was the most Machiavellian of replies and Hill, not unnaturally, was enraged. The first to score 3000 runs in Test cricket and holder of the world record score of 365 not out, Hill's average was even higher than that of Trumper, Australia's most-loved cricketer. Twelve months earlier, in his very first Test as Australian captain, Hill had made 191 against the South Africans in Sydney, Australia scoring almost 500 runs on the record-breaking opening day.

While he'd fallen cheaply to Syd Barnes twice in the previous Test in Melbourne, so had the entire Australian top-order, bar feisty Victorian Armstrong, at his best in a scrap. Barnes, with eight wickets for the game, was the matchwinner, his overwhelming first spell (5/6 from 11 overs) the most dynamic ever seen on the first day of a Melbourne Test.

Charles Macartney from NSW, 12th man in each of the first two Tests, was a genuine all-rounder and deserved a place. So did the Victorian wrist-spinner Jimmy Matthews, who'd taken 14 wickets in four preceding games, the great Jack Hobbs one of his three victims in the Victoria–MCC match.

Hill's anger magnified when the text of McAlister's telegram leaked to the newspapers. He wrote to the Board of Control complaining of McAlister's wire but received no satisfaction.

Australia lost the Test, despite a game late-match fightback, led by Hill who top-scored with 98 before falling to Barnes and his normally secure and favourite pull shot.

Approaching the all-important fourth Test, Hill met with co-selectors McAlister and Iredale (from NSW) on the second floor at Bull's Chambers in Martin Place, the NSW Cricket Association's Sydney headquarters. Their task was to pick Australia's next XII and discuss the touring team to England later in the year. Just-appointed Board of Control secretary Syd Smith was also present.

Soon into the meeting, an argument developed over Hill's leadership skills, McAlister scathing of Hill's batting order (Victor Trumper batted at No. 6 and Hill at No. 7) when the Australians were bowled out for just 133 in Adelaide, having won the toss in perfect conditions. He also felt Hill's bowling changes had badly misfired, especially his use of leg-spinner H. V. 'Ranji' Hordern as Tibby Cotter's opening partner.

Still bristling over McAlister's inflammatory telegram, Hill, who'd already been named captain of the team to England, said no Australian side would have toured England under McAlister's leadership, McAlister replying that he was a better captain than Hill and Trumper combined.

The next 15 minutes were among the most explosive in Australian cricket history. McAlister and Hill traded barbs.

McALISTER: You're the worst captain that I've seen.

HILL: If you keep on insulting me I'll pull your nose.

McALISTER: You are the worst captain I've ever seen.

According to the *Australasian* account, Hill leant across the table and struck McAlister, he said, with an open slap. Others claimed later it must have been with a fist, judging by the deep bruising under McAlister's eye. According to eyewitness reports, McAlister ran at Hill 'like an enraged bull', tables and chairs being upended and at one stage one or both almost tumbling out of an open window.

'They were both game and determined,' Iredale told the *Australasian*. 'And they went at it hammer and tongs. Very few blows were struck; it was more like a wrestling match. Smith and I did our best to separate them, but they were all over the place and when the big table was upset, I was pinned in the corner.'

After 10 minutes, maybe more, McAlister lay on his back with Hill over him, both men panting from the exertion. According to author A. G. 'Johnnie' Moyes, Smith tugged hard enough on Hill's coat tails to momentarily split the pair. Iredale then held back McAlister, who yelled 'Coward' as Hill left the room.

Hill told Smith he could no longer continue on the same selection panel as McAlister. Later that day at Hill's hotel, Smith accepted his written resignation. Iredale and McAlister then chose the fourth Test side, the South Australian Harry Blinman co-opted in case of any deadlocks.

'I would not have minded so much if he had invited me outside,' a bruised and battered McAlister told newspaper reporters on his arrival back at Spencer Street railway station in Melbourne. 'Then I would have known what to expect.'

The *Sydney Morning Herald* ran the three-deck headline: BLOOD FLOWS, VIOLENT BLOWS, HILL RESIGNS and also published pictures of the pair under a large caption: THE ADVERSARIES.

Cricket: A Weekly Record of the Game commented: 'Perhaps it was asking too much to expect Messrs Hill and McAlister to work in harmony together . . . there is an old case of friction between them.'

According to historian Rick Smith, Hill was cheered to the wicket in all his remaining innings that summer. However, he failed to make even 25 in four knocks, England winning each of the last two Tests to take the series 4–1.

Hill was never again to play for Australia. Nor would he ever again talk to McAlister.

Hill's invitation to tour England was withdrawn, along with the five other champion players, when it was clear that they would tour only under the management of Laver.

Five players new to Test cricket were blooded, Syd Gregory recalled as captain and Queensland's G. S. Crouch made manager. 'The Board of Control has acted unjustly and dishonestly and has violated its own constitution,' said the just-retired Noble.

While the inexperienced Australians easily accounted for South Africa, England won the deciding match at The Oval by 244 runs in the first timeless Test to be played in England. Barnes, in typically irresistible form, led the charge, taking five wickets in the Australian first innings to give England the edge.

Hill was selected for one more tour, to South Africa in 1914–15 – by a panel not including McAlister – but declined, along with many others including Trumper, who, tragically, was soon to die from nephritis, a disease of the kidneys. Come August the tour was abandoned, after the outbreak of war in Europe.

Hill retired, but in an ironic twist, later served on the Board of Control, as South Australia's delegate. He played his last game, a testimonial match for former team-mate Bill Howell, at the age of 47 in 1924–25, a season in which he also became Australian cricket's first expert comments radio broadcaster during the two Sydney Tests on 2BL.

DESPITE STERLING SERVICE to East Melbourne and consistent efforts at the head of the order for Victoria, including a double century on debut, aged 29, Peter McAlister's hopes for English tour selection prior to 1909 were soured by poor home seasons immediately preceding selection.

In 1901–02 he averaged only 27 and in 1904–05, 19.

In 1905, only two Victorians were chosen, Warwick Armstrong and

Charlie McLeod, plus McAlister's East Melbourne team-mate Frank Laver as manager.

In McAlister's last match before the '05 team was named, he made just eight and a first-ball duck against powerful New South Wales. He finished ninth in Victoria's averages with a highest score of 59 in eight innings.

No EARLY AUSTRALIAN cricketer made more 90s at Test level than Clem Hill. He succumbed six times in the 90s, in 1901–02 scoring 99, 98 and 97 in consecutive innings against Archie MacLaren's touring Englishmen. He made eight more 90s, too, in other first-class matches.

When controversially run out in Sydney in 1903–04, he stood his ground in an obvious show of dissent against umpire Bob Crockett, who was targeted by the crowd for the rest of the day. So angry were they that many remained behind after play waiting for Crockett to emerge. According to author Phil Derriman, Hill took it upon himself to escort Crockett through the crowd to the tram stop.

CLEM HILL'S CAREER-BEST 365 not out for South Australia against New South Wales in Adelaide in 1900–01 remained a world record for a left–hander until New Zealander Bert Sutcliffe made 385 for Otago against Canterbury in Christchurch in 1952–53. Another left-hander, West Indian Brian Lara, holds the present world record of 501 not out, while playing for Warwickshire against Durham in Birmingham in 1994.

Clem Hill stands out in my memory as the most charming and sporting personality I met in first-class cricket.   **H. V. 'RANJI' HORDERN**

I've never seen a batsman who could hit a fast bowler with greater fury than Hill.
A. G. 'JOHNNIE' MOYES

If these men were rebels, they were also gentlemen. And if there was a fault, I doubted that it was on their side.   **ARTHUR MAILEY**

CLEM HILL ALSO played Australian Rules football with South Adelaide and represented South Australia at the sport. His nickname was 'Kruger' after the Boer leader. Racing was one of his passions, and after War War I he became handicapper at the Victorian Amateur Turf Club.

SECOND XII

He was around the wicket
trying to hurt someone . . .
it was a very dangerous situation.
He was out to hurt us.
Andy Bichel on Curtly Ambrose's
fiery farewell in Perth, 1996–97

1. Fiery farewell: Curtly Ambrose

Fiery, brooding, intimidating Curtly Ambrose made sure his final fling in Australia at Perth's WACA Ground would be remembered. As cricket's most ill-tempered Test in years climaxed with umpires Peter Willey and Darrell Hair calling rival captains Mark Taylor and Courtney Walsh to order in an impromptu mid-pitch conference on the third morning, Ambrose inflamed tempers even further with a series of farewell bouncers and no-balls during an acrimonious 12-minute, 15-ball over, the longest in Test cricket annals.

FEW INTERNATIONALS HAVE been as furious or as confrontational as the final Australia–West Indies Test of 1996–97 in Perth. The 40°C heat, the parched and badly cracked WACA Ground wicket and the race to settle some old scores triggered a rare intensity from the time Matthew Hayden fell to the third ball of the match.

The sledging was open and uninhibited, especially when provocative West Indian vice-captain Brian Lara made an unscheduled visit to the wicket on the third morning, acting as a runner for his captain Courtney Walsh.

The Australians were immediately antagonistic and when Lara was accidentally bowled over as Hayden, at the bowler's stumps, took a return from the outfield, the umpires called time out and told captains Mark Taylor and Walsh that their teams were being petulant and bringing the game into disrepute.

The Australians reckoned Lara was being deliberately inflammatory and believed he'd taken a dive. Hayden stood over him and told Lara to get up. He said afterwards he'd only trodden on his toe. The contact was accidental.

The previous evening Lara had gone public against the Australians, claiming consistent intimidation of the recalled Robert Samuels which he believed was totally outside the spirit of the game.

Even Taylor, as even-tempered a cricketer as there has ever been, took umbrage and accused Lara of being an antagonist and of deliberately inciting trouble. 'He looks for things out there that get him going and get other people away from their game,' Taylor said. 'He is a good player who plays it along the lines of Arjuna Ranatunga who puts opposition players off.'

Earlier in the summer after a disputed catch at the wicket, Lara had stormed into the Australian dressing rooms in Sydney accusing wicketkeeper Ian Healy of being a cheat. 'Leopards don't change their spots,' said Healy, mindful of earlier altercations.

With Australia having retained the Frank Worrell Trophy, the Perth Test may have been a dead rubber, but it produced a series of memorable highlights, with man-of-the-match Ambrose central in the good, the bad and the ugly.

Blaming his absence (through thigh injury) from the Adelaide Test for the West Indies' series defeat, Ambrose triggered Australia's first day capitulation despite searing heat estimated at 46°C in the centre. The West Indian fast bowlers could bowl no more than one over spells before the temperature dropped with the arrival of Perth's soothing afternoon breeze, the 'Fremantle Doctor'.

So bouncy was the wicket that the ABC's Jim Maxwell speculated whether Ambrose was bowling with a rubber super ball, rather than the traditional leather Kookaburra.

Both Glenn McGrath and even the more military-paced Andy Bichel bowled bouncers which soared over wicketkeeper Healy's head and thumped against the long leg boundary.

Pivotal in the West Indies' 110-run lead, Lara played with all his irresistible flair in progressing from 15 to 103 in the mid-afternoon session. He took three fours from a Bichel over from the Swan River end and so humbled Warne that three overs cost 26, and the Australian leggie delivered a parting bouncer.

Lara's ally, fellow left-hander Samuels, chipped the ball around, scoring at no more than 14 and 15 runs per hour. At one stage he poked his tongue out at Steve Waugh, who like the rest of the Australians were rapidly losing patience.

Having been castigated by Lara in the morning newspapers, the Australians were amazed to see him re-emerge at the fall of Ian Bishop's wicket, acting as a runner for the injured Walsh.

The ill-humour of the second afternoon was repeated in the volatile opening hour, in which Ambrose, wearing two thigh pads, was struck in the ribs by McGrath before losing his wicket, run out in bizarre circumstances when his bat became stuck in one of the wicket's widest cracks. He watched helplessly as a Healy backhand flick zeroed in and broke the stumps.

Australia's hopes of saving the game all but disappeared when captain Taylor, in the middle of his infamous runless streak, was caught behind and Greg Blewett bowled first ball by a high speed, unplayable delivery which grubbed and hit his middle stump no more than two centimetres from its base.

Struggling with a bruised thigh, Ambrose spent some time off the field and on return bowled a 12-ball over, including six no-balls. Those who felt he'd been deliberately overstepping in a bid to get as close as possible to the Australian tail, especially Shane Warne, were given more proof that Ambrose was chasing more than just wickets when, in his next over, he flagrantly ignored the front line and peppered Warne and his brave partner Bichel with short-pitched deliveries.

'He was way over [the line],' said Bichel, 'I remember saying to the umpire, "He's done that on purpose." He was round the wicket trying to hit someone. At the end of the over, we more or less laughed it off, but it was pretty serious. It just so happened that it was Shane and I at the wicket.

'It was his last Test in Australia. It was hot and he was frustrated. We nicked a few and hit a few in the middle. It all came to a head. It was a very dangerous situation. He was out to hurt us. But I don't think he singled us out. Luckily no one was hit.'

Ex-Testman Dean Jones was to say on ABC Radio that he'd never seen a more disgraceful act in 20 years of Test cricket.

With Australia eight wickets down and facing a comprehensive loss, Ambrose's tactics were those of a man intent on revenge. His extended ninth over read like this on the scorecard: 1 N N . N N N (3 runs) N 3 . N N 1 N (4 runs) . – 19 runs from a record 15 deliveries.

Later, after the Windies had completed a 10-wicket victory, Taylor diplomatically side-stepped the bodyline tactics and paid tribute to both Ambrose and fellow veteran Walsh, who it was felt at the time was also on his last tour: 'I'm glad that I don't have to see you again!' he said.

Warne also fanned the ill-feeling against Lara claiming his mid-match outburst was out of place and should have been kept 'in-house'. 'I was friends with Brian Lara before the Perth Test,' he said. 'But he lost some big points with us [in Perth]. You just don't do that.'

LONGEST OVERS IN TEST CRICKET

15 balls	Curtly Ambrose (West Indies)	v Australia (Perth), 1996–97 (he bowled 9 no-balls)
13	G. O. 'Gubby' Allen (England)	v Australia (Old Trafford), 1934
		(he bowled 3 wides and 4 no-balls)
12	Ian Meckiff (Australia)	v South Africa (Brisbane), 1963–64
		(he was called for throwing four times)
12	Curtly Ambrose (West Indies)	v Australia (Perth), 1996–97
		(he bowled 6 no-balls)

2. The dirt-in-the-pocket affair: Mike Atherton

Mike Atherton has never considered himself anything but a knockabout bloke who likes a pint and the football. It was with high embarrassment that he found himself accused of cheating during the 1994 Lord's Test against South Africa in a ballooning furore that almost cost him his captaincy.

UNTIL THE 90S, when the secrets of reverse swing momentarily halted the mega scoring of the game's flat track bullies, ball-tampering had rarely been an issue. Imran Khan and fellow Pakistanis Wasim Akram and Waqar Younis broke convention and interfered with cricket's normal balance of bat over ball with their remarkable ability to prodigiously swing even the oldest of balls at high speed. So good were they that their methods were immediately questioned.

Television cameras not only were to become a 'third' umpire for run-outs and stumping decisions, they were to unveil a host of on-field misdemeanours, from bowlers notorious for illegally lifting the seam to wicketkeepers claiming catches which weren't.

No one was exempt, even the so-called 'clean-skins' like Mike

Atherton, appointed England's captain just 12 months previously as a brave new face of English cricket.

At Lord's in 1994, where South Africa played its first international at the famous old ground for almost 30 years, Atherton was accused of underhand tactics after deliberately rubbing dirt on the ball to keep it dry for second-game paceman Darren Gough.

Complicating the issue was that Atherton initially refused to admit wrongdoing when called to front International Cricket Council referee, Australian Peter Burge. Quizzed by Burge if he had anything in his pocket that could be used to alter the state of the ball, Atherton said no.

It was an answer which fuelled an already huge furore, Atherton admitting he'd panicked when interviewed by Burge, saying he'd felt like a schoolboy in a headmaster's study and hadn't been as open as he should have been.

Neither Dickie Bird nor his umpiring colleague, Australian Steve Randell, had noticed anything untoward. The condition of the ball did not point to any wrongdoing. However, television replays showed Atherton reaching into his right pocket and vigorously rubbing a substance onto the ball.

'Atherton is such an intelligent chap,' said Bird in *My Autobiography*. 'He's the last person you would think capable of doing anything underhand.'

Gough, 23, was the only Englishman able to make the ball deviate as South Africa set a massive victory target of 457 and bowled England out in its second innings for just 99.

With eight wickets for the game, several with late-swinging yorkers, Gough's figures were due to 'class bowling and nothing else', said Bird. 'It annoyed me that we had found a lad who could deliver the goods, yet his achievements were minimised and overshadowed by the ball-tampering allegations.'

In his defence, Atherton said he'd merely been trying to keep one side of the ball dry in the humid conditions on the third afternoon to aid Gough's reverse swing. But after failing to initially admit any wrongdoing, he was fined £2000 (A$4400) and widely castigated.

Referee Burge's initial statement had amazed journalists, whose offices had fielded calls from fans questioning Atherton's integrity as far away as Johannesburg: 'The match referee has investigated, under Rule 4a of ICC procedures, unfamiliar action taken by the England captain when handling the ball during the afternoon session. Consultation with the umpires and an inspection of the ball confirmed that there was nothing untoward. I also confirm that no official reports were lodged by any parties. I have accepted the explanation given and no action will be taken.'

Atherton said his less-than-open first conversation with Burge remains one of his major regrets in cricket. In an authorised biography written by David Norrie, Atherton said he didn't think he'd done anything wrong and willingly took his playing trousers with him to the interview with Burge.

'I can't deny that I panicked in there,' he said. 'If I had knowingly done something wrong, I'm sure I would have been better prepared. Suddenly I wasn't sure. I had not cheated. But had I contravened the laws? I wasn't totally truthful. Why? It was very much the atmosphere of the headmaster's study and Burge is a fairly stern bloke.

'I was not totally honest with him but I didn't feel I was withholding any evidence. He did not ask to examine my trousers. After he had asked me about the resin he asked me if I had anything in my pocket that could be used to alter the state of the ball. I didn't, but I knew that I wasn't answering his inquiry as completely and fully as he expected, or as fully as I could have. I didn't think it was crucial, but if I could change anything in the whole affair, it would be that moment.'

Atherton was fined £1000 by England's selection chairman Ray Illingworth on each 'count' of having dirt in his pocket and not being totally open when answering Burge's questions. The fine was the stiffest Illingworth could impose without Atherton being subject to a full disciplinary hearing. His action effectively ended the need for the ICC to intervene further.

Many thought Atherton's position untenable. The *Daily Mirror* headlined: THE SOILED SKIPPER. The *Daily Mail* said £2000 was a small price for Atherton to pay for 'the deceit that has sullied the honour of the English captaincy'. England could no longer pontificate to Pakistan now its own captain had been caught with dirt on his hands.

Former Pakistani captain Asif Iqbal said Atherton had betrayed his position. 'Any common man looking at those pictures will say that something was applied to the ball and it's an insult to the intelligence to argue otherwise,' he said. 'If the ICC aren't going to take any action against Atherton, it means there are double standards in world cricket and the people of Pakistan will have every right to feel cheated by what has gone on in the last few days.'

Geoff Boycott recommended Atherton should resign before the scrutiny ruined his life. 'He should quit as England captain right now,' Boycott said. 'Instead, he should concentrate on being the best batsman in the side and maybe, just maybe, consider tackling the job again in five years.'

Pakistan team manager Intikhab Alam said it was a relief to see players from other countries also cited for ball-tampering. 'We have been branded cheats on numerous occasions for a crime our bowlers never committed,' he said. 'But that's not the point. The point is we never got caught. Atherton did.'

Showing himself to be one of the game's great survivors, Atherton was to captain England in a record 52 Tests for 13 wins, 19 losses and 20 draws before being replaced by Alec Stewart. Late in England's 2000 summer, he was on target to join the elite group to play 100 Test matches.

I formed the distinct impression that had Michael Atherton smothered the ball in gooseberry jam, axle grease, HP Sauce, golden syrup, boot dubbin, Tomato

*puree, wet cement, Beluga caviar, brewers' yeast, Holy Water, high octane
aviation spirit or even Semtex, the outcome of the Lord's Test match would not
have been appreciably different.*   **IAN WOOLDRIDGE**

THE BALL-TAMPERING ALLEGATIONS which had surrounded Pakistani teams for
years were to erupt in 1988 with the release of Imran Khan's autobiography, *All Round View*. In it, Pakistan's most legendary cricketer
confessed to using a bottle top to deliberately scuff one side of the ball in a
county game with Sussex in 1981. So successful had his proteges Wasim
Akram and Waqar Younis been throughout the 80s that they were
immediately implicated and suspected of also acting illegally.

Wasim said Imran's confession put an unnecessary strain on both him
and Waqar. They spent much of their careers trying to eradicate the taint.
(In 2000, Waqar became the first to be suspended for ball-tampering.)

Wasim said Pakistani wickets are so notoriously docile that the fast and
fast-medium bowlers, to have any longevity at all, are forced to develop
extra weaponry, such as reverse swing.

Wasim reckons they never had to unfairly scuff the ball. Few batsmen
could survive against their radical new bowling technique, which allowed
them both to swing the ball back disconcertingly late. Geoff Boycott
claimed the Pakistani pair were so lethal and England's batting so inept
they could bowl the opposition out with an orange!

Soon after Imran's ball-tampering admission became public, Warwickshire captain Dermot Reeve, a known practical joker, approached Wasim
with a bottle top in his hand during a Sunday League game and said: 'Do
you want this?' Wasim was furious.

Martin Crowe, the crack New Zealander, all but accused the pair of
cheating during the 1990–91 tour of the subcontinent. Pakistan won the
series but ball-tampering allegations flew between both teams, Crowe
amazed at Lahore to inspect the ball and find it badly gouged on one side,
yet totally shiny on the other.

He said batting was particularly dangerous as even bouncers tended to veer late. 'The last over Wasim bowled to me before stumps [on day four] made me change my thinking about helmets and protection for the rest of my career,' Crowe said in *Out on a Limb*. 'Facing a bouncer, I prepared to sway inside the line of the ball, only to notice, to my horror, the ball change direction in flight and swing back towards my unprotected face.

'I wore only earpieces on my helmet [at that time]. I flung my head back outside the line to the off side, swivelling in one quick motion but only just as the ball flew past, millimetres from my mouth. I settled into my stance and prepared for the next delivery. Again Wasim bowled a bouncer. This time, though, the ball pitched on leg stump and I shaped to go outside the line, to the off side, letting the ball go behind me and over leg stump. But then the ball swung again after pitching and started heading towards where I was moving. I was trapped with nowhere to go and simply froze. Luckily for my teeth, the ball swung away so much towards the slips that it missed me again by a fraction. It was unbelievable [movement].'

Crowe said he had always admired the brilliance of Wasim and Waqar, but he lost respect for them during that tour in which they claimed almost 40 of the 60 Kiwi wickets to fall.

To even the balance between the teams, New Zealander Chris Pringle took a cut bottle top onto the field in the third Test at Faisalabad and at the fall of the first wicket, the Kiwis gathered in a tight huddle and deliberately gouged the ball. Seven wickets fell before lunch on the opening day and Pakistan was bowled out for 102, its lowest-ever score against a NZ team, Pringle's figures a career-best 7/52.

'When the umpires wanted to see the ball, we duly obliged,' Crowe said, 'only to be left under no illusion about the whole shambles when they threw the ball back saying: "Well, now it's fair for both sides!"'

'We knew we'd cottoned on to the Pakistanis' secret,' Pringle said. 'The Pakistanis do have very long, thick, sharp fingernails, but they would have to have had nails of steel to get the marks on hard leather the way that they did.'

In a controversial, ill-tempered series in which Pringle also alleged that

Pakistani captain Javed Miandad had fielded in close and repeatedly told Wasim and Waqar to 'kill him', Pakistan easily won all three Tests. Comparing the two attacks, Pringle said: 'We were triers up against sharks.'

Wasim denied that he or Waqar had gone outside the rules or the spirit of the game. He admits to raising the seam on the ball and scuffing it with dirt to aid his grip but denies that either tactic is ball-tampering. 'They're just tricks of the trade,' he said.

Reverse swing works best on dry, dusty wickets under blue skies, and Wasim was amazed during several tours of England to find these conditions – presumably created to counter the pace of the Pakistanis on green-tops, but inadvertently favouring the visiting team. Wasim said opposing teams unable to exploit reverse swing started a 'witch-hunt', trying to accuse the Pakistanis of foul play.

The most successful left-arm bowler in history, he said reverse swing is harder to bowl than traditional deliveries, as every delivery needs to be pitched on the popping crease and delivered with maximum effort. The secret of bowling it successfully is to keep one side of the ball smooth and the other rough. In England, Wasim favoured using the Reader ball instead of the Dukes ball, as it was slightly less lacquered and tended to scuff up more quickly. Instead of shining the smooth side as is traditional, the Pakistanis would try and 'weight' the ball with spit and sweat, helping it to wobble late.

So discomforted were teams that England's Allan Lamb claimed the Pakistanis were cheating. Test colleague Robin Smith said in every match he played against Pakistan in 1992, he saw 'something going on'.

NOTICE OF BOWLERS seeking advantages through unfair methods began as early as 1911–12 when Johnny Douglas, who achieved the rare distinction of captaining England in his maiden Test series, asked the umpires Bob Crockett and George Watson in Adelaide if frontline Australian bowlers H. V. 'Ranji' Hordern and Charles Kelleway were justified in using resin to obtain a better grip on the ball. He considered it an artificial aid.

The umpires said they were powerless to act, as at the time there was no law against it. They did remind Douglas, however, that wicketkeepers often smeared their gloves with birdlime, an adhesive substance, which was also outside the jurisdiction of the laws.

The medium-paced Kelleway denied any wrongdoing and was to be dropped after taking just six wickets in four Test matches. Hordern, however, claimed 12 wickets on debut and 32 for the summer with his leg-breaks and googlies. His captain, Clem Hill, said Hordern was such a renowned sportsman he doubted the truth of the allegations.

During the Bodyline series, in Adelaide, Australian Bert Ironmonger was accused by England's Maurice Leyland of using resin to improve his grip on the ball. Ironmonger turned out his pocket and Leyland was satisfied. In his other, however, was a handkerchief with eucalyptus oil, which Ironmonger claimed he used for warding off flies.

Marvelling at the big-swingers of old Derbyshire pro George Pope, who conceded he used to use Vaseline under his cap, Australian pace bowler Keith Miller regularly used Brylcreem to keep his hair in place. He admits it didn't harm his ability to move the ball either.

Ball abuse was common before the laws were changed to stop fast bowlers interfering with the seam or captains deliberately scuffing the second new ball so their spinners could continue operating.

According to historian Jack Pollard, it happened as early as the 20s, when Arthur Mailey, seeing a slow-footed batsman, rubbed the ball into the dirt. Colin McCool, another leg-spinner and one of Bradman's Invincibles, also did it, during a Sheffield Shield game for Queensland.

Richie Benaud remembers visiting West Indian captain John Goddard rubbing the second new ball into dirt patches to allow his young spin stars Alf Valentine and Sonny Ramadhin an immediate purchase on the harder ball.

In steamy Madras in 1976–77, England's left-arm bowler John Lever was accused of using Vaseline to help make the ball shinier, via Vaseline gauze that was taped onto his eyebrows to stop the sweat. When he took seven wickets for the game as India tumbled to a third consecutive loss, opposing captain Bishen Bedi accused Lever of cheating, saying he'd used the Vaseline to help make the ball swing.

In English county cricket in 1983, Imran Khan took 6/6 in a sensational 23-ball burst against Warwickshire. One of his five clean-bowled victims, ex-English all-rounder Chris Old, said that, on inspection later, the ball looked like 'a dog had chewed it'. Umpire Don Oslear complained to the Test and County Cricket Board saying there could be no explanation other than the ball had been tampered with.

Imran's Test new ball partner, Sarfraz Nawaz, was adept at wobbling the ball disconcertingly around, through saturating one side of a worn ball with sweat and saliva.

In 1995–96, the Sri Lankans were accused of deliberately scuffing the ball in the 17th over of Australia's first innings in the first Test in Perth. Captain Arjuna Ranatunga said it was a set-up. Referee Graham Dowling warned that action would be taken against the tourists if there was a repeat occurrence. Australia declared at 5/617 and won by an innings.

Later that year, in South Africa, Shaun Pollock and Craig Matthews both had to front referee Clive Lloyd and explain what seemed on television to be deliberate ball-tampering.

3. Partying in Paarl: Stephen Fleming, Matthew Hart and Dion Nash

For a weary band of jet-lagged cricketers 8000 miles from home, the lovely old guest house with its grape-vined courtyard at Paarl must have seemed like Utopia. The players had been reunited with their wives and girlfriends, and an afternoon spent at one of Stellenbosch's finest local wineries was prelude to a barbecue with all the trimmings.

IT WAS ONE of the most promising of all tour beginnings, an emphatic, against-the-odds New Zealand victory against the mighty South Africans in Johannesburg, before the touring team's partying and glaring on-field limitations were clinically exposed during a winless one-day Mandela Trophy campaign.

Leading into Christmas 1994 and the soon-to-start second Test, the New Zealand players had taken advantage of a low-key, rain-affected game against Boland to frequent wine bars and vineyards and enjoy the idyllic surroundings.

In Cape Town, South African women cavorted topless on the whites-only beach, others appeared naked in player rooms. As mid-tour reinforcement Danny Morrison noted, amid the wild holiday atmosphere, cricket was not always everyone's focus.

The world-famous wine-growing area in the rolling hills of Stellenbosch, just 45 minutes away, was a further distraction. On the first night of the otherwise-inconsequential three-day game against Boland, one player stole a bottle of spirits, despite everyone having received complimentary bottles of wine from the proprietor of the Nederburg vineyard.

Several players rampaged through the country-style guest house, Zunderlast, leaving bottles, glasses, cigar ash and port stains on age-old lounge room furniture. Chris Pringle and Richard de Groen, known as 'Grubby', admitted to having had a nightcap or three but said the side-room they'd been in was comparatively tidy when they left.

In a stern lecture the following morning, manager Mike Sandlant reminded the team they had a duty to be ambassadors for New Zealand and not behave like a bunch of pre-pubescent schoolboys on prom night.

Worse was to follow, however, after the Boland game was rained out and a large group of players again partook in local hospitality and visited another vineyard. Sandlant's lecture forgotten, the partying continued unabated back at the guest house. The atmosphere with Christmas so close was festive, and the barbecue spread immense. Clearly the players were out for a big night. Little did they know that they were about to ignite a controversy unprecedented in New Zealand cricket.

Captain Ken Rutherford spent his afternoon watching a video with his room-mate Shane Thomson. Others such as Martin Crowe lazed around the pool. It was an alibi they were glad to have. Shortly after the main meal, Rutherford noticed six or seven players and one of their partners go back upstairs, before soon afterwards re-emerging grinning and laughing hysterically. When repeat trips were made, Rutherford confronted fast bowler Chris Pringle and asked what was going on. Pringle refused to say and suggested he go up there and look for himself.

The next morning, Rutherford was informed by two players, independent of each other, that the group had been smoking marijuana at the vineyard during the afternoon and again back at the guest house that night. 'At the barbecue, the players and one partner were going upstairs and getting stoned,' Rutherford wrote in his autobiography *A Hell of a Way to Make a Living*.

He demanded action from team management, Sandlant and coach Geoff Howarth, who immediately conducted individual interviews into those who had been partaking of the illegal drug. Only three players admitted their guilt: batsman Stephen Fleming, spinner Matthew Hart and opening bowler Dion Nash. Chris Pringle was interrogated a second time and again denied all knowledge. Years later, in his autobiography, he was to admit he was also one of the seven but had lied to save his career. Three others also involved have never been publicly named.

Sandlant's immediate reaction was to send the trio who did own up home, but so close to Christmas it was impossible to get any flights, and with the Test match starting on Boxing Day, substitute players would not have been able to get to Durban in time. Instead he implemented fines, believed to be NZ$250 each, and told the group that to preserve unity and help the team again fully focus on the deciding Tests, the issue would remain in-house, without authorities back home being notified. Howarth admitted later it was naive to think that the issue would not be leaked.

The incident created clear divisions, with ill-feeling apparent against the four who hadn't owned up to their misdemeanours. And everyone wanted to know the identity of the whistle-blowers.

The Kiwis crashed to defeat in Durban and played even poorer cricket in the decider in Cape Town, becoming the first side since 1888 to lose a three-Test series after being ahead.

Leading into New Zealand Cricket's Centenary season, NZ administrators were demanding answers. Sandlant resigned, Howarth was sacked and Rutherford lasted only a few more unsteady months. By April NZ Cricket's executive director Graham Dowling had also moved on. Fleming, Nash and Hart were suspended from three one-day games back in New Zealand. Pringle was also carpeted for 'failing to adequately prepare for a Test match'.

Howarth's contract was paid out on the proviso that he not comment publicly on any issue for a three-year period, other than when defending himself from personal attacks. When the 'embargo' lifted, Howarth confirmed the story of drunken behaviour, vandalism and marijuana smoking. In *Stirred but Not Shaken*, Howarth said the final fortnight in South Africa had been hellish and many players totally undisciplined. He'd noticed clear animosity towards Pringle, who had virtually admitted his guilt when he fronted management and said he wanted to share in the fines handed out to Fleming, Nash and Hart.

'It was to come as little surprise that four years on Pringle should admit in his book to taking part in drug-taking at Paarl,' said Howarth. 'It speaks volumes of his character that he should allow his teammates to take the blame alone and not have the fortitude and honesty to admit his role in the incident at the time.'

Howarth said he was unfairly blamed for the team's run of defeats after the initial success at the Wanderers. 'We were sacrificial lambs to the slaughter,' he said. He denied suggestions he'd been a near-alcoholic throughout his career, saying he couldn't have been ranked among the top 10 batsmen in the world from 1978–83 if he'd been drinking to excess. He spoke favourably on behalf of 23-year-old Nash, whose county, Middlesex, in the face of the furore, had been considering letting him go.

Howarth believed the NZ administration at the time to be 'largely incompetent', but said it never affected his love of cricket or the pride he felt in having captained his country. At the World Cup in 1996, he wore his Kiwi blazer when introduced as one of the former international captains attending the tournament.

Fleming and Nash were both to captain New Zealand. Hart was to soon be outstripped by the fast-emerging left-arm finger spinner, Daniel Vettori. Pringle, described on tour as a law unto himself by one senior player, was to play only one more Test before being discarded, never to return.

The identity of the whistle-blowers has never been made public. However, Nash confronted Danny Morrison, accusing him of dobbing the 'smokers' in – an allegation the fast bowler vehemently denied. Elevated to the NZ vice-captaincy immediately after the scandal became public, Morrison said: 'Some of the players thought Dan had a hidden agenda. They thought I was feathering my own nest. Cricket's a gossipy environment at the best of times, but that whole scene got so political, with different information and sources moving about the team, that I think the rumour-mongering led their opinion instead of confronting me about it . . . "Ruds" [Ken Rutherford] thought I was the whistle-blower and the other players seemed to follow his lead.'

For much of the evening [at Zunderlust] I was involved in social conversation with my partner Kate and Martin Crowe. We noticed some comings and goings but thought nothing more about it. The following morning after practice was rained out, Ken Rutherford told me he suspected that some team members had been smoking dope. **New Zealand coach GEOFF HOWARTH**

Hey, this is stupid [smoking pot]. We're losing it and if we do that we're going to get in the shit here. If you keep running up here then coming downstairs laughing all the time, people are going to catch on.
Fast bowler CHRIS PRINGLE to team-mates at the pot party in Paarl

Before long, seven players were going back and forwards between the courtyard and their rooms, coming back down with that unmistakable sweet smell of marijuana around them. I could not believe how naive they were. It was blatant, in full view of a lot of people.   **DANNY MORRISON**

When it was my turn for questioning, Mike [Sandlant] informed me that three players had already owned up to smoking cannabis and that they would be reported to NZC and probably sent home. I couldn't believe it, I couldn't work out why one player would snitch on his mates and then for Ken [Rutherford] to demand an investigation of his own team while we were waiting to practise.

MARTIN CROWE

I hope their guilt stays with them for the rest of their days. They're liars and they cheated on their team-mates [by not owning up]. It doesn't get much worse than that.   **KEN RUTHERFORD**

4. Flare-up
at Faisalabad:
Mike Gatting

Cricket was never more acrimonious than when England captain Mike Gatting was sworn at and accused of being a cheat by umpire Shakoor Rana at Faisalabad in 1987–88. The pair stood toe to toe, pointing fingers and abusing each other in a furious shouting match that pushed Reagan and Gorbachev off the front pages. For Gatting, it was the beginning of his demise as English captain. Just over six months later, a much-publicised episode with a Trent Bridge barmaid provided authorities with a convenient cover. He was sacked.

FOR A LONDONER with a liking for nothing more fancy than a pie and a pint and a good time, England captain Mike Gatting found himself in troubled waters in Pakistan during the winter tour in 1987. Having triumphed in Australia 12 months earlier, the expectations were immense for Gatting and his men to continue their winning on-tour streak and extract a little revenge after Pakistan's first-ever series victory, albeit 1–0, in England earlier in 1987.

Having made a clean sweep of the one-day internationals, Gatting was shocked to see his team cave in at Lahore, amidst some startlingly fine leg-spin bowling from Abdul Qadir and a series of dubious umpiring decisions, all of which seemed to favour Pakistan. So incensed was Gatting that he broke one of his captaincy rules and delivered a rare post-match tirade against the quality of the officiating umpires, Amanullah Khan and Shakil Khan, whom he claimed had effectively stopped any chance England had of being even half competitive.

At Faisalabad, with a different set of umpires, tempers bubbled totally out of control. The Englishmen, having set themselves up in a series-squaring position, became enraged at what they saw as more blatant umpiring bias.

Gatting and the players closest to the wicket were amazed when an appeal was rejected against Ijaz Ahmed who seemed to have offered a conventional bat-pad catch. 'One rule for one and one rule for another,' said Gatting. 'The sooner we get out of this *%$#ing country the better,' said the catcher, Bill Athey.

The English claimed both comments were directed at team-mates and not at umpire Shakoor Rana, a railway engineer by trade and a member of one of Pakistan's greatest cricketing families, standing in his 15th Test. Both, however, were clearly picked up by the stump microphones, further fuelling the controversy.

With five minutes to play before stumps, Pakistan was 5/106 chasing 292, Eddie Hemmings having been told to try and push through his over to Saleem Malik, so new batsman, the inexperienced Aamer Malik, would have to face one final over. There were only several minutes left with Hemmings midway through his over when Gatting, to save time, informed Saleem that he was bringing his fine-leg David Capel up to save one. 'OK,' said Saleem. 'Right.'

Hemmings had also alerted Saleem to the alteration and was preparing to bowl when Gatting, noticing that Capel had crept in too far, beckoned him to stop. The ball had left Hemmings' hand when umpire Rana hurried in from square leg saying, 'Stop, stop.'

As his umpiring partner Khizar Hayat signalled a dead ball, Rana told Gatting, fielding close in, that it was unfair to move a fieldsman while the bowler was approaching.

'You're waving your hand,' said Rana, 'That's cheating.'

Gatting told Rana he had informed Saleem Malik of the change and had simply gestured to Capel to stay where he was. 'I'm allowed to move my fielders where I want,' he said. 'In any case I wasn't moving him. I was only stopping him.'

He told Rana to go back to his position and stop interfering. Rana then allegedly swore at Gatting, accusing him of being a cheat, the opening shot in an astonishing mid-pitch confrontation.

Given the controversies at the Gaddafi Stadium and Gatting's mounting rage against the standard of subcontinental umpiring, he admits he lost his temper. Totally. 'When it does [blow] – once every 10 years or so – it really does,' said Gatting.

A more graphic, tell-all account of the incident, planned for his autobiography *Leading from the Front*, was so disapproved of by Lord's that, in an (unsuccessful) attempt to avoid a disciplinary fine, Gatting's collaborator Angela Patmore's name went on the pertinent chapter.

'It was the last straw and it broke the camel's back,' she said. Rana and Gatting 'had locked antlers as perhaps they were intended to do' and the second Test came to a 'screeching halt'. Neither would back off and only Hemmings' over was possible. Striding from the ground, Rana told journalist Ted Corbett: 'Cheat, he called me cheat.'

The shouting match between the pair made worldwide headlines. Never before had a player so undermined the authority of an umpire, especially in a Test match. Gatting said he would only apologise if there was a reciprocal apology from Rana. With no apology from either side there was such an impasse that the scheduled third day's play was abandoned, jeopardising a continuation of the tour.

Negotiations continued into the rest day, play continuing on the scheduled fourth day only after a directive from Lord's and the Test and County Cricket Board's winter meeting which resolved that no matter the provocation, Gatting should relent for the good of the game and the tour.

He said no more than he absolutely had to in the note he handed to Rana on the fourth morning:

Dear Shakoor Rana,
I apologise for the bad language used during the 2nd day of the Test match at Fisalabad [sic], Mike Gatting. 11th Dec 1987.

In London, the TCCB's statement was clear and to the point. While mindful of the on-tour frustrations, the match and tour must go on:

It was unanimously agreed that the current Test match in Faisalabad should restart today after the rest day. The Board manager in Pakistan, Peter Lush, was advised of this decision immediately and asked to take whatever action was necessary to implement it. In reaching their decision the members of the Board recognised the extremely difficult circumstances of the tour and the inevitable frustration for the players arising from those circumstances, but they believe it to be in the long-term interests of the game as a whole for the match to be completed. The Board will be issuing a statement on the tour when it is finished, but in the meantime the chairman and chief executive will be going to Karachi for the final Test next week.

So heated was the situation that the English players, anticipating the 'play on' order, initially had refused to continue with the game. Instead, they issued a statement of their own deploring the stand-off and saying it was 'beyond dispute' that umpire Rana was the first to use 'foul and abusive language' towards Gatting. They said Gatting was prepared to apologise 48 hours earlier, had Rana done the same.

'The whole incident seemed suspicious from the start,' said Eddie Hemmings in his book *Coming of Age*, 'and when the next morning Rana refused to restart play until he got an apology from Gatting, there were other factors which confirmed my fears that we were going to be stopped from winning that Test, whatever the cost.'

It was learnt later that the Foreign Office had demanded that the game restart. A substantial amount of the tour guarantee money also remained unpaid by Pakistan at that stage; the 'long-term interests' Lord's had referred to clearly also included monetary factors.

The game belatedly continued on day four, only to end in an unsatisfactory draw, Pakistan declining a request from Gatting for a sixth day's play to be scheduled to help activate a result.

At Karachi, where Pakistan had never been beaten, Qadir increased his series haul to 30 and the match was drawn, giving Pakistan the series.

Gatting put his resignation thoughts on hold when the TCCB's chairman Raman Subba Row, on arrival in Karachi, backed him and the team and even announced £1000 tour bonuses for each of the 16 players.

Graham Gooch was amazed. In his book *My Autobiography*, he said: 'At first when I heard £1000 mentioned, I thought they meant a fine. I reckon they could sense serious rumblings of a mutiny.'

ON RETURN TO England, despite all those who sympathised with him, Mike Gatting knew he'd seriously overstepped the bounds of what was and wasn't cricket. A scandal involving a barmaid at Trent Bridge during the first Test against the West Indies the following June was enough to tip the scales. Gatting was instantly dismissed. His crime: to invite the girl up to his room for a drink.

The Board said they believed Gatting that 'no impropriety' had occurred, but he still had to go. The image of the game had been tarnished once too often. Gooch echoed the players' opinion saying his old friend had simply been sacked 'for Faisalabad in retrospect'.

The English XI had four captains that season, including Chris Cowdrey, the godson of chairman of selectors Peter May. The team lost four of the five Tests, having been saved from defeat at Trent Bridge only by rain.

Within 18 months, Gatting was surrounded by more controversy, signing to lead a rebel English tour to South Africa in defiance of the game's governing body. Only half the tour was possible after politically inspired demonstrations against the team. Like several of his fellow rebels, he returned to traditional Test cricket and played his last international, aged 37, in Australia in 1994–95.

UNTIL THE USE of neutral umpires, Pakistan had been the hotbed for umpiring dissension. New Zealander Jeremy Coney all but led his team from the field in protest at Karachi in 1984–85 and the 1988–89 Australians contemplated abandoning their tour altogether after a series of decisions they considered extraordinary.

Proud Punjabi Shakoor Rana so upset the Kiwis that their normally placid opening batsman Bruce Edgar threw his wicket on the ground in astonishment at a run-out decision at Karachi.

Later in the same game, Javed Miandad was given not out despite a unanimous appeal for a catch at the wicket. NZ captain Jeremy Coney approached Rana who said: 'I swear to Allah, I am not a cheat' before inviting Coney and the Kiwis to come off the ground and view a television replay of the incident.

Coney thought he was ending play a few minutes early to avoid further strife and was about to lead his team from the National Stadium when recalled by the second umpire, Javed Akhtar. 'It was a disgraceful piece of umpiring,' said Edgar in *An Opener's Tale*. 'Miandad was grinning like a Cheshire Cat.'

AFTER THE GATTING fiasco, it was four years before Shakoor Rana was given a further Test match, against the visiting Sri Lankans, again at Faisalabad, in 1991–92. He and Khalid Aziz, who hadn't stood in a Test since 1979–80, combined to uphold a [then] world record 14 lbw decisions!

SHAKOOR RANA WAS umpire during the 20-year-old Gatting's very first Test match, at Karachi in 1977–78. Six lbw decisions against England in its first innings equalled the world record, Gatting falling lbw twice for the match.

Rana stood in a number of English county matches in 1981 in a scheme aimed at giving overseas umpires more experience. It was such a failure than the experiment was never repeated.

A great survivor, Rana (whose brothers Shafqat Rana and Azmat Rana both represented Pakistan) was struck off a list of first-class umpires in 1989 after refusing to take a refresher course. Within weeks he was reinstated.

Asked about the Gatting incident years later, Shakoor said: 'I regret what happened. Cricket does not deserve such a thing but Mike swore at me badly. I told him that insulting a man's honour in Pakistan could lead to horrible things.'

5. Flying high: Ian Botham

On the eve of the most important match in Queensland's cricket history, the team's star all-rounder was in a Perth jail, charged under the Australian Civil Aircraft Act for unruly, offensive behaviour. His name? Ian Terence Botham.

WHEN THE LEGENDARY Ian Botham self-destructed and was sacked by Queensland after just six months of a three-year contract in early 1988, it ended the Australian sunshine state's love affair with imports and firmed Botham's standing as English cricket's most controversial figure since the great W. G. Grace.

Back-to-back Sheffield Shield losses in Launceston and Melbourne saw the Queenslanders forfeit the right to stage a home final. Instead they had to travel to Perth to meet the star-studded West Australians on a lightning-fast WACA pitch.

After a promising beginning in the first half of the season, the high-profile, controversial Englishman was struggling with a back injury, missing home and becoming increasingly hard to control.

After a one-day game, he and old foe Dennis Lillee were accused of creating mayhem in the Old Scotch Collegians dressing rooms at the historic Launceston Cricket Ground, glasses and light fittings being broken and an honourboard damaged. (Lillee later claimed any damage had been exaggerated and the rooms were run down and about to be refitted anyway.)

In the very next game against Victoria, Botham was fined $500 for language Victorian cricket's Code of Behaviour commissioner Walter Jona termed 'indecent and totally unacceptable'.

As had occurred for most of the summer, the Queensland team practised without their champion import. Having never won the Sheffield Shield before, tension was building around the team, some seeing Botham's behaviour as a remorseless flouting of authority which undermined focus and team goals. Within the XI, however, he was considered a God.

Having ignored a no-drinks directive from captain Allan Border in Melbourne, the four-hour trip on Ansett flight No. 55 from Tullamarine to Perth saw Botham once again corner the headlines. He became involved in a heated argument between Border and Greg Ritchie and when the language turned a colour of deep blue, one passenger sitting in front of Botham turned around and complained. 'C'mon, fella. Keep it down. It's becoming a bit common in here,' said Allan Winter.

His temper bubbling, Botham put his hands on Winter's shoulders and turned him around, telling him to mind his own business. He said later it was a mistake to touch the man but said he didn't harm him in any way.

Winter said Botham was telling only half the story, that he not only had gripped him firmly by the scalp and hair, he'd forcefully shook his head from side to side. He also called him an obscene name. 'It's #@&* all to do with you,' he alleged Botham had said.

When another passenger told Botham to pipe down, Botham was said to have replied: 'You! Eyes to the front. Shut up. Otherwise you'll be next.' He also abused a woman who had told him: 'You don't like freedom of speech.'

On arrival in Perth, Botham went to apologise to Winter before checking in at the team's hotel, the Merlin. Within an hour, police had arrived and arrested Botham, accompanying him to Federal Police headquarters and on to the East Perth lock-up where he was formally charged with assault and offensive behaviour.

His wife Kathy and solicitor Alan Herd had just arrived in Perth for the big match, Herd immediately being needed to help arrange bail. When Dennis Lillee was contacted, he said: 'What's the old boy been up to now?' He came down to the East Perth jail with a six-pack of beer and bailed his old adversary out on a $5000 surety.

The Queenslanders lost the final by five wickets and amidst the turmoil, which saw Ansett threaten never to again carry Botham on domestic flights, key sponsors withdrew their support and the QCA administration consulted with lawyers checking the fine print of Botham's contract. Botham remained in Perth for the court hearing and pleaded guilty as charged and was fined $800.

The prosecutor, Jeff Scholz, said throughout much of the flight Botham used obscene language which frightened many of the passengers. He said Botham's language degenerated even further in an argument with Border.

Afterwards Border claimed the ongoing police inquiries and actions against Botham and batsman Greg Ritchie (also charged with offensive behaviour) had been distracting and a clear factor in his team's defeat.

Botham was overseas on a charity walk when the Australian Cricket Board announced a $5000 fine and an emergency meeting of the QCA rescinded his contract. From Perpignan in southern France, Botham said he was unconcerned by the additional fine: 'Five thousand dollars is about 50 quid at the present rate of sterling!' he said.

He was disappointed, however, not to be returning to Queensland to fulfil the remaining two years of his agreement. He regarded

Australia as a home-away-from-home, regardless of the backlash against him. He was critical of cricket legend and member of the ACB, Greg Chappell, being central in the QCA decision, given that he had ordered the infamous underarm delivery to be bowled in Melbourne seven years previously.

As several key sponsors withdrew their support, including the Carphone Group and the London *Sun* newspaper, Chappell said Botham had fallen on his own knife. 'When you go around behaving like him in public, you are looking for trouble,' he told newspapermen.

Not everyone, however, agreed with his sacking. Lillee described Botham's sacking as 'very, very harsh'. Ex-international Geoff Dymock, who managed several Queensland teams on tour during the 1987–88 season, said Botham was a popular team man, who invariably was first to bed the night before a game. 'I've seen other players do worse things and use extremely foul language and they have not even been reprimanded,' he said.

Sheffield Shield attendances at the 'Gabba more than doubled during Botham's time in Brisbane. With 646 runs (average 34), 18 catches and 29 wickets (at 27.75), Botham's presence was pivotal in Queensland's top two placing. He polled five votes in the Sheffield Shield Player of the year, won by teammate Dirk Tazalaar (with 19 votes).

I'm not surprised by anything Ian Botham does really, either on the field or off the field. I think he has been allowed to start believing that he is above the law.
IAN CHAPPELL

As far as I was concerned, a trifling little matter had grown out of all proportion. I knew that I had powerful enemies at Queensland. **IAN BOTHAM**

6. Rendezvous in Singapore: rebel tours of South Africa

At first glance, it seemed to be little more than a fortnight of goodwill, a one-day tournament to celebrate the Golden Jubilee of India's Ranji Trophy, a chance for some valuable match practice leading into the high-octane meetings with the world-champion West Indians.

But when key members of the victorious Australian team stopped over in Singapore, to join others who had just flown in from the south, it suddenly assumed fresh significance. Another raid was being made on Australia's playing elite.

IT WAS 11 P.M. and the receptionist at Singapore's Paramount hotel was working overtime. 'Dr Ali Bacher's suite? Yes sir,' she said.

She'd had inquiries for several days, all of them from strong, athletic types with broad accents.

Upstairs in the biggest room he could book, Bacher, the recruiting power behind the South African Cricket Union's rebel tours, was looking to consummate a two-year agreement for a long-awaited Australian visit to the Republic. He'd gone close in 1983 before negotiations stalled. This time he had a A\$3 million budget, with large advances payable to the 14 or 15 players prepared to sign.

South Africa had been out of bounds, at least to sportsmen, for years. While its cricket administration had a reputation for its indefatigability and was much admired for at least trying to maintain a profile via international tours – not that their peers would publicly admit it – it seemed they were fighting an impossible cause.

Attitudes were hardening. The South Africans had been denied a hearing by the game's rulers, the International Cricket Conference and shortly three of their key administrators were to be refused visas to even enter Australia.

When three countries broke ranks and toured South Africa in the early 1980s, Australia's cricket-loving Prime Minister Bob Hawke met leading Australian players at The Oval during the 1983 World Cup and reminded them of his Government's continuing stand against South Africa. Until the abolishment of apartheid he wanted no sporting associations at all with the Republic. He asked the players if they knew the last two lines of their passports: THIS PASSPORT REMAINS THE PROPERTY OF THE AUSTRALIAN GOVERNMENT, a not-so-veiled threat of Government intervention should any player turn renegade.

Almost the same week, across town in upmarket Mayfair, Bacher was having a series of meetings with the Aussies, who were showing great enthusiasm for a tour and tax-free monies – if not for South Africa's politics or the potential bans they faced.

While Australia's top-ranked 16 players were enjoying greater security via a newly implemented contract system – three-tiered, with the best on $65 000 – the rest were still playing for a pittance.

Some, such as seasoned trio Graham Yallop, Rodney Hogg and Carl Rackemann, were Test regulars, when fit. Others, like Rod 'Puppy' McCurdy, were on the fringes, having worn only the canary yellow uniform of the Australian one-day team. The barrel-chested Victorian felt this may be his only opportunity to represent Australia, even if it was just the 'A' team. Members of the inaugural rebel squad, Graham

Gooch's Englishmen, had been outlawed for three years, but at 24, McCurdy had age on his side should a similar ban be applied by Australian authorities. More important, in his eyes, was the need to fend for his wife and their young son. He knew that the squad to the West Indies just six months earlier had grossed little more than $10 000 per player. Bacher was offering him $200 000 for two seasons. Any tax would be paid by the Union. The Pup couldn't sign quickly enough.

Most of the rebel players believed the Australian Cricket Board's contractual hold extended for only a further 12 months, taking in the 1984–85 international season and the 1985 Ashes tour to England. From 1 November 1985, they regarded themselves as free agents. Their lawyers considered the ACB's additional option clause tenuous.

The meeting in Singapore with Bacher went for five hours and after a break, resumed again at 10 a.m. The former South African cricket captain was determined and persuasive. The night before, he'd taken the New South Wales contingent to Raffles, Singapore's most famous hotel, and shared with them his dream of a new South Africa in which a truly multi-racial game could thrive in the townships and black communities. Only then, he believed, could South Africa ever again hope to re-enter official ranks. At the time, the rebel tours were intrinsic in promoting the game's continuing profile. He didn't want a generation to be lost to cricket.

Bacher said the Australians would not only be handsomely rewarded and play against some of the world's best at some of the game's most-esteemed venues, they would be challenging Apartheid by direct contact rather than ostracism.

Seated next to him was his Australian agent Bruce Francis from Sydney, a former Test player, who for years had been advocating sporting links with the Republic. It was Francis who'd made the initial contacts with players just weeks earlier during a training camp in Canberra. He'd worked for the South African Rugby Board and in

1973 he toured with Derrick Robins' XI, the first multi-racial cricket team to visit South Africa.

Before the meeting started, Bacher took David Hookes aside and offered him the captaincy. Events were to preclude Hookes' eventual involvement – his trip resulted only in the embarrassment of being late to the South Australian Cricket Association's Bradman Medal count, having rushed straight back from Adelaide airport.

The assembled players were keen and attentive. In what was a very informal gathering, many of the players were stretched out on the carpeted floor. At one stage Francis pointed out that the higher profiled, those with considerable Test experience, should receive more than others. He suggested a sliding scale of payments. But Bacher intervened, claiming this untenable and spoke of the problems a similar system had caused when Lawrence Rowe's West Indians toured two years earlier.

Asked by Carl Rackemann what guarantee the Australians had of being paid, Bacher, for once, was lost for words. 'I had no answer,' he said. 'Nobody had ever asked that question before.'

With Bacher and Francis out of the room, the players took a vote and agreed that fees of $200 000 each were fine – if they could be guaranteed. The Union had agreed to bear all tax liabilities in South Africa and up to 60 cents in the dollar in Australia. On Bacher's return, they emphasised the importance of an upfront component.

When Jeff Thomson's solicitor, Andy Hewlett, expressed concern that Thomson's sizeable provident fund monies may be at risk, lessening his client's enthusiasm for the tour, Bacher called a 10-minute interlude and immediately telephoned Terry Alderman in Perth. It was midnight and Bacher said he'd like Alderman to get on the next available plane. If one fast bowler was going to be a dissenter, he wanted to know that a more-than-able replacement was standing by. Alderman assured Bacher of his interest – he was receiving only match payments from the ACB – but it wasn't practical for him to leave straight away. He asked to be kept informed.

Bacher left Singapore truly believing for the first time that an Australian tour could take place.

The players flew back to Australia, determined that the arrangement was 'one-in, all-in'. They agreed to keep the arrangements secret. Many of the players aspired to one last English tour. If there was a leak, it would blow everyone's cover. In 1977, all but four of the chosen 17 had signed with Kerry Packer and were well into their tour before the story was revealed. Maybe they could be as lucky, go to England and if necessary, straight on to South Africa.

Nine of those present in Singapore were shortly to be named in Australia's first Test team in Perth. Kim Hughes was another rebel – not that he knew it at the time. He was to resign his captaincy in tears just two Tests into the summer and, after also being omitted from the 1985 touring party to England, was grateful for the invitation. With Hookes' withdrawal, he was to be captain.

For much of the summer, there were veiled hints that another major revolution might be brewing in Australian cricket. Senior players seemed particularly anxious to check provident fund entitlements – Hughes, for example, was entitled to more than A\$75 000. By early March, just after the team to England had been announced, the rumours were confirmed when the ABC's Jim Maxwell broke the story on national radio. He'd been at a dinner with a former Test player, privy to the offer. Within 36 hours, it was front page news, everywhere.

It was like a bomb going off. World Series Cricket all over again – except this time Packer was in bed with the ACB. Believing they'd been undermined by cricketers too mercenary for their own good, the ACB threatened 10-year bans on prospective rebels who refused to sign statutory declarations saying they wouldn't tour South Africa. They denounced the South African Cricket Union, saying it was as culpable as the players.

The politicians stoked the fire, Prime Minister Hawke accusing the rebels of so prejudicing the future of cricket in Australia that other Test-playing countries may consider their own boycotts. Feeling betrayed, an angry Mr Hawke promised that every rebel's personal finances would be investigated and even suggested – if he could force through the legislation in time – that extra income tax may be payable.

There was no such inquisition on trade with South Africa, of course. That was considered an entirely different matter. In the first 11 months of 1984, exports had soared 80 per cent to more than A$200 million. Mr Hawke also conveniently ignored public opinion polls, where 80 per cent were in favour of the link with South Africa – even if it wasn't officially condoned.

So hysterical was the Government response that Immigration Minister Mr Hurford initially blocked entry visas for Bacher and fellow Union heavyweights Geoff Dakin and Joe Pamensky, who needed time in Australia to prepare their defence of writs issued by the ACB against Francis and eight of the players. Several days later the Foreign Minister, Mr Hayden, countermanded the order, saying it was undemocratic and contravened natural justice.

Meanwhile seven of the 17-man Ashes squad were confirmed as having signed with Bacher's breakaways. In a day of almost unprecedented drama for the Australian cricket community, four players – Dirk Wellham, Wayne Phillips, Graeme Wood and Murray Bennett – did an about-face, signed the ACB's declaration and withdrew from the tour.

The remaining three, Rackemann, McCurdy and Alderman, stood firm, Rackemann charging those who had withdrawn with disloyalty and endangering the tour. He told Trevor Grant of the *Age*: 'By bailing out they have made it harder for the other guys . . . it seems they have been bought out. If it is true it is interesting to note that the people who run Australian cricket consider there are some players worth buying out and others who are not.

'None of the four consulted with the others or the organisers before they reversed their decisions. When we originally signed, we all pledged we would stand firm, no matter what. We have had to depend on the South Africans honouring their side of the bargain. In fact, one thing which worried us was if the going got tough, would the South Africans stand by us? But the net result is that a few of us haven't stood by the South Africans.'

Wellham was one of five promising young cricketers immediately rewarded with a $45 000 three-year scholarship from Packer's PBL Marketing. Another was Victorian Dean Jones, who'd also received an initial South African offer.

Much of the doings of the patched-up and underachieving 1985 Ashes squad in England were given scant treatment by newspaper editors, while the latest developments concerning the rebel tour were eagerly reported. The headlines continued right through until August when lawyers agreed to an out-of-court truce.

After weeks of legal manoeuvring, the South Africans agreed to pay A$120 000 of the ACB's legal costs and had to promise there'd be no more raids. Two more players outside the ACB's contracts list were allowed to join rebel ranks, however: South Australian Michael Haysman and Tasmania's Peter Faulkner.

Victorian Sheffield Shield player Mick Taylor was another late beneficiary. He was earning $75 000 a year as an AMP agency manager, and while his business career was to take a step backwards, he says he'd do it all over again. 'Almost everyone was very supportive of me,' he said. 'Only two or three said I wasn't doing the right thing. I'm not so sure, though, they'd walk away from an opportunity like the one I had.'

While bans were to be imposed, they were only for three years from Test cricket and two from the Sheffield Shield. Given that the rebels were unavailable anyway for two of the years, it hardly seemed a penalty at all. Several of the World Series players who had been ostracised in 1977 were amazed at the leniency afforded the rebels.

One accused the ACB of hypocrisy when one of the team, Queenslander Trevor Hohns, later became Australia's selection chairman.

Of the 16 rebels to South Africa in 1985–86, Alderman, Hohns and Carl Rackemann were the only players to represent Australia at Test level again, Hohns for the first time.

I was 29 at the time and hadn't played for Australia. There were no state contracts in place. I had nothing to lose. The opportunity to go on a tour like this was a career highlight. I would have gone for free.

Australian 'rebel' team batsman MICK TAYLOR

WHEN THE INTERNATIONAL Cricket Council declared South Africa a 'no go' zone, Ali Bacher and other administrators decided if South Africa wanted to maintain any sort of international presence, the only way to maintain the game's profile was via unauthorised tours.

In a nine-year period, seven touring teams visited from four countries, playing against some of the world's best, including champion all-rounder Mike Procter and the great Graeme Pollock. In 16 unofficial Tests from 1982 to 1987, Pollock scored five centuries and averaged 65, including 143 on his last appearance, in home town Port Elizabeth at the age of 43.

The teams not only figured in some of the best cricket of their lives, they acted as ambassadors, involving themselves in multi-racial games which softened world opinion.

England, the West Indies and Australia all toured twice, and Sri Lanka once. All players were banned from official Test cricket, the Englishmen and the Australians for three years, the Sri Lankans for 25 years and the West Indians for life.

In a giant public relations exercise to celebrate its centenary year of Test cricket in 1989, the South African Cricket Union invited former players and journalists from around the world to share in the gala occasion. Hong Kong was a popular stopover point, and spending money was even provided.

Among those present were ex-Test captains 87-year-old Bob Wyatt from

England, Lindsay Hassett, Ian Craig, Ian Johnson and Neil Harvey (Australia) and Walter Hadlee and John Reid (New Zealand).

Members of the Australian Cricket Board were also invited. When all declined, some very reluctantly, South African Cricket Union president Joe Pamensky said: 'Our international critics ignore the glaring defects around the world and direct their venom at us. We can never be satisfied with the pace of change in South Africa, but surely only the most cynical would dare to deny that sweeping change is taking place here, especially in the world of cricket.'

Evidence of this was the dozens of games going on in a huge clearing in Soweto, and the passion for the game in other black townships like Alexandria. While the whites only facilities were eye-opening, all-race cricket teams were being promoted and it was clear that cricket was a pacesetter in much of the bridge-building slowly reunifying South Africa, after the shunning of black and coloured communities for years.

WHEN GRAHAM GOOCH defied authority and led the first rebel team to South Africa in early 1982, he hoped the tour would be treated on its merits as a sporting venture, rather than a political issue. While the monies pocketed were handsome, averaging around £45 000 per man, Gooch and the other 14 players were each banned from Test cricket for three years.

The controversy caused uproar in the House of Commons, Gooch's team being labelled as 'The Dirty Dozen'. British Prime Minister Margaret Thatcher condemned the venture. Sports Minister Neil McFarlane accusing the team of 'deception'.

When they arrived, 12-strong, in Johannesburg, they had no idea who they were going to play against, or when. The program was frenetic, with only a day's break in between games, and three reinforcements were summoned from England. Three tests were eventually played and in front of captivated crowds, South Africa winning the series 1–0.

Gooch was shocked at his ban. 'Sure, I might have been naive, but I thought back to the attempted ban on the men who joined World Series

Cricket, rescinded in some embarrassment and at great cost to cricket after a stormy court case, and I honestly believed the Test and County Cricket Board would be neither wise nor justified in trying the same treatment again,' he said in *Out of the Wilderness*.

The rebel teams to South Africa were:

1981–82, ENGLAND (toured in March 1982): Graham Gooch (captain), Dennis Amiss, Geoff Boycott, John Emburey, Mike Hendrick, Geoff Humpage, Alan Knott, Wayne Larkins, John Lever, Chris Old, Arnie Sidebottom, Les Taylor, Derek Underwood, Peter Willey, Bob Woolmer.

1982–83, SRI LANKA (toured from October to December 1982): Bandula Warnapura (captain), Flavian Aponso, Ajit de Silva, Bandula de Silva, Hermanthe Devapriya, Lanthra Fernando, Mahes Goonatillake, Nirmal Hettiaratchi, Lalith Kaluperuma, Susanthe Karunaratne, Tony Opatha, Bernard Perera, Anura Ranasinghe, Jerry Woutersz.

1982–83, WEST INDIES (toured from January to February 1983): Lawrence Rowe (captain), Richard Austin, Sylvester Clarke, Colin Croft, Herbert Chang, Alvin Greenidge, Bernard Julien, Alvin Kallicharran, Collis King, Everton Mattis, Ezra Moseley, David Murray, Derek Parry, Franklyn Stephenson, Ray Wynter.

1983–84, WEST INDIES (toured from November 1983 to January 1984): Lawrence Rowe (captain), Hartley Alleyne, Faoud Bacchus, Sylvester Clarke, Colin Croft, Alvin Greenidge, Bernard Julien, Alvin Kallicharran, Monte Lynch, Collis King, Everton Mattis, Ezra Moseley, David Murray, Albert Padmore, Derek Parry, Franklyn Stephenson, Emmerson Trotman.

1985–86, AUSTRALIA (toured from November 1985 to February 1986): Kim Hughes (captain), Terry Alderman, John Dyson, Peter Faulkner, Michael Haysman, Tom Hogan, Rodney Hogg, Trevor Hohns, John Maguire, Rod McCurdy, Carl Rackemann, Steve Rixon, Greg Shipperd, Steve Smith, Mick Taylor, Graham Yallop.

1986–87, AUSTRALIA (toured from November 1986 to February 1987): Kim Hughes (captain), Terry Alderman, John Dyson, Peter Faulkner, Michael Haysman, Tom Hogan, Rodney Hogg, Trevor Hohns, John

Maguire, Rod McCurdy, Carl Rackemann, Steve Rixon, Greg Shipperd, Steve Smith, Mick Taylor, Kepler Wessels, Graham Yallop.

1989–90, ENGLAND (toured from January to February 1990): Mike Gatting (captain), Bill Athey, Kim Barnett, Chris Broad, Chris Cowdrey, Graham Dilley, Richard Ellison, John Emburey, Neil Foster, Bruce French, David Graveney, Paul Jarvis, Matthew Maynard, Tim Robinson, Greg Thomas, Alan Wells.

OVERALL, SOUTH AFRICA won eight, lost three and drew eight of the 19 unofficial Tests in the Republic from 1982–90.

The defeats were all to the West Indies, one in 1982–83 and two in 1983–84. One of the highlights came with the inclusion of Cape Coloured spin bowler Omar Henry in two Tests against the Australians in 1986–87. When first told of his selection, Henry thought it a hoax. 'The moment of glory wasn't just for me,' he said in *The Man in the Middle*, 'it was for the non-white community of South Africa. If cricket, by then, was open, in everyday life there remained a gulf between the whites and non-whites.'

7. Political storm: Basil D'Oliveira

Ever since emigrating to England from racially oppressive South Africa to fuel his cricketing ambitions, Basil D'Oliveira's long-time wish was one day to return to his heartland with a white man's dignity and status. It would have been a glorious victory for sport over politics and a thoroughly deserved honour for the unassuming, kindly all-rounder from Cape Town whose only handicap was being born into a white man's autocracy.

IT WAS A MARATHON selection meeting, fully six hours. No panel had ever faced a greater dilemma. Should Marylebone Cricket Club include 27-year-old Basil D'Oliveira among the best 16 players in the country, ignoring the politics and running the risk of having their wintertime tour to South Africa disrupted? Or should they sidestep a showdown with their second-oldest cricketing rival and omit him for reasons of colour?

On the very night that England had squared the Ashes with just minutes to spare at The Oval, across town at Lord's the five-man selection committee had shortened its celebrations to deliberate over their 16-man squad.

D'Oliveira's domineering 158 followed by a crucial wicket in the gripping final half-hour had been all-important in one of England's most famous postwar victories. If the team was to be chosen on merit, he surely had to be an automatic choice.

But there was a complication. D'Oliveira was Cape Coloured, and under South Africa's abhorrent apartheid laws, a second-class citizen, not able to be served in a white man's hotel, travel in the same train carriages or swim at his beaches. At the time, apartheid was at its most sinister, noted activist Nelson Mandela having only just started a 27-year jail term on Robben Island.

As the first non-white South African to play professionally in England, D'Oliveira yearned for the day when cricket could be free of political interference and when matters of race were no longer as important. The son of a tailor, who learned his cricket on the streets of Signal Hill, Cape Town, he felt a debt to the people who had championed him and raised the fare for him to go to England and take up his first £450 appointment in the Lancashire Leagues. He hoped more of his people could also go to England and enjoy the privileges of a true democracy.

From bitter experience, the white man was not to be trusted, and D'Oliveira was initially hesitant even to enter a white man's house. He was amazed to see whites driving buses and serving in hotels – jobs which had been strictly reserved for the coloureds back home.

Without the encouragement of the famed English writer and commentator John Arlott, his star would almost certainly have petered out. He'd scored more than 50 centuries in non-white cricket, including one knock of 225 in just 70 minutes. Considering that matches in Cape Town were almost exclusively on coir matting or rough earth pitches, his performances were exceptional.

When Middleton dismissed its West Indian professional Roy Gilchrist on the eve of the 1960 season, D'Oliveira began his first headlining steps of a professional career which had seemed worlds away growing up in rental accomodation in Signal Hill's bleak Malay quarter.

Having made 119, including 96 in boundary shots, for Arthur Gilligan's XI against the 1964 Australians at Hastings and fulfilled his residential qualifications, D'Oliveira debuted for Worcestershire in 1965 and was one of only two batsmen (along with champion veteran Tom Graveney) to score more than 1500 runs in the English season. On debut he made 106. He was picked for England (aged 34), met The Queen and named for his first representative tour, to the West Indies in 1967–68.

Until then, he'd played with exuberant abandon, a man making up for lost time, being as noted for lifting the new-ball bowlers back over their heads as he was with his delicate back cut, which traditionalists claimed was worth the price of admission alone.

With the scheduled tour of South Africa less than 12 months away, he began to feel the pressure of his position. He was good enough to play for England, but would he be acceptable to South Africa and its vitriolic Prime Minister Dr John Vorster?

So affected was he by the impeding showdown with the South African Government that he lost his place in England's XI and struggled even at county level. Some friends wondered if his form slump was deliberate.

Having averaged just 16 for much of the '68 summer, it was with much surprise and relief that he was reinstated in England's team for the deciding fifth Test on the withdrawal of batsman Roger Prideaux.

Putting a lucrative offer on hold to return to South Africa as a cricket coach to the non-white population, he marched back into prominence, albeit with a large slice of luck – he scored his second Test century after being dropped on 31 by the normally sure Australian wicketkeeper Barry Jarman from the bowling of leg-spinner Ian Chappell.

On the last afternoon, when Australia looked likely to draw the game and win the Ashes 1–0, his late-afternoon dismissal of Jarman triggered the collapse in which Derek Underwood took five wickets in six overs as England won with just five minutes to spare.

Having been dropped earlier in the summer, despite making 87 not out at Old Trafford in the opening Test, his return was both triumphant and timely, with the South African touring team to be chosen. He celebrated with a century against Sussex.

At the time both D'Oliveira and the selectors were unaware that Prime Minister Vorster had as early as March told Viscount Cobham, a former MCC president, that D'Oliveira, as a Cape Coloured, would be unacceptable. The message had been passed back to a select few at MCC. Inexplicably, the selectors hadn't been told and it created a furore in itself.

Despite his qualifications as one of England's rising international newcomers, D'Oliveira was omitted from the squad, a harassed selection chairman Doug Insole saying his bowling did not rate highly enough for him to be considered a genuine all-rounder. Roly-poly opener Colin Milburn was another surprise absentee.

There were howls of protest within England and abroad, most believing the selectors had allowed political pressures to affect their judgement. Politicians rowed, administrators resigned and a protest group was established.

A week later when injured medium pacer Tom Cartwright withdrew, D'Oliveira was named, only for the South Africans to immediately interject and for the tour to be cancelled. D'Oliveira was in Plymouth having dinner with his wife and some friends when he heard the news. 'It was the greatest moment I can remember,' he said in *The D'Oliveira Affair*. 'I think I knew then in my heart, however, that the tour would probably not take place.'

BASIL D'OLIVEIRA'S MEETING with the great South African speedster Peter Pollock in a game at Scarborough at the end of 1966 triggered banner headlines. In the very first over from Pollock, D'Oliveira received a high speed beamer which he only just kept out of his face. When Pollock made no gesture of apology, a livid D'Oliveira lifted the next delivery high back over his head for six.

It wasn't until two years later that the pair talked during the World Championship of Cricket in Australia in 1968, and Pollock admitted it had been accidental and he'd had no intention of hitting him.

'Suddenly we were all talking,' said D'Oliveira, 'Graeme Pollock, Peter Pollock, Trevor Goddard, Denis Lindsay and I. They all said how sorry they were that it had happened [the tour cancellation]. I remember Denis saying: "Sorry about all this, Bas. We would have loved to have had you and seen you playing out there. There was nothing we could do about it." '

8. Watering the wicket: Melbourne 1954–55

Melburnians had never before experienced such murderous heat. It was 104 degrees one day and 107 the next. Even at midnight on the rest day of the Test, the temperature touched 96. So parched and cracked was the wicket at the Melbourne Cricket Ground that first-game curator Jack House watered it in mid-match and senior Australian officials, highly embarrassed by the furore, considered calling it a 'no match'.

IN THE DAYS BEFORE the 1956 Olympics and the transformation of the Melbourne Cricket Ground into a coliseum, passing peak-hour traffic in adjacent Brunton Avenue often slowed to a standstill, fans enjoying the opportunity of seeing a ball or two bowled. The flattening of the Public Stand on the northern flank in preparation for the new Olympic stand further exposed the grand old ground, even allowing spectators in Jolimont Park a peek.

Len Hutton's 1954–55 Englishmen had squared the series in Sydney, giving the third Test an extra edge.

The game started in heatwave conditions on New Year's Eve, the soaring temperatures continuing unabated for 48 hours, the northerly wind so fierce that temperatures unprecedented in Melbourne's history were recorded.

So hot was it on the Saturday that England bowled just 54 eight-bowl overs in five hours, Hutton employing deliberate go-slow tactics to conserve the strength of his bowlers and irritate the Australian top order into false shotmaking.

With Australia 8/188 chasing England's 191, the game was delicately poised but seemed unlikely to go beyond four days, given the enormous cracks in Melbourne's much-vaunted Merri Creek wicket, which were wide and deep enough for the fattest of fountain pens to disappear.

So rock-hard was the wicket by the second morning that Frank Tyson's pace partner Brian Statham twice skidded and fell in his delivery stride. Batsmen running up the pitch could hear their boot spikes clatter on the surface as if they were wearing tap shoes.

The wicket had been damp early, Keith Miller producing one of his greatest spells: 9–8–5–3 pre-lunch on the first day, less than 24 hours after having his injured knee rejuvenated by one of his mate Scobie Breasley's horse-racing doctors.

Playing his first Test match, Victorian Len Maddocks was relieved to see off the menacing Tyson and Statham and go to stumps on the Saturday night unbeaten on 36. Batting for the first time in his career with a thigh-pad, borrowed from Yorkshireman Vic Wilson, Maddocks had the major share of an important 37-run unbroken stand for the eighth wicket with captain Ian Johnson. 'Virtually every ball I faced from Tyson, if I'd missed it, it would have drilled me in the throat,' said Maddocks. 'I don't claim him to be the best bowler ever, but he could well be the fastest ever. I'd step behind it, hold my bat in front of it and hope that it would hit a bottom edge and go for one. He didn't bowl any half-volleys.'

Describing the wicket as like concrete in the final session on Saturday night, Maddocks and his captain were amazed on Monday morning to see the transformation. The cracks had all but closed. It was almost like a first day wicket all over again, only wetter.

'We went out to open the batting on the Monday and it was like walking on cheese,' said Maddocks, 'Your spikes were making a popping sound. The curator [Jack House] had watered it to try and hold it together. It was virtually a sticky [wicket] before falling apart again.

'Without the extra water the Test would never have lasted five days. It would have been all over in four. By the last day there were cracks going up and down and across the pitch that were literally inches wide. Depending on whether Tyson landed on the off-side or the leg side, you'd get a fast, lethal leg- or off-cutter, or if he landed on the cracks going across, it either hit you on the foot or threatened to take your head off. It was impossible to bat on. Once the cracks opened, we fell apart.'

With 7/27, Tyson totally decimated Australia's top order, giving England a 2–1 series lead with two Tests to play. It took England just 75 minutes to bowl Australia out on the final morning.

Just weeks before, the wicket had crumbled badly in the Victoria v MCC game, and curator House was co-opted to assist in helping prepare the best possible wicket for the Test match, the last at the ground for four years. He normally looked after the Albert Ground, the cricket club's No. 2 ground, also in inner Melbourne,

With the fierce northerly sending the temperature gauge soaring to 105 degrees, the wicket cracked badly, and by the rest day House decided he must do something drastic, even if it meant flouting convention. Flying in the face of Marylebone Cricket Club regulations forbidding any watering of the wicket once a game starts, House turned on the hose and showered the wicket for some minutes. Others went home to avoid being implicated.

Percy Beames, a former Victorian captain, covering the match for the Melbourne *Age*, was working in his Collins Street office late on Sunday afternoon when he learnt of House's actions.

He went to his sports editor Harold Austin and told him of the scandal.

'Is it legal?' asked Austin.

'No.'

'Will it be good for cricket?'

'No.'

'Well, we'll put it aside then, but get all the facts together.'

Alongside Beames' Sunday night copy, Austin included a paragraph, in reverse type, about how it was illegal to water wickets. Come the following morning, it was clear that the story had substance, despite the emphatic denials from the Melbourne Cricket Club. Beames made a full exposure in Tuesday morning's paper.

'The game wouldn't have lasted,' said Beames. 'The curator was overseeing his first Test. It was illegal but he did it with every good intention to save face. He wanted the game to go the full distance.

'We wrote that it had been watered and they [the Melbourne Cricket Club] threatened to sue us. But you could tell the way the spikes sunk in [that it had happened].'

A groundsman, an old football team-mate of Beames, had alerted him to the story of a lifetime. But so open was the MCG that dozens of passers-by late on Sunday must also have seen it.

The furore saw the Australian Cricket Board of Control go into damage control and consider offering Marylebone a replay had their own team won.

The Melbourne Cricket Club, led by secretary and ex-Testman Vernon Ransford, strenuously denied the allegations and collected statutory declarations from staff including House, saying the pitch had not been tampered with. All sorts of theories were advanced, from the apparent presence of an underground stream to abnormal sweating under the covers triggered by Monday's cool change.

The Australians established a 40-run lead, the courageous Maddocks finishing with 47, before England experienced the best batting conditions of the match and made 279, despite five wickets from Bill Johnston, extracting sharp turn with his left-arm orthodox slows.

Set 240, Australia tumbled from its overnight 2/75 to be all out for 111, the last eight wickets falling for 34 runs, with Tyson taking 6/16 from 51 balls. As spectators ate their lunches on early trains back home, Tyson and his MCC team-mates celebrated in the bowels of the Grey Smith Stand. For the second time in consecutive Tests, Australia had been bowled out cheaply despite being set only modest fourth-innings totals.

In his autobiography, *A Typhoon Called Tyson*, Tyson said the abnormally hot conditions had so panicked House that he believed the match would finish in four days, if not earlier.

'If one put oneself in Jack House's shoes on that black Sunday, it must have seemed logical to water the wicket,' he said. 'He had been brought in to prepare the Test wicket, expressly to prevent the recurrence of the crumbling wicket of the Victorian game [a fortnight previously]. Had he not acted there can be little doubt that there would have been hardly any wicket left on the Monday.'

The much-vaunted Australians may have again been humbled, but the crowds were enormous, more than 300 000 seeing the five days, including 50 483 on the final day, some of whom scampered onto the ground afterwards and secured a souvenir piece of centre wicket turf.

While House may have brought the game into infamy, the financial benefit was enormous, with gate receipts totalling almost £50 000. Despite the loss of reserved seat revenue from the demolished Northern Stand, the tourists' half share of the gate was £23 966, the largest cheque ever paid to a visiting team for a single game. And the Victorian Cricket Association's share of the receipts was almost £9000, just under half its total income for the 1954–55 summer.

THREE DOCTORED WICKETS

1956   **Old Trafford England defeated Australia by an innings and 170 runs.**

Jim Laker's match. The Surrey off-spinner took 19/90, all from the Stretford end on a red dustbowl of a wicket, described by Neil Harvey as a 'mockery of everything the game of cricket stands for'.

He said the Australians had to endure shockingly substandard wickets for each of the final three Tests. 'They turned bowlers into magicians and class batsmen into helpless puppets,' he said in *My World of Cricket*.

1975   **Headingley   Drawn**

Vandals sabotaged the Rugby end of the pitch with knives and oil, forcing the fifth day's play of the third Test to be abandoned with Australia 3/220 chasing 445.

1996–97   **Delhi   India won by seven wickets**

A dry, cracked pitch spun markedly from the first day, Australia hamstrung by the loss of the injured Shane Warne. The curator at the Feroz Shah Kotla Stadium was later accused of malpractice by match-fixing authorities.

9. The day the Don went on strike: Don Bradman

Don Bradman on strike! It seems inconceivable, but Australia's sporting icon was not making any idle threats. It almost saw him miss the most infamous summer of all, the 1932–33 Tests against Douglas Jardine's visiting Englishmen.

DON BRADMAN'S LIFE changed irrevocably from the time he made a double century in his fairytale maiden appearance in England, at Worcester in 1930. Bursting like a meteor onto the world cricketing stage, his triumphant solo through England totally overshadowed Australia's Ashes-winning feats and made him the ultimate sports hero for thousands struggling through the Depression.

In amassing a record-breaking 974 runs in five Tests, including double centuries at Lord's and The Oval and a triple at Headingley, Bradman scored virtually when he pleased at a run every 1.62 balls, an astonishingly fast rate. He was immediately flooded by a string of lucrative offers which were particularly enticing given the depressed economic climate.

Wrongly denied part of his 'good conduct' bonus of £50 – almost 10 per cent of his total tour fee – for breaking tour regulations when extracts from his life story, *Don Bradman's Book*, were printed between the fourth and fifth Test matches, Bradman was further irritated when the Board effectively blocked his move to play the first of two seasons with Lancashire League club Accrington in 1932.

The £600 per year contract, likely to be supplemented by newspaper work and other endorsements, was indeed handsome. However, it contravened Bradman's 1930s tour contract which stated he could not return to England to play for a period of two years. If the clause was broken the Board could exercise its right to block Bradman's selection for Australia. At a time when work opportunities were strictly limited, it made the English advances even more attractive.

The opportunity for Bradman to remain and work in Australia came via a three-tiered contract with the Sydney *Sun* newspaper, radio station 2UE and sporting retailers F. J. Palmer & Son. While it wasn't as lucrative, it did avoid any immediate showdown with officialdom. Bradman was well aware, however, that Board members frowned on players writing articles for newspapers.

Bradman was at the peak of his form and fitness against the visiting South Africans, the first to Australia in more than 20 years. He'd married Jessie Menzies, also from Bowral, and they'd enjoyed an extended honeymoon to North America as part of Arthur Mailey's private touring side.

On return, on the eve of the arrival of the Englishmen, Bradman's articles in the *Sun* became a more serious issue. Seeking official permission from the Board to continue his involvement with the *Sun* – a request he thought was a formality – he was stunned to learn of Board chairman Aubrey Oxlade's refusal, on the flimsy grounds that journalism was not his sole occupation. The regulations allowed latitude only to those, like Jack Fingleton, who were full-time writers.

'I must earn my living,' Bradman told pressmen, 'and if cricket interferes with my living then I must give up cricket. If the Board has said its last word, I shall not be available for the Test matches.'

BRADMAN BOMBSHELL exploded the newspaper headlines, both in Australia and in London. The game's newest, most-glittering star was at war with his own Board and threatening to stand out of the game for up to two years. Rating Bradman one of the greatest personalities of his time, 'ranking with Lindrum, Mussolini, Gandhi, Hitler, Lindbergh, Kingsford Smith and the Prince of Wales', the editor of the *Australian Cricketer* magazine, H. Drysdale Bett, said the game could not afford to lose a player of his stature, especially as he gave fresh hope and inspiration to all affected by the Depression.

Bradman was adamant that he would not back down. 'I promptly did what any man of integrity would do,' he said in *Farewell to Cricket*, '[and] announced that I would honour my contract and therefore, if the Board was adamant, I would not be available for the Test matches. Not only did it foreshadow the prospect of no Tests for me in 1932–33, but there was the 1934 tour of England in the background.'

Complicating the issue were lucrative offers to cover the Ashes series for newspapers in London.

Given his playing exertions in America (51 innings in 10 weeks, for 3782 runs with 18 centuries), Bradman may have been wiser to bypass an opportunity for an early look at the touring English. However, he, Fingleton and Stan McCabe accepted an offer to play in Perth for a combined Australian XI. Bradman amassed a century: 2/106 from 19 overs of leg spin! Furthermore he found the 10-day return train trip across the continent exhausting. So run down and distracted was he by the furore raging over his availability that he missed the opening Test in Sydney. He attended the game and completed his daily commentaries, but did abide by the Board's edict not to write.

Bradman's withdrawal from the XI was greeted with disbelief. It had been kept from the public until the day before the game. One writer suggested Australia's champion batsman had had a nervous breakdown. Another ventured that his absence was diplomatic, so frightened was he of England's express bowler Harold Larwood, who had unveiled deliberate leg-theory for the first time just a fortnight previously.

The impasse with the Board wasn't settled until the day before the second Test in Melbourne, when a motion urging that the player–writer rule be altered was defeated. Associated Newspapers, owners of the *Sun*, its managing director Sir Hugh Denison and its editorial director Frank Packer (Kerry Packer's father) immediately released Bradman from his contract, cleverly avoiding any backlash from the Sydney public and clearing Bradman's way to play again.

Relieved, but still far from happy with Board bureaucracy, Bradman vented his anger via a press release:

> Through the generosity of the Associated Newspapers of Australia, who requested me to play for Australia instead of occupying a seat in the press box, I have been enabled to play in the second Test. To the great cricket-loving public of Australia, may I express my extreme pleasure at being thus able to represent my country once more.
>
> Even though the Board of Control continues to prevent me from earning an honourable and permanent living from journalism, it allows other members of the Australian XI to broadcast comments freely, despite the fact that broadcasting to them is only a temporary occupation.
>
> Again the difference between journalism and radio work is so small as to make the distinction appear ridiculous.
>
> The Board have all the facts before them at their meeting and their legislation means that they are able to dictate to players the means by which they shall earn their living . . .
>
> I must emphatically protest against the Board of Control being allowed to interfere with the permanent occupation of any player. To my mind the Board was never meant to have powers directing the business activities of players. It is certainly no encouragement

to any player to remain in Australia when such restrictions are brought in.

If Bradman's response was provocative, his return to cricket in Melbourne was nothing short of triumphant. He followed a first-ball duck with one of his most glorious centuries which helped Australia win its only match of the infamous summer, soon to become known for one word: Bodyline.

DON BRADMAN WAS not the only frontline Test player to fall into dispute with the Australian Board of Control over playing and writing. Leg-spinner Arthur Mailey retired from Tests on the eve of the 1928–29 Ashes series when the Board objected to him pursuing his profession in journalism and commentating on matches in which he appeared. Although he was 42, he had appeared in Australia's previous 14 Tests and in his final game at The Oval in 1926, famous for Wilfred Rhodes' comeback at the age of 48, he claimed 6/138 and 3/128.

To my astonishment the Chairman of the Board ruled that I could not write and play because the Board regulations only gave that latitude to anyone whose sole occupation was journalism . . . you can imagine my mental state when that decision was conveyed to me.   **DON BRADMAN**

Here was a pretty 'how d'you do'. An Australian XI without Bradman! It was unthinkable and the public and the newspapers lost no time in saying so.

JACK FINGLETON

AN ON-FIELD SCANDAL engulfed Bradman upon his postwar return to the crease. His ethics and sportsmanship were questioned in the very first Ashes Test after the war in Brisbane when he refused to walk, having swished at a full-length delivery from Bill Voce straight to Jack Ikin at second slip.

Bradman claimed a 'bump' ball, saying he'd first edged the ball into the ground before it had been taken by Ikin. But the Englishmen were so sure it was a catch that they initially didn't even bother to appeal. Only when it became obvious that the experienced George Borwick wasn't going to give Bradman out, did the English appeal. Bradman was just 28 at the time and went on to make 187.

England's captain Walter Hammond walked past Bradman at the change of ends and said: 'A fine &%#! way to start a series.'

Leading batsman Denis Compton said: 'We were stunned and felt a great injustice had been done.'

Captain-to-be Norman Yardley also believed it was out. 'I was in the best position on the field, even better than the umpire himself, to see exactly what happened,' he said. 'I watched the ball bounce from the turf to the top edge of the bat and go from there straight to Ikin's hands. According to the Laws of Cricket he was out.'

Bradman said had he failed in his first comeback Test, he was undecided whether he'd continue in the series. He'd agreed to play only to help cricket get started again after the war.

10. Out of the race: Jack Marsh

Full-blood Aboriginal fast bowler Jack Marsh was so fast the 1901–02 Englishmen refused to play against him. Ranked among the leading express bowlers of the Golden Age, Marsh so delighted in his blue NSW state cap he'd wear it around the streets. He never got to don a baggy green cap, however, his name being scratched from the list of players who could practise even with the New South Wales squad at the SCG by officials blinded by the racial customs of the day.

HAD JACK MARSH been born white, he could easily have played for Australia. For three years the outstanding strike bowler in Sydney, the power base of Australian cricket, Marsh's exploits were phenomenal.

Strong and highly athletic, he was a professional runner and hurdler of note, competing professionally in three states before being 'discovered' by an official of the South Sydney Cricket Club throwing a boomerang for holiday makers at La Perouse.

His double-jointed, wristy bowling action was dubious and resulted in early no-ball calls against him at grade and state trial level. But when he bowled just as fast with his arm encased in splints, it was clear that prejudices outside cricket were clouding his advancement.

Marsh was the find of the 1900–01 Australian season, in which he claimed 24 wickets in four matches, but was also no-balled for throwing 19 times in two matches by the Victorian umpire Bob Crockett.

His debut game, in Adelaide, was memorable for Clem Hill amassing 365 not out, the world record first-class score. But Marsh took 5/181 and followed with six wickets against Victoria, a game in which he was first called by Crockett, the umpire saying later he was concerned at the twist in his wrist, rather than his elbow.

A campaign against throwers had been waged in England and Crockett was the first Australian umpire, at representative level, to make a stand. He no-balled Marsh both in Melbourne and Sydney and Marsh became so exasperated that he deliberately threw three balls.

Long-time critic J. C. Davis (under the nom de plume 'Not Out' in *The Referee*) admitted that 'there was an undoubted and definable difference between the manner in which those balls were thrown and the usual delivery. The difference was so plain that many who had previously held the opinion that Crockett was right, now began to doubt it.'

Cricket historian Bernard Whimpress said Crockett, on the verge of his first international selections, may have deliberately set out on a personal crusade to outlaw Marsh and increase his chances of highest honours, after 10 years spent exclusively at intercolonial level. Umpires who had stood up to throwers had been applauded in England.

The controversy so affected Marsh's standing within the NSW XI that it was 15 months before he was selected again and only when M. A. 'Monty' Noble, NSW's just-appointed sole-selector, was on his way to England with the 1902 Australians and didn't have a say. Noble, one of the ultimate power-brokers in Australian cricket, had blocked Marsh's initial selection only to be overruled by co-selectors Tom Garrett and Ted Briscoe.

Despite his boom first year, Marsh was bypassed for further representative honours until February 1902 when named by the Western Cricket Union to play against Archie MacLaren's English team in Bathurst, only for MacLaren to so object that he threatened to call off the game.

Several citizens' meetings were called at which the pro-Marsh lobby was strong. They firmly believed there were reasons of colour behind MacLaren's stand and his objections that his batsmen risked being injured by Marsh in a second-class game was merely a blind. Many felt Marsh unfairly condemned and that his suspect action was no more than a diversion for a darker conspiracy against him to take the heat off others. Noble, for example, had been labelled a thrower himself, by Sammy Woods, a notable all-round sportsman who represented both Australia and England in Tests.

England was trailing 1–2 in mid-series and Marsh supporters felt MacLaren fearful of Marsh's inclusion as it would highlight Australia's superiority and depth of quality reserves. Though Marsh didn't play, England lost the last two Tests anyway and Marsh drifted into oblivion, playing only sporadically at the highest level, notably when Noble was committed elsewhere.

Marsh led the Sydney grade averages for three years in a row, and may have again in 1904–05 but for missing a portion of the season and touring with the Hippodrome circus, giving bowling exhibitions throughout NSW and Queensland country centres.

In his solitary 'international' for a Bathurst XV against the 1903–04 Englishmen, he took 5/55 and bowled with such variation, curve and break-back that many of P. F. 'Plum' Warner's tourists considered him the finest bowler they had faced on tour, superior even to the great Victorian Hugh Trumble. Warner lost his middle stump to Marsh and claimed later, however, that Marsh threw as many as three balls per over.

'I've never seen anyone throw so deliberately,' said team-mate

Reggie Foster. 'It was a good wicket and he was turning the ball up to a yard at times.'

By now, Marsh had dropped pace and preferred to experiment with seam and spin changes rather than blasting opponents out and running the risk of being targeted by ambitious umpires. He was also rapidly losing heart with the system and especially with Noble, who not only thought him a chucker, but believed he lacked sufficient 'class' to mix in cricketing circles.

Warner made it known that he would strongly resist any moves by the Australians to play Marsh in the remaining two Tests that summer. According to author Anthony Meredith: 'Warner, not to be trifled with in negotiations at any times, was always in belligerent mood when playing second-class matches.'

Crockett's presence as umpire in all five of the summer's Tests was a further deterrent against Marsh's inclusion.

Whimpress says Marsh was 'undoubtedly the victim of racism over selection matters' as well as accusations against the validity of his action. Fellow historian Ray Webster says one of the stamps of the Aboriginal race has been their loose-limbed flexibility and this has led to unorthodoxy, particularly as Aborigines were denied the formal early coaching of their white counterparts.

When it was suggested that Marsh should be considered for the 1905 Australian tour of England, prominent doctor and NSW cricketer L. O. S. 'Les' Poidevin said it was a long shot, 'probably because the absurd White Australia policy has touched or tainted the hearts of the rulers of cricket, as it has the political rulers'.

Years after Marsh's brutal death, aged 42, in a street fight in the New South Wales country town of Orange, former Australian batsman and Test selector Warren Bardsley said Marsh was the best bowler he ever faced, ahead even of the famed Englishman Syd Barnes. 'The reason they kept him out of big [Test] cricket was his colour,' he said.

Author Phil Derriman found an old cutting from the *Bulletin* calling Marsh 'the greatest bowler NSW ever sheltered'. On his death, it said: 'But he was a darky troubled with manners which white brothers found it impossible to put up with.'

ABORIGINES TO PLAY FIRST-CLASS CRICKET

Men:	Johnny Cuzens	Eddie Gilbert
	Johnny Mullagh	Ian King
	Twopenny	Roger Brown
	Albert 'Alec' Henry	Michael Mainhardt
	John 'Jack' Marsh	Jason Gillespie
Women:	Faith Coulthard	Edna Crouch
	Alison Bush	Mabel Campbell

The first black man to play for Australia was Samuel Morris, born in Hobart of West Indian parents, who played one Test in Melbourne in 1884–85.

11. Kidnapped: W. G. Grace and Billy Midwinter

It was an extraordinary scene: Billy Midwinter was padded up and practising with the 1878 Australians ready to open the innings against Middlesex at Lord's when the all-powerful W. G. Grace arrived, claiming 'Middy' was needed elsewhere, and promptly bundled him off in a cab!

YOUNG WILLIAM MIDWINTER was just nine when he joined his family on the *Red Jacket* to Australia, along with hundreds of other struggling Britons smitten by the lure of gold fever. His father, William snr, was first a goldminer before working as a butcher in the Bendigo and Eaglehawk area where William jnr was soon noted as a cricketer of uncommon promise, playing at A grade level from the age of 13.

Scorer of the first recorded double century in Australian cricket, 256 for Bendigo United against Sandhurst in 1869–70, Midwinter's friendship with Harry Boyle, Bendigo's most famous cricketer, saw new opportunities open in Melbourne.

At 191 cm (6'3") and 89 kg (14 st.), Midwinter was a giant of a man, who became a headliner virtually overnight when, representing XVIII of Victoria against the touring Englishmen, he bowled

W. G. Grace and his brother, G. F. Grace (the then holder of the world record first-class score of 154) at the Melbourne Cricket Ground.

A member of the inaugural All-Australia XI which played All-England in March 1877, a game later recognised as the first Test match, Midwinter was one of seven of the Australian team born outside the colonies. Handy in the middle order, he particularly impressed with the ball, taking 5/78 and 1/23 from 73 economic overs of medium pace and almost immediately was offered terms by his county-of-birth, Gloucestershire, captained by legendary W.G.

Not as self-confident as some – he once almost withdrew from an important match because he felt he was not in sufficiently good form – Midwinter was also prone to temper, as shown in Bendigo club cricket in 1876–77 when he was reported for threatening to strike a North Bendigo opponent.

The first in a line of cricket mercenaries to play professionally, six months in England and six in Australia, Midwinter represented Gloucester from 1877–82 and became the first to play Test cricket both for *and* against Australia.

Enticed by the £700 on offer, per man, with Dave Gregory's 1878 Australians, Midwinter looked to alter his cross commitments, the prospect of benefit matches in Melbourne and Sydney more appealing and far more lucrative than the £8, plus expenses, he was pocketing per game from Gloucester. According to Tom Horan ('Felix') in the *Australasian*, Midwinter 'didn't seem to know his own mind for two minutes together'.

Having already helped the colonials to their first-ever victory at Lord's, 'Middy' was preparing to open the batting with famous stonewaller Alick Bannerman against Middlesex when W.G. – pumped-up, to use the modern vernacular – arrived with his closest friend, Gloucestershire county wicketkeeper and rugby international Arthur Bush, on a 'piratical raid' – as described by Grace's most recent biographer, Simon Rae.

After 15 minutes of argument, persuasive to the extreme, back into the cab the two Englishmen stepped – with Midwinter beside them, the sweet-talking Doctor having convinced Midwinter of the importance of Gloucester's match with Surrey, just 30 minutes away across London at Kennington Oval.

Grace was the giant of the game, who had agreed to come to Australia several years earlier only after a £1500 fee and honeymoon expenses were negotiated – not bad for the leading amateur of the day. In an extraordinary week of scoring, in August 1876, he'd amassed 839 runs for only twice out, including an unbeaten 318 against Yorkshire.

When told earlier that 20 June morning of Midwinter's decision to remain with the Australians, Grace lost his temper and abused Australian manager John Conway and fast bowler Boyle, saying they were 'a damn lot of sneaks'.

With Bush as his ally, Grace made his infamous dash across town, picked up Midwinter and within an hour of the start of Gloucestershire's game, had re-entered the field, with Midwinter, and, hardly pausing to find out the score, come on at first change. It had been quite a morning. 'Midwinter is a Gloucester man who had promised Mr Grace to play in all county matches,' said one source.

The Australians and particularly Conway were appalled and considered boycotting the fixture against Gloucestershire later in the season. With Midwinter safely back on full-time county duty, Grace admitted to 'unparliamentary language' towards Conway, an old adversary, and hoped that the Australians would reconsider as they'd 'meet a hearty welcome and a good ground at Clifton'. The game was duly played, a thumb injury conveniently sidelining Midwinter and the match being easily won by the Australians without incident.

In the early 1880s, Midwinter was one of the outstanding all-rounders in the world, and named for Alfred Shaw's English team to Australia in 1881–82, he played in all four Tests against his old team-mates. He also shared in a partnership of 454 in five and a half hours with champion all-rounder William Barnes, for MCC versus Leicester, and counted every run as he went. Once when he was accorded a collection at Scarborough, he carried the money away in a carpet bag. The total proceeds totalled £30, mostly in coppers and it took him two hours to count it all. Asked if he would have preferred a cheque, he said: 'Not a bit of it. I would have to take a cheque to the bank. But the stuff is here and I can do what I like with it.'

According to historian Jack Pollard, when Midwinter arrived back in Australia after the 1882 English season, he said he objected to being called an Anglo-Australian. He considered himself Australian to the core. 'Are we to submit to another season of vagueness from this very slippery cricketer?' asked 'Censor' in the *Sydney Mail*. 'One day he is Australian and the next day an English player.'

After his eyesight began to fail, Midwinter quit the game, passing up the opportunity to tour England one last time in 1888, and became the owner of the Victoria Hotel in inner Melbourne. He died at 39 in a mental asylum, after the tragic early death of his wife Elizabeth and two young children, Elsie and Albert, and the collapse of his family's stockbroking firm. He'd become paralysed from the waist down and lapsed in and out of consciousness. His pauper's grave at the Melbourne General Cemetery in Carlton for years was marked only 'L286' before being found and restored by the Australian Cricket Society in 1982.

A plaque was unveiled as part of a brief service:

WILLIAM EVANS MIDWINTER
The only cricketer to play for Australia v England (eight Tests)
and England v Australia (four Tests)
The Australian Cricket Society in association with the
Victorian Cricket Association, February 1982.

AUSTRALIAN TEST PLAYERS WHO ALSO PLAYED TEST CRICKET
ELSEWHERE

Player	Country/Span	Place of birth	Aust Mts	Total
Jack Ferris	England (1), 1891–92	Sydney (NSW)	8	9
Billy Midwinter	England (4), 1881–82	St Briavels (Eng.)	8	12
Albert Trott	England (2), 1898–99	Abbotsford (Vic.)	3	5
Kepler Wessels	South Africa (16), 1991–94	Bloemfontein (RSA)	24	40
Sammy Woods	England (3), 1895–96	Glenfield (NSW)	3	6

WHILST REVERED, W. G. GRACE was not immune to scandal. He was accused of sharp practice during the 1882 Ashes Test at The Oval when he claimed a run-out against Australian No. 8 Sammy Jones who, after completing a run, had left his crease to do some 'gardening'. One version has Jones looking at Grace and nodding, implying a tacit agreement between them that he was clear to leave his crease. Another was that the ball was unmistakably still in play. Jones and the Australians were astonished when Grace lifted the bails and appealed.

Initially Robert Thoms, one of England's most highly rated umpires of the time, made no move, seeming to be as stunned as the Australian. He asked Grace if he wanted a decision and on Grace saying 'yes' replied: 'It is not cricket, but I must give the batsman out.'

So infuriated was Australia's 'demon' bowler Fred Spofforth by what he considered poor sportsmanship that he bowled like a man possessed, taking 7/44, to go with his 7/46 in the first innings.

England lost by seven runs, prompting the celebrated mock obituary notice in the *Times* saying the body of English cricket would be cremated and taken back to Australia.

12. Cricket's first riot: Sydney 1879

Recent match-fixing and gambling scandals have shaken the foundations of cricket, but they are foundations that have stood up to such shenanigans before. Gambling was at the root of cricket's first riot, in Sydney in 1879 when English captain Lord Harris was attacked with a stick and one of his team punched, amidst reports that the team had deliberately 'played dead' in earlier matches on tour. The furore so stigmatised Australia's 1880 tour to England that the team had to advertise for matches.

WARNINGS AGAINST THE detrimental effect gambling was having on important cricket matches freely circulated more than 100 years ago. Newspapers such as the Sydney *Echo* said that betting 'threatened to eat the heart out of many of our sports'.

Gambling was such an integral part of early Australian cricket that 19th-century annuals regularly including rules for betting. Advertisements were also included from leading city hotels, which boasted 'direct telephone facilities to the Melbourne Cricket Ground and Victoria Racing Club'.

The arrival of teams from England intensified the public interest and large wagers at club and international level were commonplace. When the fourth Lord Harris (Robert George Canning) led a semi-representative side on tour in 1878–79, there were joyous celebrations after the Australian XI defeated his Gentlemen of England in Melbourne in a game later recognised as cricket's third Test match. Even then, cricket was more than just the national pastime.

Soon afterwards a New South Wales XI team also defeated the tourists and come the return fixture in February 1879 at the Association Ground (now the Sydney Cricket Ground), bookmakers looked for more spoils. Despite the earlier English loss, money was again plentiful for England at better odds, even though the world's No. 1 bowler Fred 'Demon' Spofforth was available again for NSW after having missed the first match through injury.

By late on the second day, the local XI had followed on 90 runs in arrears and were sliding to defeat. Bookmakers in and around the pavilion stood to lose the fortune they'd made earlier in the year, as loyal English supporters outnumbered those who had backed NSW. There'd been several big bets on England on the very eve of the game.

The bookmakers' agitation was heightened when first-innings star Billy Murdoch was ruled run out by the tourists' nominated umpire, 22-year-old George Coulthard from Victoria. In a tremendous furore, 2000 invaded the ground and surged to the centre. Most had come from the direction of the terrace area, later to become the ground's famous Hill, where several bookmakers were fixed. Many alleged that Coulthard was incompetent, several accusing him of deliberately cheating.

In the commotion, Lord Harris was hit across the body by a stick. A team-mate, the popular Lancastrian A. N. 'Monkey' Hornby, was punched. His shirt was also torn after he'd grabbed a man he thought was Lord Harris' assailant. Only later, at a much-publicised court case, did the authorities discover that Hornby had collared the wrong man.

According to Spofforth, the crowd refused to vacate the oval until a new umpire was appointed. 'Let an Englishman stand umpire,' they said, 'We won't have a Victorian!'

The melee lasted for 30 minutes and made even bigger headlines than the bank raid bushranger Ned Kelly made on the NSW country town of Jerilderie on the very same day.

Throughout the riot, a grim and determined Lord Harris kept his players on the field, not wanting the New South Welshmen to claim the game. The NSW captain Dave Gregory told Harris he wanted Coulthard replaced and when Harris refused, Gregory claimed the match over and was only persuaded to continue after discussions with the other umpire, Edmund Barton, whose diplomatic skills were later to help him become Australia's first Prime Minister.

Harris understood the emotional reaction to the run-out of Murdoch, the local hero, but fairly bristled at suggestions that his team's sudden improvement in form was because of the generous odds on offer. A great cricket enthusiast and regarded at home as an ambassador, the playing hours never seemed long enough for Lord Harris.

He said such a demonstration wasn't warranted. It demeaned the game and after all, wasn't cricket a game for gentlemen? As to the so-called controversial nature of Murdoch's run-out, two of his fielders square on to the wicket said Coulthard's decision was justified.

Play was abandoned for the day when it became obvious that Harris would not back down and allow a replacement for Coulthard. He admitted Coulthard had made mistakes but they had balanced out. A 5 p.m. restart was aborted.

The *Sydney Morning Herald* described the riot as 'a national humiliation'. And it fearlessly cited Gregory as 'aiding and abetting' the disturbance.

In a letter to the London *Daily Telegraph*, Harris maintained his rage, accusing the Australians of being 'poor losers'. A lengthy reply from the NSW Cricket Association's secretary J. M. Gibson was also published, in which it was claimed Harris had deliberately suppressed some important facts.

Harris again scoffed at suggestions that Coulthard had backed England to win, or that his two professionals, Yorkshiremen George Ulyett and Thomas Emmett, had sullied the game by deliberately performing below their normal standards in earlier matches to make a killing later in the tour.

However, there was no doubt that the bookmaking fraternity was threatened with large losses if England won. 'One well-known betting man acted as a fugleman,' said the *Sydney Morning Herald*. 'The crowd, encouraged by his bad example, worked themselves into a state of violent excitement. A large number of larrikins sitting within the boundary fence made a rush for the centre of the ground and were quickly followed by hundreds of roughs who took possession of the wickets.'

Historian Jack Pollard reported that the men who had struck Lord Harris and Hornby, William Rigney and John Richards, were each fined £2, plus 25 shillings in costs. A Victorian bookmaker had his 1879 membership fees returned and was barred for life. However, other bookmakers continued to gain admittance and freely operated at the ground, despite signs forbidding their presence.

Insulted by what he described as 'a howling mob', Lord Harris withdrew from the scheduled second match against all-Australia in Sydney and on return to London angrily defended his team of accusations that they'd been 'strolling actors rather than a party of gentlemen'. He refused to meet the 1880 Australians on their arrival in England, the team having to advertise for matches.

It wasn't until the influential W. G. Grace, the great Surrey administrator C. W. Alcock and Victorian and Australian all-rounder George Alexander became involved that a full international was arranged, in London. 'W. G.' made the first Test century by an Englishman, Harris was captain and the politics which had dogged the early weeks of the tour were momentarily forgotten amidst the euphoria of a magnificent English victory.

It was a scene of confusion and blows were received and returned. As a general melee was now imminent a number of gentlemen from the pavilion and grandstand hurried to the assistance of the English team who otherwise might have been seriously maltreated. The small body of police who were present were too late to get to the centre of the ground when the rush occurred and subsequently found it difficult to make their way through the crowd.

The *Echo* newspaper

BETTING WAS COMMON practice in England from the earliest times. Wagers on matches in Kent occurred as early as 1646. In the 1730s, the Prince of Wales had played cricket for large bets.

In 1817, England's leading professional player, William Lambert, was said to have sold the match between England and Twenty-two of Nottingham, at Forest Ground. A rough diamond, he was forbidden from ever again playing at the home of cricket, Lord's.

Just weeks earlier, he'd become the first player in the game's history to score centuries in each innings of a match.

Before Lambert's warning-off, which later also spread to the bookmaking element (notorious for sitting in front of the pavilion at Lord's, making odds and taking wagers), cricket and its leading players were becoming increasingly susceptible. According to author Patrick Morrah, young professionals up from the country, living beyond their means in London, were easy game for bookmakers and punters alike.

Big bets, too, were commonplace in Australia. Leading into the first intercolonial between New South Wales and Victoria in Melbourne in 1856, the Victorians wanted to have a side stake of £500, but NSW preferred to play for honour.

Early newspapers often carried the odds, as did the 1859 *Australian Cricketer's Guide*.

A timeline
of trouble

June 1873: Surrey's Edward Pooley is suspended for the remainder of the season for throwing a match against Yorkshire at Sheffield.

March 1877: In the game's first major player dispute, Sydney's Fred 'Demon' Spofforth, the colony's No. 1 fast bowler, withdraws from the inaugural Test after a Melburnian, Jack Blackham, is chosen to keep wickets.

October 1878: A near riot takes place in Germantown during a match between the Gentlemen of Philadelphia and the touring Australians after the visitors refuse to accept decisions by the local umpires.

February 1879: English captain Lord Harris is attacked with a stick and one of his team punched in the face during cricket's first riot at the Sydney Cricket Ground. The invasion comes after NSW XI opener Billy Murdoch is given run out by a Victorian umpire, George Coulthard. Play is abandoned for the day, big betting punters unhappy at the local team's position. Some of the agitators allege the visitors deliberately 'played dead' in earlier matches on tour.

September 1880: Seven of Nottinghamshire's finest players refuse to play for their county unless their demands for a guaranteed benefit and the right to organise their own matches are met. They include notable duo Alfred Shaw and Arthur Shrewsbury who are to stand out of county matches throughout the following English season.

December 1881: Allegations are made in Cootamundra that three of Alfred Shaw's touring English team were to be paid to perform badly in the game with Victoria. The players said to be under the influence of bookmakers are opening bat George Ulyett, No. 3 John Selby and No. 8 William Scotton. England win an extraordinary game after being forced to follow on. Captain Shaw later comments, after witnessing certain cases of misfielding, that 'the rumours were not without foundation'. Ulyett makes 2 and 4, Selby 6 and 23 and Scotton 28 and 2.

December 1884: The entire Australian XI withdraws from the second Ashes Test after an impasse in the distribution of gate receipts between Arthur Shrewsbury's touring Englishmen and Billy Murdoch's Australians, who seek 50 per cent of the takings. Nine players new to Test cricket are chosen for the Melbourne Test, five representing Australia for the one-and-only time.

February 1885: After a mid-match blow-up with captain Arthur Shrewsbury, England's leading wicket-taker for the series, the rumbustious William Barnes refuses to bowl in either Australian innings of the third Test in Sydney.

June–August 1893: During a tour of England fouled by allegations of drunkenness, brawling and financial disputes, Bill Bruce threatens to pull the nose of his captain, fellow Victorian Jack Blackham. The players rebel against manager Victor Cohen, whom they regard as a spy for the Australian Cricket Council.

August 1896: Looking to double their match fees of £10, five Englishmen threaten strike action before the start of the deciding Test match against Australia at The Oval. Robert Abel, Tom Hayward and Tom Richardson relent and take their places, but dual international William Gunn and paceman George Lohmann refuse to play.

August 1897: Champion bowler Bobby Peel is suspended by Yorkshire after arriving onto the field drunk at Bramall Lane. He expressed his readiness to bowl but proposed to do so facing the pavilion rather than the stumps. His captain Lord Hawke leads Peel from the ground and out of big cricket. 'It had to be done for the sake of discipline and for the good of cricket,' he says.

December 1897: A prominent member of G. F. Vernon's English tourists, Billy Bates, taker of the first Ashes hat-trick in Australia, is struck in the eye at net practice in Melbourne, ending his first-class career at 32.

December 1903: English captain P. F. 'Plum' Warner all but leads his side from the field after a noisy demonstration against umpire Bob Crockett, following the run-out of Clem Hill in Australia's second innings during the first Ashes Test in Sydney. Attempting a fifth run from an overthrow, Hill lingers at the crease, adamant he had made his ground. Later he helps escort Crockett out of the ground past the angry mob.

May 1906: With the control of cricket in Australia still in the hands of the Melbourne Cricket Club, the NSW Cricket Association suspends 10 big-name players known to have signed with the club for coming internationals against an English touring team. The ban is quickly lifted again when leading cricketers from Melbourne and Adelaide retaliate by threatening never to play in Sydney again.

March 1908: The Australian Cricket Board of Control refuses to endorse a Fijian tour of Australia, saying it is against the White Australia Policy. The

Melbourne Cricket Club takes over as underwriter. None of the four important games are given first-class status.

January 1912: Australian captain Clem Hill is involved in an extraordinary fist fight with selector and longtime adversary Peter McAlister in the Sydney offices of the New South Wales Cricket Association. A table is upturned during the fight, McAlister claiming that Hill, after a disagreement over the composition of Australia's third Test team, had thrown the first punch before wrestling him to the ground. Hill said he had acted under high provocation, after McAlister referred to him as the 'worst captain in Australian cricket history'.

February 1912: Industrial action is threatened by Australian trade unions against the staging of the fourth Test in Melbourne if Australia names Queensland fast bowler John McLaren, who'd acted as a special constable in a strike earlier that year. McLaren is omitted from the XI and plays his one and only Test a fortnight later in Sydney.

July 1921: After a rain delay and heated debate over a declaration at Old Trafford, Australia's captain Warwick Armstrong becomes the first to bowl two overs in a row in a Test match.

August 1922: Hampshire stalwart Jack Newman is ordered from the field at Trent Bridge by his captain The Hon. Lionel Tennyson for refusing to bowl while the crowd is barracking. He kicks down the stumps in his anger on his way to the pavilion.

March 1923: Victoria's Arthur Liddicutt sends down an underarm in exasperation in Melbourne after English pair Geoffrey Wilson and Wilfred Hill-Wood bat through the entire third and final day's play.

October 1930: Don Bradman is fined £50 after excerpts from *Don*

Bradman's Book are published during the 1930 tour. After a further dispute, he threatens to withdraw from the 1932–33 Tests.

December 1932–January 1933: England captain Douglas Jardine orders his battery of pacemen to bowl deliberate leg-theory at the Australians. G. O. 'Gubby' Allen, an amateur, refuses and dares Jardine to send him home. The Bodyline controversy comes to a head soon afterwards in Adelaide when Australian captain Bill Woodfull, struck earlier in the game by Harold Larwood, tells the MCC management, that 'One [team] is playing cricket. The other is not.' For a time Anglo-Australian relations are strained after the Australian Board of Control issues a telegram saying that Bodyline bowling contradicts the spirit of cricket.

June 1936: India's leading all-rounder Lala Amarnath is sent home from his first tour of England on disciplinary grounds a week before the first Test, after using bad language in the rooms during an inconsequential county match at Lord's. Mushtaq Ali described his team-mate as 'quick to love and quick to fight'.

December 1936: MCC captain Gubby Allen is promised £475 by way of a bribe if he would divulge the composition of England's first Test team for the opening Ashes match in Brisbane . . . providing the recipient won the first prize outright in the forecasting competition run by the local Brisbane *Courier-Mail* newspaper. He refuses.

January 1937: Four Australian players, Stan McCabe, Bill O'Reilly, 'Chuck' Fleetwood-Smith and Leo O'Brien are asked to front the Australian Board of Control at the Victorian Cricket Association's city headquarters. Insubordination and unfitness are mentioned by Board chairman Dr Allen Robertson, but when O'Reilly, a schoolteacher, intervenes and asks if the four players are central in the allegations, Dr Robertson says 'no' and the meeting breaks up. Told to keep the meeting quiet, the quartet emerge into Exhibition Street to the *Herald* newspaper banner proclaiming BOARD CARPETS FOUR TEST MEN. O'Reilly always claimed sectarianism was the real issue, the four enlisted all being Irish Catholic. (Australia was to go 61 years between Catholic captains: Percy McDonnell in 1888 and Lindsay Hassett in 1949–50.)

September 1937: Less than 12 months before England amasses the world record score of 7/903 declared at The Oval, Australian Board of Control chairman Dr Allen Robertson announces: 'I doubt whether England will ever produce a team to make an even go with Australian cricketers – in my lifetime they are not going to produce a team equal to ours.'

November 1945: Thousands of incensed Indians march in protest against free-hitting hero Mushtaq Ali's non-selection for India against the Australian Services XI in the second international in Calcutta. The decision is reversed and Mushtaq plays.

December 1945: Umpire Jack Scott asks for an apology from colourful Australian Services all-rounder Cec Pepper who remonstrates with him after an lbw appeal is rejected against Don Bradman in Adelaide. Cricket writer R. S. 'Dick' Whitington helps Pepper compose the apology, but the Australian Cricket Board of Control say the letter is never received and Pepper, a Test prospect, refuses to send another. Instead he severs all ties with Australian cricket and shifts to England.

November 1946: In a controversial resumption of Test cricket after the war, Don Bradman refuses to walk in Brisbane after Englishman Jack Ikin claims a catch at second slip.

December 1947: Without warning, Australian opening batsman Bill Brown is run out for backing up too far by the Indian Vinoo Mankad in Sydney. Weeks earlier, representing the Australian XI, he had fallen in an identical manner in Melbourne. On that occasion Mankad had previously issued a warning.

May 1948: Lionel Lord Tennyson, a former captain of England, accuses Don Bradman of being a 'mannerless little man' after his request to make a courtesy call is denied during the Australians–MCC game at Lord's.

September 1948: Don Bradman is accused of a protocol faux pas by walking with his hands in his pockets with King George VI at Balmoral at the conclusion of the all-conquering 1948 tour. The King, in fact, had told Bradman and the team to be totally relaxed.

March 1949: Keith Miller is sensationally dropped and Sid Barnes and Don Tallon make themselves unavailable for selection for Australia's tour of South Africa. Miller's axing is said to be for reasons other than cricket. According to Jack Fingleton, it's 'one of the worst selection blunders in Australia's cricketing history'. Ray Robinson calls it 'an ugly blot'. Barnes claims he can't afford time away from his family and business. Later it's revealed that the Australian Board had wanted a £450 limitation on the player bonus, so increased fees would not be payable in home Tests. Members of F. G. 'Tufty' Mann's MCC side to South Africa had received £600 per player 12 months earlier.

December 1951: Controversial Sid Barnes is excluded from Australia's team for the third Test against the touring West Indians for reasons other than cricket. He is later to take the Australian Board of Control on – and win.

February 1952: Prompted by some fiery spells from New South Wales paceman Alan Walker, Australian authorities move to outlaw intimidatory bowling at Sheffield Shield level by recommending a change of laws empowering umpires to intervene in the case of 'unfair bowling pitching in line with a batsman in his normal stance'. Walker had struck South Australia's Bruce Bowley on the back of the head.

February 1954: A shower of bottles, boxes and other debris thrown onto the ground halts play during the West Indies v England Test in Georgetown. England captain Len Hutton refuses to take his team from the ground, saying, 'We want another wicket or two this evening.' Police reinforcements restore order.

December 1954: England's Frank 'Typhoon' Tyson is knocked unconscious by a Ray Lindwall bouncer at the Sydney Cricket Ground, having bounced his fellow fast bowler previously in the opening Test in Brisbane.

January 1955: The Melbourne Cricket Ground pitch is illegally watered on the rest day of the third Ashes Test.

May 1955: Jamaican Leslie George Hylton, 50, is executed for the murder of his wife. He'd played six Tests for the West Indies between the wars.

February 1956: Several members of a Marylebone Cricket Club team, in the presence of their captain, Donald Carr, pour a bucket of cold water over one of the umpires, Idris Begh, during the third international in Peshawar. What was meant as a joke becomes a diplomatic incident, fuelled by criticism of several umpiring decisions earlier in the match. Feelings run so high that MCC offers to abandon the tour. There is further trouble in the remaining unofficial Test, when one of the home batsmen, Imtiaz Ahmed, accuses the English fieldsmen of abusive language towards himself and the umpires.

July 1956: With the Ashes series all-square after three Tests, Bert Flack, the head groundsman at Old Trafford, admits he'd been instructed to deliberately prepare a dusty wicket to help England's finger-spinners Jim Laker and Tony Lock. Laker grabs 19 wickets in an extraordinary match which England wins by an innings.

December 1957: A South African Test umpire confides to an Australian pressman that the action of Australia's Ian Meckiff is illegal. Asked why he didn't no-ball him, he said he and South African cricket didn't need the controversy.

August 1958: Johnny Wardle's invitation to tour Australia is withdrawn by the MCC after a controversial series of articles are published in which Wardle criticises his Yorkshire county captain Ronnie Burnet, who had been lifted direct from club ranks into county cricket. 'For years I've said that Yorkshire is run by a lot of people who think that their old fashioned methods are good enough to cope with modern cricket,' he says. 'A rot has set in with Yorkshire.'

January 1959: Following a selection disagreement, P. R. 'Polly' Umrigar resigns as Indian captain the night before the fourth Test against the West Indies in Madras.

January 1960: Disappointed by their own team's performance, Trinidadians riot midway through the Test against England, at Port-of-Spain. For a time Peter May and his English players remain on the field, huddled around the pitch, before opting for the safety of the pavilion. Seeing all the bottles and debris on the field, next-man-in Wes Hall turns back to the pavilion, saying, 'I'm not going out there for anybody's money, man!' Tear gas is used by police and play is abandoned for the day.

May 1960: The publication of Jim Laker's controversial autobiography *Over to Me* so upsets Surrey and officials that his honorary membership of MCC is withdrawn.

January 1961: Australian captain Richie Benaud is roundly booed and jeered for the remainder of the third day of the second Test by sections of the 65 000 Melbourne crowd, having successfully appealed for hit wicket against West Indian opener Joe Solomon whose cap fell on his wicket.

December 1963: The central victim in a clean-up campaign against throwing, Ian Meckiff, is no-balled out of cricket in the Australian summer's opening Springbok Test in Brisbane. He is the first Australian since Ernie Jones in 1897 to be called at Test level. Years later he concedes, 'The more I hear, the more I believe it was got up to put me out of business.'

September 1966: Publisher Stanley Paul withdraws Bobby Simpson's book *Captain's Story* by order after a controversial section on throwing is particularly critical of ex-team-mate Ian Meckiff. The book is later re-released as a paperback, without the offending Meckiff material. In the original, Simpson refers to the Meckiff influence on youngsters 'when he was throwing at his spectacular best'.

December 1966: South African umpire Hayward Kidson has to raise his finger twice and motion Australian opening batsman Bill Lawry towards the pavilion after giving him out caught behind in the second Test in Johannesburg. Lawry had made 98.

January 1967: After administrators had oversold seating allocations, spectators riot at Calcutta, several trying to damage the pitch and others hurling chairs and benches onto a midfield blaze during the second India v West Indies Test. The second day's play is abandoned as fearful players flee the ground. The army is called in to restore order.

January 1968: In-form fast bowler Graham McKenzie is dropped from Australia's Test team for the final two Tests against India, so the selectors can trial new-ball back-ups for the 1968 Ashes tour.

February 1968: Hundreds of bottles are thrown onto Sabina Park on the third day of the second Test against England. The trouble is triggered by star West Indian batsman Basil Butcher's dismissal to a controversial low-down catch by England wicketkeeper Jim Parks. Play is held up for 75 minutes while bottles are removed and riot police summoned.

September 1968: The MCC abandons its scheduled tour of South Africa after Prime Minister Dr John Vorster objects to the selection of Cape Coloured all-rounder Basil D'Oliveira in England's 16-man squad.

January 1969: Australian opener Ian Redpath is run out 'Mankad' style, without warning, by West Indian fast bowler Charlie Griffith in Adelaide. In the next Test in Sydney, he again wanders absent-mindedly down the wicket. Wes Hall stops at the crease but does not raise the bails.

March 1969: A 17-year-old Viv Richards is banned from cricket for two years after disputing a decision which triggers a riot. It was his debut match for Antigua.

March 1969: The third Pakistan–England Test in Karachi is abandoned early on the third day after a mob of 600 youths invades the ground. The tour, which had struggled along against a continuous background of political turmoil, student protests and general breakdown of law and order, is immediately called off and the English players hurriedly leave for home.

October 1969: Play on the third day of the third India v New Zealand Test in Hyderabad is abandoned after a youth, who had come onto the ground during a determined last-wicket stand by Srini Venkataraghavan and Bishen Bedi, is struck on the face by a lathi (heavy police club) wielded by a guard. The crowd react angrily, throwing chairs onto the ground and lighting fires in the stands.

November 1969: After India's Srini Venkataraghavan is controversially given out caught behind during the first Test against Australia in Bombay, bottles were thrown onto the outfield and chairs and canvas awnings set on fire in protest. Play continues, however, amid all the noise and smoke.

December 1969: Australian captain Bill Lawry is accused of striking an Indian photographer in mid-pitch during a 15-minute break in play with Australia tantalisingly close to victory in the fourth Test in Calcutta. Hundreds of fans had spilled onto Eden Gardens after being pelted by oranges and fruit from upstairs stands. During the delay, several photographers come onto the field to obtain close-up photos of Lawry and his opening partner Keith Stackpole. Lawry pushes away a particularly intrusive photographer who falls heavily, leading to accusations of assault which inflame an already tense situation. After the match the Australian team bus is stoned as it makes its way to the airport.

February 1971: Bill Lawry is sacked as Australia's captain with one Ashes Test to play, the climax of his controversial leadership period. Several of his teammates to India and South Africa had expressed misgivings about his leadership.

February 1971: Without consultation with umpires Tom Brooks and Lou Rowan, England captain Ray Illingworth leads his team from the Sydney Cricket Ground in protest after cans are thrown onto the field and fast bowler John Snow manhandled by a spectator in front of The Hill. Snow had earlier been warned for intimidatory bowling after striking tailender Terry Jenner in the head with a lifting delivery. Fourteen fans are arrested for offensive behaviour during a day without precedent in Australian Test cricket. After being warned by the umpires that they risked forfeiting the match, the England team returns to the field after a break of seven minutes.

July 1971: John Snow is suspended for a Test after shouldering India's Sunil Gavaskar in the opening Test at Lord's. He relays a message to the English selection hierarchy: 'Tell them they can stuff themselves.'

January 1973: Saeed Ahmed is banned for life on return from Pakistan's tour of Australia, having cited a back injury as his reason for not wanting to open the batting in the third and final Test on a green Sydney wicket. He refused a call to return home immediately, and was to be sacked (only to have the ban lifted again soon afterwards). Injured team-mate Mohammad Ilyas is also told to come home, but also refuses, instead seeking citizenship in Australia and ending the summer opening the batting in Sydney grade ranks.

March 1973: Riots and field invasions result in the loss of nearly two hours in playing time during the third Pakistan v England Test in Karachi.

June 1973: Having conceded 19 runs from one of his wayward overs, Derbyshire's Alan Ward is sent off the field by his county captain Brian Bolus at Chesterfield after refusing to bowl again on the final day of the county game against Yorkshire.

August 1973: In a self-protest against the dissent of West Indian captain Rohan Kanhai over a ruling in favour of Geoff Boycott during the second Test at Edgbaston, umpire Arthur Fagg refuses to stand for the first over of the third morning, Alan Oakman taking his place.

August 1973: A bomb threat sees 85 minutes lost on the third day of the England v West Indies Test at Lord's. A telephone call to say that a bomb had been planted at the ground came at a time when the IRA was waging a terrorist campaign in London. The authorities order the crowd of 28 000 to leave the ground while the stands are searched. Many spectators spill onto the playing area. The call proves to be a hoax.

October 1973: The South African Government agrees to allow Pakistan's Younis Ahmed (Saeed's brother) and West Indian John Shepherd to join Derrick Robins' touring team. Younis in particular is castigated as a mercenary for accepting 'honorary white' status. 'He has disgraced not only his country but also his race,' says Pakistan cricket writer Anwar Husain.

February 1974: Alvin Kallicharran is run out while walking back to the pavilion after the final ball of the second day's play in the opening Test against England at Port-of-Spain. Tony Greig had noticed him out of his crease at the non-striker's end and on throwing the wicket down, umpire Douglas Sang Hue gave Kallicharran out. 'It was the dirtiest trick I have seen on a sport's field,' says Errol de Santos, president of the Queen's Park Club. Greig's appeal is withdrawn overnight and on recall, Kallicharran goes from 142 to 158.

March 1974: Ian Chappell has his infamous mid-pitch run-in with New Zealand's Glenn Turner during the second Test in Christchurch. 'I made the comments purely because he annoyed me,' said Chappell. So great was the abuse, Turner claims, that he vows never to change in the same dressing room as the Australian. 'I'm sure that if each series were played in the way this one was I personally wouldn't remain in the game very long,' he says.

July 1974: After complaining about a wide call in a John Player League match at Edgbaston by sticking up two fingers and abusing West Indian-born umpire Peter Wight, Surrey's Geoff Arnold is suspended for two matches.

January 1975: Ninety minutes of playing time is lost after tea on the second day of the fifth India v West Indies Test when the crowd riot following the assault of a youth by police. The youth had run onto the ground when West Indies batsman Clive Lloyd reached his double century.

February 1975: Doubt surrounds the credibility of the toss at Lahore, the first of two Tests between Pakistan and West Indies. Clive Lloyd reportedly returned to the West Indian dressing rooms saying: 'Do you know what? I just lost the toss and was told by the other captain [Intikhab Alam] I'd won!'

February 1975: Ewen Chatfield's heart stops beating after he deflects a bouncer from England's Peter Lever onto his temple in Auckland. His life is saved by England's physiotherapist Bernard Thomas, who runs onto Eden Park and revives the stricken New Zealander, who has a hairline fracture of the skull. As Chatfield lies motionless, Lever slumps to his knees in disbelief and starts crying. 'I thought I'd killed him,' he says.

August 1975: Vandals pour a gallon of oil and gouge three large holes in the Headingley wicket, forcing the final day to be abandoned. England was in sight of its only victory of the summer after setting Australia 445 to win in the fourth innings. Responsibility is claimed by a group attempting to have convicted criminal George Davis released.

January 1976: Indian captain Bishen Bedi accuses England new-ball pair Bob Willis and John Lever of using Vaseline to help shine the ball during England's winning tour, their first to India in more than 30 years. Within 48 hours, the International Cricket Conference replies to Bedi's official complaint, clearing the two Englishmen of any 'sharp practice' and saying the Vaseline-fastened gauze strips used by Lever and Willis to keep the sweat from their eyes were totally appropriate for the sweltering conditions.

April 1976: Five Indians are recorded 'absent hurt' against the West Indies as the fourth Test ends in acrimony on a bouncy, unprepared Sabina Park wicket. The Windies take only 11 wickets yet win the game in four days by 10 wickets. Captain Bishen Bedi and fellow spinner Bhagwat Chandra-sekhar do not bat in either innings. All 17 of India's touring party field at some stage of the game as injuries and illness take their toll.

August 1976: Play is held up late on the third day of the fifth Test between England and the West Indies when a large number of spectators invade the field and trample the pitch, after the dismissal of England captain Tony Greig.

May 1977: In the biggest sporting scoop of the decade, Australian cricket writers Peter McFarline and Alan Shiell break news of the breakaway World Series Cricket movement under the funding of Australian media tycoon Kerry Packer. .

September 1977: Cricket's most dramatic court case begins with Packer's World Series Cricket Pty Ltd and three key players Tony Greig, John Snow and Mike Procter seeking orders to prevent the Test and County Cricket Board and the International Cricket Conference from applying Test and county bans. The case is to go for seven weeks, Justice Slade ruling in favour of WSC and the trio. The bulk of the court costs, estimated at more than $300 000, are awarded against the ICC and the TCCB and its counties, whose annual dividends are affected. In summing up, Justice Slade says, 'A professional cricketer needs to make his living as much as any other professional man.'

February 1978: New Zealand's Ewen Chatfield 'Mankads' Derek Randall after he backs up too far, late in the second Test in Christchurch.

May 1978: Umpire Ralph Gosein and standby umpire John Gayle refuse to stand on an unscheduled sixth day to allow a finish to the fifth Test between the West Indies and Australia at Kingston. Play had been abandoned the night before after a crowd disturbance with the West Indies facing likely defeat, at nine wickets down, with 6.2 overs still to be bowled. The crowd hurls bottles, stones and other debris onto the ground after tailender Vanburn Holder lingers at the wicket having been given out caught behind. West Indies officials agree to extend the match into an extra day to make up the time lost. However, the umpires are apparently not consulted and decline to officiate.

October 1978: Umpire Shakoor Rana warns India's Mohinder Amarnath for damaging the pitch in his follow-through during the first Test against Pakistan at Faisalabad. Sunil Gavaskar is furious and the fifth day starts 11 minutes late with the umpires making a stand against what they considered to be insulting language from the Indian captain.

December 1978: The fifth day of the second Test between India and the West Indies in Bangalore is abandoned after rioting in the city.

January 1979: Rick Darling is carried unconscious from the Adelaide Oval after blacking out, having been hit under the heart by Bob Willis' fifth delivery of the Australian first innings. In the same game, Australian captain Graham Yallop confronts Rodney Hogg as the fast bowler heads for the dressing rooms having bowled just four overs on the third morning. 'At one stage Hogg suggested we survey the back of the Adelaide Oval – and I don't think he had a tennis match on his mind,' says Yallop.

March 1979: Relations between Australian and Pakistani players plunge to a new low in a series of incidents sparked by Javed Miandad's run-out of Rodney Hogg while doing some 'gardening' in mid-pitch in Melbourne. In the next Test in Perth, Alan Hurst 'Mankads' Sikander Bakht and Sarfraz Nawaz appeals successfully against Andrew Hilditch when he picks up the ball and throws it back to the giant Pakistani. In the press box, Bill O'Reilly dubs it 'the ugliest act of reprisal I have ever seen'.

March 1979: The second Supertest in Bridgetown is abandoned on the fifth day when bottles are thrown onto the field following West Indian Roy Fredericks' debatable lbw dismissal. After a break of 50 minutes while the ground is cleared, the players return. Many in the crowd had been chanting: WE WANT FREDERICKS. When Clive Lloyd – and not Fredericks – resumes, there is a second volley of bottle throwing and a section of the crowd spills on to the field, ending the game.

March 1979: Just a fortnight afterwards, a more serious riot takes place in Guyana. The start of the fourth Supertest is delayed for two days by heavy rain, but a return to fine weather leads to an official announcement that play would commence on time the following day. When damp run-ups cause another delay, sections of the large crowd, which had grown increasingly restive and frustrated by the lack of action, erupt into violence. Fences are pushed over and chairs, benches, bottles and other missiles hurled onto the field. Radio booths and the press box are attacked. The mob even storms the pavilion, looting and smashing glass. Fearing for their lives, the Australian and West Indian teams barricade themselves in their dressing rooms. It takes riot police two hours to restore order.

June 1979: Somerset is disqualified from the Benson & Hedges one-day cup competition on charges of bringing the game into disrepute. Looking to keep his team's imposing run-rate after three consecutive victories, captain Brian Rose had declared his innings closed at 0/1 after just one over of the game against Worcestershire. 'It's a great pity when the supreme game of cricket is brought down to this level,' says Worcestershire chairman Geoffrey Lampard.

November 1979: In his farewell first-class season, Ian Chappell is suspended for 21 days for abusive language against umpires in a Sheffield Shield game in Devonport. Later in the summer, during South Australia's international against England, he again runs foul of the umpires and receives a suspended sentence.

November 1979: In a bizarre conclusion to a thrilling World Series match in Sydney, English captain Mike Brearley placed his entire field, including 'keeper David Bairstow, around the boundary with the West Indies needing three to win from the final ball.

December 1979: Dennis Lillee scores his first runs with an aluminium bat in the non-Ashes Test match against England in Perth. Tempers rage when

English captain Mike Brearley objects to its use, saying the ball is being unfairly battered. After a 10-minute delay, Australian captain Greg Chappell finally persuades Lillee to use a conventional blade. Lillee's bat conformed in every way with the definition of a bat as laid down in the then laws – being no more than four and a half inches at its widest and not more than 38 inches long. Cricket's lawmakers amend the rules immediately after the incident, adding a clause that bats must be made of wood.

February 1980: In the first Test at Dunedin, West Indian paceman Michael Holding kicks down the stumps in anger after having a caught behind appeal disallowed against New Zealand's John Parker. At the end of the match, when the last New Zealand batsmen run a leg-bye to give their team a boilover one-wicket victory, Gordon Greenidge deliberately kicks over a stump at the 'keeper's end.

February 1980: As a protest against the competency of New Zealand's senior umpire Fred Goodall, the West Indian team emerges 12 minutes late after the tea interval on the third day of the second Test against New Zealand at Lancaster Park. On the fourth morning, fast bowler Colin Croft deliberately cannons into Goodall after he'd rejected an lbw appeal against Richard Hadlee. Earlier, he'd shown his displeasure at one of Goodall's decisions by flicking off the bails at the umpire's end. At first slip West Indies captain Clive Lloyd makes no effort to intervene. Croft says of the nightmarish tour in which the world champions suffer a rare defeat: 'If I was shipwrecked a mile from the coast of New Zealand, I'd turn around and swim past the sharks to Australia.'

August 1980: Umpire David Constant is jostled in front of the Long Room by some MCC members, frustrated at a lengthy stoppage during the Centenary Test.

January 1981: Heckled beyond endurance by fans who hurl oranges and other missiles at him, West Indian fast bowler Sylvester Clarke throws a brick into the crowd, seriously knocking a student leader unconscious at Multan during the acrimonious fourth Test with Pakistan. His captain Alvin Kallicharran appeals to the Qasim Bagh crowd on bended knee to help restore order.

February 1981: Australian captain Greg Chappell instructs his brother Trevor to bowl an underarm to New Zealand No. 11 Brian McKechnie to finish a one-day international in Melbourne. Chappell admits later he was mentally exhausted and not fit to captain Australia that day.

February 1981: Indian captain Sunil Gavaskar motions his batting partner Chetan Chauhan to also walk off with him in protest against an lbw decision against him in Melbourne. Chauhan is stopped at the gate by the team's tour manager Wing Commander S. K. Durrani, who tells him to resume his place at the wicket for fear of the Indians forfeiting the game.

February 1981: England withdraws from the second Test match against the West Indies in Georgetown after permission for fast bowler Robin Jackman to stay in Guyana is revoked, because of his previous association as a player and coach in South Africa.

July 1981: Dennis Lillee and Rod Marsh bet against Australia winning the Leeds Test – and win A$15 000 after an astonishing second-innings collapse. When Lillee confesses all in his autobiography, future contracts are to forbid any Australian player or associate gambling on games.

September 1981: Imran Khan uses a bottle top to scuff the ball in a county game between Sussex and Hampshire at Hove.

November 1981: Dennis Lillee is fined and suspended for two one-day internationals after kicking Pakistan's Javed Miandad during the first Test at the WACA Ground. Javed shapes to strike Lillee in retaliation, saying: 'I lifted my bat to ward him off and to tell him that if he hit me, I'd hit him,' said Javed, who claimed Lillee had kept saying 'dirty words' to him.

February 1982: The first New Zealand v Australia one-day international is marred by repeated pitch invasions. When Australian captain Greg Chappell comes out to bat, a lawn bowl is rolled across the outfield towards the pitch.

March 1982: The first Pakistan v Sri Lanka one-day international in Karachi is reduced to a 33-over-a-side match by crowd disturbances and repeated field invasions.

April 1982: Members of Graham Gooch's rebel English XI which toured South Africa are given a three-year ban from Test cricket. Twelve months later, Sri Lankan rebels are to be banned for 25 years and West Indian rebels for life.

October 1982: Following several interruptions, the third Pakistan v Australia one-day international in Karachi is abandoned after only 12 overs. Geoff Lawson is struck by a missile and other boundary riders only narrowly escape being hit.

November 1982: Australian fast bowler Terry Alderman dislocates his shoulder while attempting to tackle a spectator who had invaded the field during the first Ashes Test in Perth.

May 1983: Rod Marsh breaks his 44-can beer-drinking record from 1977 by downing a 45th just before arrival at Heathrow with the 1983 Australians for cricket's third World Cup. Very much worse for wear, he is transported at least part of the way into the terminal on a luggage trolley.

July 1983: Australia's vice-captain David Hookes is fined A$1200, a quarter of his World Cup tour fee, for breaching the ACB's code of behaviour in his criticism of his captain Kim Hughes in a radio interview on Adelaide radio station 5DN. Asked about the captaincy, Hookes says: 'I guess I'm echoing a lot of players' thoughts in that I believe Rod Marsh would be an excellent captain of Australia.'

December 1983: Enraged by India's poor showing after it is dismissed for 90 by the West Indies in the second innings in Calcutta, spectators throw bottles, fruit and stones onto the field and later attack the team bus, breaking several windows and injuring one of the Indian players and an Indian official. Soon afterwards in the sixth Test in Madras, West Indian fast bowler Winston Davis is struck by a missile thrown from the stands causing West Indies captain, Clive Lloyd to lead his team from the field. Only after receiving assurances that extra police had been enlisted does Lloyd return his team to the ground after a half-hour delay.

January 1984: Police arrest 70 fans for wild behaviour on the Sydney Hill during a World Series game between Australia and the West Indies.

March 1984: Riot police are called in on the final day of the first Sri Lanka v New Zealand Test in Kandy, to quell crowd demonstrations after the home side is dismissed for 97 in its second innings.

March 1984: Rodney Hogg defuses speculation of a rift between himself and captain Kim Hughes despite almost punching Hughes after he'd taken Gordon Greenidge's wicket at Port-of-Spain. 'I was off the planet, my eyes were spinning. I was that glad to take the wicket,' says Hogg. 'I didn't know who was next to me even though I almost knocked his head off.'

November 1984: Kim Hughes resigns the Australian captaincy in tears in Brisbane, saying, 'The constant criticism, speculation and innuendo by former players and a section of the media over the last four or five years have finally taken their toll.'

December 1984: The fourth Pakistan v New Zealand one-day International in Multan is reduced to 35 overs per side following a delay at the start of the game when spectators clash with ground staff.

December 1984: Jeremy Coney all but takes his NZ team from the field, following heated exchanges after controversial umpire Shakoor Rana rejects an appeal against Pakistan's Javed Miandad during the third Test in Karachi.

December 1984: After 65 consecutive Tests and leading India to the 1983 World Cup triumph, Kapil Dev is dropped from the third Test against England at Eden Gardens, scapegoat of India's loss in the previous Test in Delhi when he self-destructed in India's second innings.

December 1984: Australia's Geoff Lawson is fined $500 and placed on a $1500 good behaviour bond after an incident with West Indian Gordon Greenidge serious enough to warrant an official protest from the tourists during Melbourne's Christmas Test.

January 1985: After a flare-up between Australian wicketkeeper Steve Rixon and Viv Richards which also sees Allan Border become involved, 'Smokin' Joe' Richards invites Border behind the Sydney Cricket Ground grandstand at the end of play to 'sort it out'.

January 1985: Two die and 20 are injured when a temporary stand collapses during the fourth India v England one-day international in Nagpur.

February 1985: Pakistan's Abdul Qadir is ordered from the field on the last afternoon of a drawn game against Wellington by stand-in captain Zaheer Abbas, having shown 'a disinterested attitude' in the field. He is immediately sent home.

April 1985: The Australian Cricket Board issues nine Supreme Court writs against South African Cricket Union president Geoff Dakin, his Australian agent Bruce Francis and seven rebel players in order to stop their involvement in the first of two unauthorised tours to South Africa. Sixteen Australians are to be banned for three years from official Test cricket and for two years from interstate cricket.

February 1986: Play in the first Sri Lanka v Pakistan Test in Kandy is held up for 30 minutes on the final day after the umpires and Sri Lankan batsmen return to the pavilion in protest at abuse from the Pakistan fieldsmen after an appeal for a catch against Arjuna Ranatunga is rejected.

March 1986: A spectator throws a stone at Javed Miandad after he disputes his dismissal, lbw, during the second Sri Lanka–Pakistan Test in Colombo. The Pakistanis are so incensed they consider abandoning the tour.

May 1986: On the verge of surpassing Dennis Lillee's world record for most wickets in Test cricket, Ian Botham is suspended for two months after confessing to smoking pot. He is to miss five of the summer's six Tests. Police had originally raided his Epworth home and found some marijuana in a bedroom drawer on New Year's Eve. Botham claims it had been given to him by a supporter some years before and he'd simply forgotten about it.

February 1987: Pakistan's Qasim Omar is banned for seven years by the Pakistan Cricket Board after accusing team-mates in *People* of drug-taking in the first of a long line of stories-for-cash peddled by the disgraced middle-order batsman.

March 1987: Play in the fourth Test at Ahmedabad is held up for 50 minutes on the fourth day after spectators throw stones at Pakistan fielders. On resumption six fieldsmen wear helmets onto the field.

April 1987: A New Zealand tour of Sri Lanka is abandoned after a bomb blast kills more than 100 people at crowded Pettah bus station, where the team had been just 30 minutes before.

May 1987: Police reinforcements are called to Edgbaston after a series of ugly incidents erupt between English and Pakistani supporters during the third one-day international.

July 1987: Ian Botham has to be separated from Pakistani wicketkeeper Salim Yousuf by umpire Ken Palmer after Yousuf had claimed a bump ball as a catch during the third Test at Leeds.

November 1987: So dismayed is England opener Chris Broad at being given out in Lahore by umpire Shakil Khan, caught at the wicket, he refuses to leave the crease for a full minute. 'Like it or lump it, I'm not going,' he says heatedly to Pakistani close-in fieldsmen. He is finally led away by his partner Graham Gooch. Miraculously, he escapes with a stern reprimand. After the dramatic match, which England loses by an innings, English captain Mike Gatting accuses the umpires of cheating.

December 1987: Mike Gatting clashes with umpire Shakoor Rana in a toe-to-toe tirade late on the second day of the second Test in Faisalabad. Shakoor refuses to officiate for the rest of the game unless he receives an apology from Gatting. One finally comes after a direction from the Test and County Cricket Board in London and the game resumes a day late.

January 1988: Given out lbw by umpire Mel Johnson, David Boon reacts angrily and repeatedly shouts at the umpire as he makes his way back to the pavilion during a one-day international in Brisbane. He escapes with a reprimand, but not without a phone call from his mother in the dressing room saying he should never react like that again.

January 1988: In another display of dissent, English batsman Chris Broad swipes out his leg stump with his bat after being bowled and is fined £300 during the Bicentenary Test in Sydney.

February 1988: Ian Botham and Dennis Lillee are fined almost $4000 between them after the Launceston Cricket Ground's visitors' dressing room is wilfully damaged at the conclusion of a McDonald's Cup match between Tasmania and Queensland.

March 1988: Ian Botham's controversial one-and-only season with Queensland ends in acrimony when he is fined $500 on a charge of assaulting a passenger on a plane trip from Melbourne to Perth. He's fined a further $300 for offensive behaviour and later another $5000 by the Australian Cricket Board on code of behaviour violations. '$5000 is about 50 quid sterling so I'm not really too bothered,' says Botham.

April 1988: Pakistan captain Imran Khan protests to the umpires after Viv Richards angrily waves his bat at 'keeper Salim Yousuf after what he considered an unnecessary appeal during the Test in Port-of-Spain.

April 1988: Frustrated by the rejection of several appeals against Jeff Dujon, Pakistani leg-spinner Abdul Qadir becomes involved in a confrontation with a heckler on the boundary in Bridgetown. The spectator is struck during the tangle and in an out-of-court settlement, $1000 is paid to relieve Qadir of assault charges and allow him to leave Barbados with the team.

August 1988: Mike Gatting is fined £5000 (A$11 000) by the Test and County Cricket Board for unauthorised remarks made in his autobiography *Leading from the Front*. It eclipsed the fine of £2000 (A$4250) imposed on Yorkshire's Chris Old in 1982 for a contentious newspaper article.

September 1988: After losing the first Test in Karachi by an innings, the

Australians complain bitterly of an unacceptable pitch and biased umpiring by Mahboob Shah and seriously consider abandoning their tour.

December 1989: Indian fieldsmen are twice forced to leave the field after stones and other missiles are hurled at them in Karachi during the third one-day international. The game is abandoned after only 14.2 overs.

January 1990: Pakistan's Wasim Akram cannons into Australian fast bowler Merv Hughes in mid-pitch in Adelaide, prompting a furious war of words and intervention from umpire Tony Crafter. 'It was a clash of the heavyweights,' said Crafter. 'I was stuck in the middle.'

December 1990: Sixteen are arrested and one policeman hospitalised during a violent brawl on the Sydney Hill during a World Series game between England and New Zealand.

January 1991: India's ill-tempered Duleep Trophy final between North Zone and West Zone is abandoned after an enraged Rashid Patel attacks North Zone batsman Raman Lamba with a stump at Jamshedpur. Lamba had baited Patel, hoping he'd lose his line. The bowler responded by striking Lamba during the incident, described by writer Rajan Bala as 'the most inglorious act ever perpetrated in Indian cricket'. Patel is suspended for 13 months and Lamba for 10.

March 1991: West Indian captain Viv Richards refuses to call Dean Jones back to the wicket at Bourda in a gross act of poor sportsmanship. Bowled by a Courtney Walsh no-ball, Jones is walking back to the pavilion when Allan Border at the non striker's end yells at him to get back in his crease. Before he makes his ground, the wicket is broken (again) and umpire Clive Cumberbatch gives him run-out, when, in fact, the ball should have been called 'dead'. Cumberbatch is not to stand in the rest of the series.

November 1991: Frustrated by the home side's batting collapse during the first one-day international, a section of the Karachi crowd invades the field. West Indies player Philo Wallace has to leave the field with a bruised shoulder after being struck by a missile.

January 1992: England's Phil Tufnell is abused by the crowd and pelted with fruit as he fields near the boundary in the first one-day international in Auckland.

January 1992: Play in the fifth one-day international between Pakistan and Sri Lanka is held up for 30 minutes while Rawalpindi police attempt to control an unruly crowd with baton charges and tear gas.

March 1992: Pakistan pair Aamer Sohail and Moin Khan and Australia's Mike Whitney become the first players to be charged under the International Cricket Council's new code of conduct. Each is found guilty and fined – Sohail for showing dissent after an appeal against David Boon is disallowed, and Moin and Whitney over a confrontation late in Australia's innings when Moin claims a catch behind.

July 1992: Former Pakistan fast bowler Sarfraz Nawaz sues Allan Lamb for libel following the English Testman's accusations that Pakistani pacemen were 'known ball-tamperers'. Lamb's revelations follow the acrimonious Lord's Test when umpires are forced to change the ball during the English innings. Denying that he is going public for his own monetary gain, Lamb donates his £5000 fee received from a London newspaper to charity.

November 1992: Five members of the New Zealand team and coach Warren Lees return home early from Sri Lanka after a suicide bomber assassinates four naval personnel only 50 metres from the Colombo hotel where the New Zealand players are staying.

December 1992: Pakistan's Aaqib Javed becomes the first player to be suspended by the ICC after his abuse of New Zealand umpire Brian Aldridge during a one-day international in Napier.

December 1992: India's Kapil Dev 'Mankads' South Africa's Peter Kirsten during a one-day international at St George's Park, prompting Kepler Wessels to retaliate with a clip with his bat to Kapil's shins, while running between wickets. Earlier on the tour, Kapil had warned Kirsten for backing up too far. For his reaction, Kirsten is fined half his match fee. Wessels escapes penalty.

March 1993: Zaheer Abbas is tied up and blindfolded during an armed robbery at his home in Karachi. His cook finds two children at the door asking for a glass of water. As he opens the door, two armed men and a woman enter, threatening Zaheer and his wife, Najma, and stealing money and jewellery. Two weeks later, another ex-Pakistani Test player Sadiq Mohammad is robbed of his car at gunpoint.

March 1993: A metal bolt, thrown from the boundary edge, only narrowly misses England's Devon Malcolm as he chases a ball in the outfield at Jamshedpur during the fourth one-day international.

March 1993: Merv Hughes triggers fury in the New Zealand camp after spitting at opening batsman Mark Greatbatch at Eden Park. 'If it was within the rules to get physical, Merv would have done it,' claims Greatbatch.

April 1993: Four Pakistanis, including captain Wasim Akram and vice-captain Waqar Younis, are arrested on a beach at St George's, Grenada, and charged with 'constructive possession of marijuana'. Three of the four, included in the match against the West Indian Under 23 side, play the match on bail. The charges are dropped at the completion of the game, Wasim saying, 'We are accused of things wherever we go. Last year in England it was ball-tampering and now this, which was 20 times worse. We are not bad human beings. We don't make trouble. All we are is good cricketers. Why are some people jealous of that?'

November 1993: Play in a Hero Cup match is held up for 40 minutes after spectators in Ahmedabad, frustrated at India's batting collapse, pelt stones, firecrackers and plastic bottles at West Indian fieldsmen.

March 1994: Australia's champion leg-spinner Shane Warne tells South Africa's Andrew Hudson to '&%#@ off' after bowling him behind his legs during the third Test at Johannesburg. He admits to having become a victim of pressure, his mood not being improved after a shocked Australian Cricket Board fines him his entire match fee of $4400. Merv Hughes is fined a similar amount after separate misdemeanours.

March 1994: Pakistan's Ata-ur-Rehman is struck on the head by a bottle thrown from the crowd during the second one-day international in Auckland. Players leave the field for 11 minutes.

July 1994: England captain Mike Atherton admits to storing dirt in his pocket and rubbing it across the ball to help dry it during the first Test against South Africa at Lord's. He's fined £2000 but maintains that he was ignorant of the law and had never knowingly cheated at cricket.

October 1994: Crowd violence mars the seventh one-day international in Peshawar. Australians Michael Slater and Shane Warne are struck by missiles while fielding while team-mate David Boon and South Africa's Daryll Cullinan have firecrackers thrown at them.

December 1994: New Zealand's Ken Rutherford is found guilty and fined for attempting to intimidate an umpire to uphold an appeal against Sri Lankan's Hashan Tillekeratne during a Mandela Trophy match in East London.

December 1994: Three young New Zealanders, Stephen Fleming, Matthew Hart and Dion Nash, admit to smoking marijuana at Paarl during the team's tour of South Africa. They are fined and, on return to NZ, are suspended for three one-day internationals.

February 1995: Pakistan captain Saleem Malik is central in bribery accusations brought against him by Australian trio Shane Warne, Tim May and Mark Waugh. Australian Cricket Board executive director Graham Halbish dubs it 'cricket's greatest crisis in 20 years'.

March 1995: West Indian cricket great Viv Richards accuses Steve Waugh of cheating in that he claimed a juggling catch at Bridgetown to dismiss Brian Lara which he knew had hit the ground. 'If I had doubts,' says Waugh, 'I would have called him back.'

June 1995: In one of the most controversial UK tours for years, West Indian tourist Winston Benjamin is sent home in mid-tour on fitness and disciplinary grounds. Shortly afterwards, master batsman Brian Lara briefly goes AWOL, saying cricket has ruined his life. When Carl Hooper also leaves the tour early, both he and Lara are fined 10 per cent of their tour fee. Curtly Ambrose and Kenny Benjamin suffer similar fines for poor behaviour and attitude. Lara is so angered by his fine that he withdraws from the team's one-day tour of Australia later in the year.

November 1995: A wall of a newly-extended stand collapses at Nagpur, killing 12 spectators and injuring 61 during the luncheon interval of an India v New Zealand one-day international.

January 1996: After an ill-tempered and incident-ridden final, the Sri Lankan players refuse to shake hands with Australian captain Mark Taylor at the World Series presentation ceremony in Sydney.

March 1996: After seeing Pakistan eliminated from the World Cup, a fan from Islamabad shoots his TV set and then himself with a rifle.

March 1996: A riot ends a World Cup semi-final in Calcutta after Indian supporters, enraged by a batting collapse by their side, throw bottles onto the outfield and light fires in the stands. Sri Lanka, which had been in a commanding position when the riot broke out, are declared the winners by default.

June 1996: During a routine drug test at Tunbridge Wells, Sussex and England 'A' fast bowler Ed Giddins tests positive to cocaine in his bloodstream and is suspended for 18 months. He claims a drink had been spiked. He's the first player, after Yorkshire's Richard Stemp (in 1992), to fail a drug test.

August 1997: Shane Warne is given police protection after a county game at Taunton in which Australia's acting captain Steve Waugh halts play and asks security men to stop a torrent of abusive barracking. In the Trent Bridge Test which follows, a rowdy element continue their Warne baiting asking, 'Everyone who hates Shane Warne, stand up.'

September 1997: Taunted by a Toronto spectator who, through a megaphone, had been constantly calling him a potato, Pakistan's Inzamam-ul-Haq leaves the field while the Sahara Cup match against India is in progress to remonstrate with the man. Play is held up for almost an hour. Meetings between the two fierce rivals had for years been drawn on neutral soil to avoid crowd disturbance.

November 1998: Dismayed at their demands for increased pay and across-the-board benefits for all of its members, the Australian Cricketers' Association agrees to boycott four of the summer's one-day internationals on 4, 7, 9 and 14 December. 'The only way to convince the ACB that we actually believe in our own proposals is for us to demonstrate a contingency of striking,' says wicketkeeper Ian Healy. The strike is averted after the Board reopens discussions.

December 1998: Australian fast bowler Glenn McGrath is reported for sledging England's tail-end batsman, Alan Mullally, and given a heavy suspended fine.

January 1999: Sri Lanka's captain Arjuna Ranatunga is reported on a host of charges after umpire Ross Emerson no-balls Muttiah Muralitharan for throwing. Ranatunga leads his players to the edge of Adelaide Oval as an angry Ranatunga debates the incident with match referee Peter Van der Merwe. After finally agreeing to return, Ranatunga is involved in another angry confrontation with Emerson over where he should stand in relation to the stumps when Muralitharan is bowling. After engaging a firm of Melbourne lawyers, Ranatunga is given a suspended ban and a light fine. Later in the match there is a further controversy when Sri Lankan batsman Roshan Mahanama appears to deliberately collide with Englishman Darren Gough as he runs a quick single.

January 1999: Ricky Ponting is suspended for three one-day internationals and issued with a suspended $5000 fine by the Australian Cricket Board's code of conduct commissioner Rick Lewis after an altercation in a Sydney night club which left Ponting with a blackened eye. Ponting admits to an alcohol problem for which he is to receive counselling.

April 1999: Having spat seemingly in the direction of West Indian opening batsman Adrian Griffith, Australian fast bowler Glenn McGrath is severely reprimanded and has a previous $2250 suspended fine implemented during the fourth and deciding Test in St John's.

April 1999: The fifth Australia v West Indies one-day international in Guyana is ruled a tie after a crowd invasion. With four runs needed to win from the last ball, 2000 spectators swarm the field as Steve Waugh strikes the final ball of the match to deep midwicket. The batsmen complete two runs and are attempting an unlikely third run for a tie when they are engulfed and jostled by intruders. The stumps are stolen and the Australians harassed and threatened as they return to the pavilion.

April 1999: During the seventh one-day international in Bridgetown, local hero Sherwin Campbell reluctantly departs having been given run out after a mid-pitch collision with giant Australian fast bowler Brendon Julian. Bottles and other missiles are thrown, one bottle narrowly missing Australian captain Steve Waugh as he heads for the dressing room. After a 45-minute stoppage, during which the local police commissioner tells Waugh he cannot guarantee the team's safety if the match is abandoned, the Australians reluctantly agree to reinstate Campbell and the match continues.

May 1999: In his column in the London *Times*, Shane Warne vents his anger against old adversary Arjuna Ranatunga. 'Sri Lanka and the game of cricket would be better off without him,' he says. Warne is issued with a suspended fine of $1800 and a suspended two-match ban for contravening clause 8 of the ICC code of conduct. Ranatunga returns the fire. 'I've done more things than he's done,' says Ranatunga. 'The comments show more about Shane Warne and the Australian culture. We come from 2500 years of culture and we all know where they come from.'

May 2000: Herschelle Gibbs is fined 15 000 rand (A$3750) and given a three-match suspended sentence for conduct unbecoming after an incident in Durban on the eve of a ODI against Australia in mid-April 2000. Ten thousand of the 15 000 rand fine is suspended, pending Gibbs' good behaviour for 12 months.

June 2000: In England during his debut year of county cricket with Hampshire, Shane Warne admits to having phone sex with 22-year-old single mother Donna Smith from Leicester. Two months later he is stripped of his Australian vice-captaincy.

June 2000: Dean Jones refuses to name an Indian cricketer he knows has direct links with match-fixing. 'I don't want to be involved in a situation where I jeopardise the safety of my family or myself,' he tells Melbourne's Channel 10.

July 2000: After years of suspicion, Pakistan fast bowler Waqar Younis becomes the first cricketer to be suspended for ball-tampering during the Singer Cup one-day series in Colombo. He is fined 50 per cent of his match fee and banned for one match. Only a month earlier he'd joined the elite band of bowlers to take 300 Test wickets. Team-mates Azhar Mahmood and captain Moin Khan are also cited by the match referee John Reid, Azhar fined 30 per cent of his match fee and Moin severely reprimanded for 'allowing the spirit of the game to be impaired'. Both Waqar and Azhar are caught tampering with the ball via television.

September 2000: Three Pakistanis, Shahid Afridi, Hasan Raza and Atiquz Zaman are fined $1570 and suspended for one tournament on misconduct charges after women had been found in their rooms in Lahore on the eve of their team flying out to Singapore for a tri-series.

February 2001: The English Cricket Board rules unprovable allegations of match-fixing in the Lancashire v Essex games at Old Trafford in August 1991. Essex won the three-day Britannic Assurance county game by eight wickets with three balls to spare after being set a generous 270 from 67 overs; their win taking them to the top of the championship table and ultimately a £44 000 (A$85 000) first prize. Lancashire needed to win their one-day game on the Sunday to remain in contention to win the Refuge Assurance League. They did by five wickets, but still had to settle for second place overall, and a £13 000 (A$24 000) prize pool. One of Saleem's Essex team-mates, Don Topley, later declared that the games had been fixed on an 'exchange' basis.

April 2001: English-born Duncan Spencer, a West Australian Mercantile Mutual Cup fast bowler, becomes the first Australian cricketer to be suspended for failing a drug test. Spencer, 29, tests positive to the banned anabolic steroid nandrolone and is banned for 18 months from state and international cricket.

May 2001: In his autobiography *Retired Hurt*, ex-Sri Lankan captain Roshan Mahanama accuses Australian fast bowler Glenn McGrath of racially abusing team-mate Sanath Jayasuriya. The alleged incident was said to have occurred in the second final of the World Series Cup in Sydney in 1995–96, the most ill-tempered of all one-day internationals. McGrath denies the charge, but Mahanama insists it was 'the truth, the whole truth and nothing but the truth'. 'I like Glenn McGrath and think he's a fine bowler, but that doesn't mean I condone his sledging,' says Mahanama.

May 2001: Herschelle Gibbs and four members of the South African touring cricket team in the West Indies are disciplined after admitting to smoking marijuana at the luxurious Jolly Harbour resort in Antigua following South Africa's Test series victory in early April. Paul Adams, Roger Telemachus, Andre Nel and Justin Kemp are each fined 10 000 rand (A$2500), as is team physiotherapist Craig Smith. In a tour where misbehaviour was commonplace, Telemachus had earlier been fined 2000 rand (A$500) for twice verbally abusing team-mates. One of those, batsman Daryll Cullinan, was fined 2000 rand (A$500) for leaving the field without the consent of captain Shaun Pollock.

Big bets
1980–2001

1980

January: In his farewell Test match, a drawn encounter at Eden Gardens, Calcutta, Pakistani captain Asif Iqbal is accused of losing the toss 'under curious circumstances'. Additionally, his first-innings declaration at 4/272, 59 runs behind India's first innings, is considered so suspicious that Bombay bookmakers cancel all bets. When it is suggested that large bets have been placed on India's first-time captain Gundappa Vishwanath winning the toss and India gaining a first-innings lead, Asif denies any wrongdoing. 'I didn't even know betting existed then,' he tells author Jack Bannister in *Tampering with Cricket*. 'As for the people who made the allegations about the toss – were they there when the coin was up? As far as declaring is involved, the players had a chat and we felt that losing the series 3–0 is little different to 2–0. Anyway, we dropped a couple of catches.' Vishwanath claims Asif said, 'Congratulations' while the coin was still airborne.

1983

May: Worcestershire's leading batsman, Younis Ahmed, is dumped after backing Leicestershire to beat his team in a John Player League match. Younis, previously sacked in controversial circumstances by Melbourne sub-district club Malvern, claims he placed the bet at generous odds as a way of covering his win bonus if Worcestershire lost. Ironically, the game in question is washed out.

June: An unnamed subcontinent fan wins £50 000 after wagering £1000 at 50/1 on outsiders India winning the 1983 World Cup.

1987
September: Pakistani players are alleged to have been paid 30 million rupees (around A$1 million) to lose their World Cup semi-final against Australia in Lahore. Ex-captain Asif Iqbal is again said to be linked.

1991
October: Pakistan captain Imran Khan is told that four members of his team have been approached to throw a one-day international against arch-rivals India in Sharjah. He insists that every player commit his match wage to form a US$20 000 kitty, which is then placed on Pakistan to win. They do so comfortably by 72 runs, doubling their money. Fast bowler Aaqib Javed takes a rare and distinguished hat-trick of lbws (Ravi Shastri, Mohammad Azharuddin and Sachin Tendulkar).

1992
August: Ex-Pakistani Test bowler Sarfraz Nawaz claims the Texaco Cup match at Trent Bridge, in which England completes a clean sweep against Pakistan by 198 runs, is fixed. Pakistani journalist Fareshteh Gati-Aslam says the performances of Wasim Akram (11 overs, 1/55) and Waqar Younis (11 overs, 4/73) are particularly questionable. England scores a record 7/363 from its 55 overs.

September: Early in Australia's tour of Sri Lanka, an Indian bookmaker (understood to be M. K. Gupta) offers Dean Jones a cake tin containing A$66 000 in unmarked notes, in return for providing inside information on the state of the pitch and the fitness of players. Jones rejects the offer and immediately reports the incident to Australian team manager Cam Battersby.

1993

August: Ex-Pakistani captain Mushtaq Mohammad denies that a A$1 million offer to Allan Border to lose the fifth Test at Edgbaston during the 1993 Ashes series was anything more than a party joke. Asked if he intended the offer, made on the fourth night of the match, to be a bribe, Mushtaq says: 'No, no, no, no, no, no.'

1994

March: Pakistan's Rashid Latif claims to have been approached by his captain Saleem Malik on the eve of the fifth and final match of the Bank of New Zealand ODI series at Lancaster Park and offered one million rupees (A$32 350) to play badly. Wasim Akram is alleged to have asked fast bowler Ata-ur-Rehman to bowl opposite to the field placings in the same game. Rehman turns out to be the most expensive of the Pakistani attack, conceding 44 runs and taking just one wicket from nine overs. Unbeaten to that point, Pakistan loses the match by seven wickets.

August: Warwickshire committeemen win £100 000 (on their original stake of £82) after their team wins three of the four English domestic competitions.

September: Indian all-rounder Manoj Prabhakar claims to have been offered A$10 000 to throw a one-day match in Colombo. (Later he names the legendary Kapil Dev as the man who offered the bribe.) Prabhakar says the approach came at the team's hotel, the Oberoi. He immediately reports the incident to manager Ajit Wadekar and captain Mohammad Azharuddin, who recommend that he forget it and concentrate on India's next match.

September: During a short tour of Sri Lanka for a four-nation one-day tournament in Colombo, the Singer World Series, Mark Waugh and Shane Warne meet an Indian bookmaker at a casino and are offered money in exchange for information on pitch and weather conditions. They accept and are paid US$6000 and US$5000 respectively.

September: An Indian bookmaker, Saleem Pervez, is said to have paid six million rupees (A$192 000) each to captain Saleem Malik and star spinner Mushtaq Ahmed to ensure that Pakistan loses a Singer World Series match against Australia in Colombo. In the game, a low-scoring affair on an underprepared Sinhalese Sports Club wicket, Pakistan loses by 28 runs. Saleem is unusually slow, taking 51 balls to make 22 before a wild slash to cover. He also fills in as a sixth bowler, having five overs. Mushtaq takes 2/34 from 10 overs. 'That night after the game there was some talk in the bar that something wasn't right,' says Australia's David Boon. Team-mate Steve Waugh, who took 3/16 from 10 overs, concurs. 'I've played cricket for 30 years and I know when things aren't quite right,' he tells the Australian Broadcasting Corporation's *Four Corners* program in July 2000. 'It was the way the opposition were playing. A couple of players, in particular, didn't appear to be playing the way they normally would.'

September: After allegations of big bets during the Colombo tournament, the International Cricket Council (ICC) instructs match referee John Reid to be particularly alert to gambling and game-fixing while officiating at the Pakistan v Australia series.

October: Mark Waugh, Shane Warne and Tim May are offered US$200 000 each by Saleem Malik to throw matches during Australia's tour of Pakistan.

October: At Lahore, South African umpire Cyril Mitchley is offered US$50 000 (A$84 000) to influence the result of the Test Pakistan's way. He says, 'I reported the matter immediately to match referee John Reid and went back and showed him where the man was standing, but he obviously didn't have much luck investigating it.'

October: Needing nine runs an over to win an ODI in Kanpur, Indians Manoj Prabhakar and Nayan Mongia are suspected of chicanery when they score just 16 from the final 43 balls. The West Indies win by 46. So dissatisfied is match referee Raman Subba Row that he implements an unprecedented two-point fine on the Indians. Prabhakar and Mongia are immediately dropped.

November: Pakistan players are ordered to take an oath on the Holy Koran that they will not accept bribes to throw matches or perform poorly during their forthcoming tour of South Africa and Zimbabwe.

1995
January: Hansie Cronje is involved in attempted match-fixing when an Indian or Pakistani bookmaker Cronje later names as 'John' offers him US$10 000 to throw the first final of the Mandela one-day trophy. After discussing the offer with South African veteran Pat Symcox, he turns it down.

January: Pakistan's Aamer Sohail denies all knowledge of a conversation with the *Australian*'s Adam Shand in which he supposedly pointed out during a training session at the Harare Sports Club team-mates known to have taken bribes. 'It's getting so bad it's giving the guys who don't do it a bad name,' he says.

February: Saleem Malik angrily denies any involvement in match-fixing. 'I think it's shameful,' he says from Harare. 'Seventy thousand dollars. I wish I had that sort of money. I never spoke to anybody like this. I will speak to my lawyer and will take legal action.'

February: The Australian Cricket Board (ACB) secretly fines Mark Waugh $10 000 and Warne $8000 over their involvement with John the book-maker. Neither the fines nor any aspect of the affair are recorded in the Board's minutes.

February: Rashid Latif and Basit Ali leave Pakistan's tour of Zimbabwe and fly home to Karachi, saying they are no longer prepared to play under Saleem's captaincy.

March: Saleem Malik and Pakistani coach Intikhab Alam are suspended from any role at international and first-class level pending an inquiry into match-fixing. Saleem is, however, allowed to play domestic cricket.

March: In sworn statements to the ICC, Mark Waugh, Warne and May repeat their allegations of foul-play attempts by Saleem. The ACB rejects requests for the trio to fly to Pakistan and appear before the inquiry. 'They have nothing to add to their statements and there is no need for them to go,' says the ACB's chief executive officer, Graham Halbish. 'It is an internal Pakistan matter.'

October: A Pakistani inquiry led by retired Judge Fakhruddin G. Ebrahim exonerates Saleem and finds the Australians' allegations 'unbelievable'. Saleem says Warne's charges were concocted 'as he could not take my wicket once in the series'. Intikhab is reappointed manager for the Australian tour and for the 1996 World Cup.

1996
February: At the orders of president Farood Ahmed Khan Legari, Pakistan's Federal Intelligence Agency begins bugging phones at hotels in which the Pakistani team stay in the lead-up to the 1996 World Cup. Farood has been tipped off that players have remained in contact with big-spending Indian bookmakers since the Saleem affair.

March: Pakistan team physiotherapist Dan Kiesel tells journalist Fereshteh Gati-Aslam that Wasim Akram faked a shoulder injury that kept him out of Pakistan's losing World Cup quarterfinal against India at Bangalore. 'I do not deserve this,' the all-rounder says. 'I have received death threats and my family is getting abusive phone calls. I have always played my best for Pakistan. I am ready to swear over the Holy Koran that I do not get involved in betting and that I am clean.'

March: Former Pakistan opening batsman Qasim Omar claims to be a 'middleman' in bribery scams involving 15 Test players. He tells the *People* newspaper that corruption infiltrates every level of Pakistan cricket, often with official knowledge and acceptance.

April: Former Pakistani team manager Khalid Mahmood says the living standards of many Pakistani players have so dramatically improved that their involvement in gambling 'seems to be closer in fact'.

December: Introduced by Mohammad Azharuddin to bookmaker Mukesh Gupta, Hansie Cronje is asked to ensure that South Africa loses the deciding Test match. He accepts US$30 000, saying he will talk to the team about it, but does nothing. South Africa loses by 280 runs. The same week, Cronje is offered US$250 000 to fix 'Jimmy' Amarnath's benefit match at Mumbai at the end of the tour. Cronje discusses it with several of the team. One player jokingly says, 'Let's see if we can get more.' Cronje picks up the phone and negotiates an extra US$100 000. The plan is denounced by coach Bob Woolmer and leading players including Andrew Hudson and Daryll Cullinan, and the game given full ODI status. At that stage the South Africans have no idea that Cronje is crooked and has been for several years. Ironically, the match is Cronje's 100th at ODI level and his 50th as captain.

1997

January: For the first two return Tests against India, Hansie Cronje supplies information to bookmaker Mukesh Gupta for an unspecified sum, indexed to Gupta's winnings. Team selection and when and at what score Cronje will declare are supplied. Cronje's share is US$50 000. Gupta offers Cronje US$300 000 for South Africa to lose the third Test, but he rejects the offer. The match is drawn, but only just, thanks to some stormy weather and late-match resistance from Daryll Cullinan (122 not out) and Lance Klusener (49).

1998

August: Experienced Pakistani umpire Javed Akhtar angrily denies suggestions that he has been paid off to help England win the deciding Test against South Africa at Leeds. He gives nine lbws, seven against the Proteas, in a low-scoring game that England wins by 23 runs.

September: A three-member Pakistani Cricket Board (PCB) committee headed by Justice Chudhary Ejaz Yousuf declares Saleem Malik, Wasim Akram and Ijaz Ahmed guilty of match-fixing and recommends they be banned from Test cricket. Before referring the matter to a High Court judicial inquiry, however, the PCB says that all players under suspicion should remain eligible for the Test series against the visiting Australians.

October: Mark Waugh, captain Mark Taylor and ACB chief executive Malcolm Speed agree to attend an in-camera hearing with Lahore High Court judge Justice Malik Mohammad Qayyum inquiring into match-fixing allegations against Pakistani players. Waugh does not reveal his involvement with bookmakers; nor does Speed, who has been informed of Waugh's association with John the bookmaker.

December: Shane Warne and Mark Waugh's payments from the Indian bookmaker are made public by Malcolm Speed after *Australian* cricket writer Malcolm Conn invites Speed to comment on a story he is about to publish regarding Mark Waugh's involvement with an illegal bookmaker. Speed confirms the facts and says a second Australian player, Shane Warne, is also involved. At a press conference Warne and Waugh admit they were naive and stupid for accepting the money. Former ACB chairman Alan Crompton says the matter was deliberately kept silent at the time because it was regarded as an internal disciplinary matter.

December: Ricky Ponting reveals he was offered money by a Sydney bookmaker 12 months previously to provide confidential information about the team. He rejected the offer.

December: The ACB launches it own inquiry into betting, headed by Brisbane criminal lawyer Rob O'Regan, QC.

2000

January: Captains Nasser Hussain and Hansie Cronje agree to contrive a result in the final Test at Centurion Park. England forfeits its first innings and South Africa its second. Unbeknown to Hussain, Cronje has been offered 500 000 rand and a leather jacket to initiate a result. South Africa loses. Several players, on both sides, are amazed at Cronje's generosity. In the one-day series which follows, Cronje is introduced to Hamid Cassim, a friend of Mohammad Azharuddin. Hamid introduces Cronje to a man called Sanjay, who asks him to throw a game. Cronje refuses. He is handed a box containing at least US$10 000 in case he changes his mind.

February: Now trapped into a web of systematic corruption through his previous dealings with illegal bookmakers, Hansie Cronje admits the pressure on him to manipulate results is suffocating. He offers newcomer Pieter Strydom money to throw the first Test in Mumbai. Lance Klusener, Mark Boucher and Jacques Kallis rebuff his advances before the following Bangalore Test; they think he is joking. South Africa wins both games. More Cronje bribe attempts are made during the ODIs. Herschelle Gibbs and

Henry Williams agree to a fix before the fifth match: Williams is to bowl poorly and Gibbs to make less than 20. All bets are off by lunchtime as South Africa scores 320, its highest ODI score against India. Gibbs makes 74. Cronje also accepts US$8200 from a bookmaker for information leading into the ODI series between Zimbabwe and England.

April: Just four days after denying any involvement with match-fixing, Hansie Cronje breaks down and admits to a liaison with bookmakers. He says that in a moment of weakness he allowed 'Satan and the world to dictate terms'. He asks his wife, Bertha, to search for money stashed in many hiding places throughout their Bloemfontein house. 'I had that nauseous feeling in my stomach,' she says. 'I was anxious and confused. I counted half of it all wrong, stopped and took it all to Bloemfontein.' In two transactions, lawyers deposit more than US$50 000 into a trust account. Bertha tells Liz Hayes of Channel Nine's *60 Minutes* (in a paid interview) that she still loves her husband. 'He will always be my hero.'

April: Indian bookmaker Rajesh Kulra, the first man arrested in conjunction with match-fixing, claims that bookies paid $670 000 to fix the ODI series in March between India and South Africa. He confirms that spread betting – betting on small matters within a game – is rapidly matching the turnovers of match results.

May: After a 20-month judicial investigation in Lahore, Justice Qayyum hands down a 91-page report recommending life bans for Saleem Malik and former team-mate Ata-ur-Rehman – Saleem for match-fixing and Ata-ur-Rehman for perjury. 'Everyone seems to name him [Saleem] as the main culprit in match-fixing, Imran Khan, Javed Miandad, his own coaches, managers and fellow players,' says the judge. His recommendations are immediately activated by the PCB. Six others – Wasim Akram, Mushtaq Ahmed, Saeed Anwar, Inzamam-ul-Haq, Akram Raza and Waqar Younis – are also found by the Commission of Inquiry to have been caught in a web of deceit. They are fined for various offences, from associating with gamblers to withholding evidence. Judge Qayyum recommends that Wasim forfeit the captaincy. He says Wasim has avoided a suspension only because Ata-ur-Rehman's testimony against him could not be believed. 'He [Wasim] cannot be said to be beyond suspicion,' says the judge, '[and] it is therefore recommended that he be censured and be kept under strict vigilance.' Saleem again professes his innocence. 'My hands are clean,' he says. He adds that he will appeal through his lawyers within 48 hours. He doesn't.

May: Accused again by Manoj Prabhakar of being a key Indian player in match-fixing, Kapil Dev breaks down in tears in a television interview where he denies any such involvement. 'Why would I offer him money to play badly?' he says. 'He was never such a good player for me to offer him money to play badly.' Kapil takes legal action against Prabhakar and the owners of www.tehelka.com, the Internet company that assisted Prabhakar in producing some controversial match-fixing interviews on tape.

June: Herschelle Gibbs and Henry Williams admit their guilt at South Africa's King Inquiry in Cape Town. Both are given indefinite suspensions. In return for immunity from prosecution, Hansie Cronje reveals his dealings with illegal bookmakers, which go back five years. He exposes Mohammad Azharuddin and Saleem Malik, as others to have had dealings with bookies.

July: When noted No. 11 Glenn McGrath makes his maiden first-class half-century in a county game for Worcestershire, Shane Warne collects $1000 from Mark Waugh in an off-beat side bet made five years previously.

July: Azharuddin is named by the ABC's *Four Corners* as having pocketed unprecedented riches through his association with illegal bookmakers.

August: During nationwide raids, Indian tax officials seize unaccounted-for wealth worth more than A$1.5 million from the homes of top Indian cricketers and officials. Among the search targets are houses belonging to Mohammad Azharuddin and Kapil Dev.

August: Herschelle Gibbs and Henry Williams are suspended from international cricket until 1 January 2001 over their match-fixing involvement. They are, however, allowed to continue in South African domestic ranks from October.

November: Six Indian players, including ex-captains Azharuddin and Ajay Jadeja, are officially accused of wrongdoing in the Indian Central Bureau of Investigation report, *Cricket Match-Fixing and Related Malpractice*. The CBI also raids 25 homes and offices of those alleged to be implicated in fraudulent cricket broadcasting deals from 1996 to 1999. Six executives are said to have sold rights into private hands for personal gain.

December: India becomes the third country to impose the highest penalty against players found guilty of match-fixing. Azharuddin and Ajay Sharma are banned from first-class cricket and all administrative posts for life. Jadeja, Manoj Prabhakar and India's physiotherapist Ali Irani are given five-year bans. Two others implicated in the CBI report, Nayan Mongia and New Delhi groundsman Ram Adhar, are exonerated.

2001
February: Told that he would be stood down if he continued to refuse to talk to Sir Paul Condon's ICC Anti-Corruption Unit, Mark Waugh agrees to be interviewed and takes his place in Australia's teams for the Carlton Series one-day finals and for the tour of India.

June: Having unsuccessfully tried to interview bookmaker Mukesh Gupta to detail charges against players he had alleged to have bankrolled, Sir Paul Condon and his ICC Anti-Corruption Unit give Gupta two additional weeks in which to cooperate and substantiate his allegations before the Unit would move on to concentrate on protecting the future of the game. Gupta preferred to remain silent, effectively clearing Mark Waugh, Martin Crowe, Alec Stewart and Co.

Further reading

BOOKS

Arlott, J., *Basingstoke Boy* (Guild, 1990)

Bailey, P., Thorn, P. & Wynne-Thomas, P., *Who's Who of Cricketers* (Newnes, 1984)

Beecher, E., *The Cricket Revolution* (Newspress, 1978)

Bhogle, H., *Azhar: The Authorised Biography* (Penguin, 1994)

Botham, I., *My Autobiography* (CollinsWillow, 1994)

Bowen, R., *Cricket: A History of Its Growth and Development Throughout the World* (Eyre & Spottiswoode, 1970)

Bowes, W., *Express Deliveries* (Stanley Paul, 1949)

Brearley, M., *Phoenix from the Ashes: The Story of the England–Australia Series 1981* (Hodder & Stoughton, 1982)

Cairns, L., *Give It a Heave* (Moa, 1984)

Campbell, R.H., *Cricket Casualties* (ABC, 1933)

Cashman, R., *The 'Demon' Spofforth* (University of New South Wales Press, 1990)

Chappell, I., *Chappelli: The Cutting Edge* (Swan, 1992)

Chappell, I. with McFarline, P. & Beecher, E., *Chappelli: Ian Chappell's Life Story* (Hutchinson, 1976)

Compton, D., *Testing Time for England* (Stanley Paul, 1947)

Crowe, M., *Out on a Limb* (Reed, 1995)

Derriman, P., *The Grand Old Ground: A History of the Sydney Cricket Ground* (Cassell, 1981)

—— *The Top 100 and the 1st XI* (Fairfax Library, 1987)

D'Oliveira, B., *The D'Oliveira Affair* (Collins, 1969)

Down, M., *Archie: A Biography of A.C. McLaren* (Allen & Unwin, 1981)

Farnes, Kenneth, *Tours and Tests* (Lutterworth Press, 1940)

Fiddian, M., *A Miscellany of Left-Handers* (South East Newspapers, 1998)

Frindall, B., *The Wisden Book of Test Cricket,* vols 1 and 2 (Headline, 1995)

—— *Limited-Overs International Cricket: The Complete Record* (Headline, 1997)

Gatting, M., *Leading from the Front* (Queen Anne Press, 1988)

Gavaskar, S., *Idols* (Allen & Unwin, 1984)

Gooch, G. & Keating, F., *Gooch: My Autobiography* (CollinsWillow, 1995)

Gooch, G. & Lee, A., *Out of the Wilderness* (Guild, 1985)

Griffiths, E., *Kepler: The Biography* (Pelham, 1994)

—— *Jonty: Fruits of the Spirit* (CAB, 1998)

Haigh, G., *The Cricket War* (Text, 1993)

Harris, J. & Wust, K., *Bendigo District Cricket 1853–1990* (Crown Castleton, 1991)

Hartman, R., *Hansie and the Boys* (Zebra Press, 1997)

Harvey, R. N., *My World of Cricket* (Hodder & Stoughton, 1963)

Henry, O. with Graham, K., *The Man in the Middle* (Queen Anne Press, 1994)

Hobbs, J.B., *Recovering the Ashes: An Account of the Cricket Tour in Australia, 1911–12* (Sir Isaac Pitman & Sons, 1912)

Hookes, D. with Shiell, A., *Hookesy* (ABC, 1993)

Hordern, H.V., *Googlies* (Angus & Robertson, 1932)

Howarth, G. as told to Hepenstall, I., *Stirred but not Shaken* (Hodder Moa Beckett, 1998)

Imran Khan, *All Round View* (Chatto & Windus, 1988)

Jaggard, E., *Garth: The Story of Graham McKenzie* (Fremantle Arts Centre Press, 1993)

Kippax, A., *Anti Body-Line* (Sydney & Melbourne Publishing Company, 1933)

Larwood, H., *Bodyline* (Elkin, Mathews & Marrot, 1933)

Larwood, H. with Perkins, K., *The Larwood Story: A Cricketer's Autobiography* (W.H. Allen, 1965)

Lillee, D., *Lillee: My Life in Cricket* (Methuen Australia, 1982)

Mahony, P., *Mary Ann's Australians* (Cricket Lore, 1996)

Mailey, A., *And Then Came Larwood* (John Lane The Bodley Head, 1933)

Marsh, R., *The Gloves of Irony* (Lansdowne, 1982)

—— *Gloves, Sweat and Tears* (Penguin, 1984)

Marlar, R., *The Story of Cricket* (Marshall Cavendish, 1979)

Martin-Jenkins, C., *Ball by Ball: The Story of Cricket Broadcasting* (Grafton, 1990)

McGilvray, A., with Tasker, N., *Backpage of Cricket* (Lester Townsend, 1989)

McGregor, A., *Greg Chappell: Cricket's Incomparable Artist* (William Collins, 1985)

McHarg, J., *Bill O'Reilly: A Cricketing Life* (Millennium, 1990)

Meher-Homji, K., *Cricket's Greatest Families* (Rupa & Co., 1981)

Morrah, Patrick, *Alfred Mynn and the Cricketers of His Time* (Eyre & Spottiswoode, 1963)

Morrison, D., *Mad as I Wanna Be* (Hodder Moa Beckett, 1997)

Mosey, D., *Laker: Portrait of a Legend* (Queen Anne Press, 1989)

Moyes, A.G. Johnnie, *A Century of Cricketers* (Angus & Robertson, 1950)

—— *Australian Cricket: A History* (Angus & Robertson, 1959)

Norrie, D., *Athers: The Authorised Biography of Michael Atherton* (Hodder Headline, 1997)

Oldfield, W.A., *Behind the Wickets* (Hutchinson & Co., 1938)

Oslear, D. & Bannister, J., *Tampering with Cricket* (CollinsWillow, 1996)

Patherya, M. & O'Brien, B., *The Penguin Book of Cricket Lists* (Penguin, 1987)

Pawle, G., *R.E.S. Wyatt: Fighting Cricketer* (Allen & Unwin, 1985)

Peebles, I., *Straight from the Shoulder* (Hutchinson & Co/The Cricketer, 1968)

Piesse, K., *Warne: Sultan of Spin* (Modern Publishing, 1995)

—— *One Day Magic* (Australian Publishing, 1996)

Piesse, K. & Hansen, B., *Wildmen of Cricket,* vol. 1 (Brian Hansen, 1997)

Pollard, J., *Bumpers, Bosies and Brickbats* (Murray, 1966)

—— *Australian Cricket: The Game and the Players* (Hodder & Stoughton, 1982)

—— *Australian Cricket 1893–1917: The Turbulent Years* (Book Company, 1996)

Pollard, J. (ed.), *The Primary Club's Middle and Leg* (Macmillan, 1988)

Pollock, P., *The Thirty Tests* (Don Nelson, 1978)

Pringle, C., *Save the Last Ball for Me* (Celebrity Publishing, 1998)

Procter, M. & Murphy, P., *South Africa: The Years of Isolation* (Queen Anne Press, 1994)

Rae, S., *W.G. Grace: A Life* (Faber, 1998)

Redpath, I., with Phillipson, N., *Always Reddy* (Garry Sparke, 1976)

Richardson, V. with Whitington, R., *The Vic Richardson Story* (Rigby, 1967)

Robinson, R., *From the Boundary* (Collins, 1950)

—— *The Wildest Tests* (Pelham, 1972)

—— *After Stumps are Drawn: The Best of Ray Robinson's Cricket Writings, as Selected by Jack Pollard* (Collins, 1985)

Rutherford, K., *A Hell of a Way to Make a Living* (Hodder Moa Beckett, 1995)

Scott, J., *Caught in Court* (Andre Deutsch, 1989)

Sharpham, P., *Trumper: The Definitive Biography* (Hodder & Stoughton, 1985)

Simpson, R., *Captain's Story* (Stanley Paul, 1966)

Smith, I. as told to Brittenden, R., *Smithy: Just a Drummer in the Band* (Moa, 1991)

Smith, R., *Cricket Brawl: The 1912 Dispute* (Apple, 1995)

Sutcliffe, H., *For England and Yorkshire* (Edward Arnold, 1935)

Swanton, E.W., *Gubby Allen: Man of Cricket* (Hutchinson, 1985)

Synge, A., *Sins of Omission* (Pelham, 1990)

Tatz, C., *Aborigines in Sport* (Australian Society for Sports History, 1987)

Tatz, C. & Tatz, P., *Black Diamonds* (Allen & Unwin, 1996)

Tennant, I., *Imran Khan* (H.G. & F. Witherby, 1994)

Tennyson, L., Lord, *Sticky Wickets* (Christopher Johnson, 1950)

Turner, G., *My Way* (Hodder & Stoughton, 1975)

Tyson, F., *A Typhoon Called Tyson* (William Heinemann, 1961)

—— *The Century-Makers: The Men Behind the Ashes 1877–1977* (Hutchinson, 1980)

Wardle, J. as told to Thomson, A., *Happy Go Johnny* (Robert Hale, 1957)

Warner, P.F., *Long Innings* (Harrap, 1950)

Webber, J.R., *The Chronicle of W.G.* (Association of Cricket Statisticians, 1998)

Webster, R., *First Class Cricket in Australia Vol. 1 1850–51 to 1941–42* (R. Webster, 1991)

—— *First Class Cricket in Australia Vol. 2 1945–46 to 1976–77* (R. Webster, 1997)

Whimpress, B., *Passport to Nowhere: Aborigines in Australian Cricket 1850–1939* (Walla Walla Press, 1999)

Whitington, R.S. & Hele, G., *Bodyline Umpire* (Rigby, 1974)

Wynne-Thomas, P. & Arnold, P., *Cricket in Conflict* (Newnes, 1984)

MAGAZINES & ANNUALS

Australian Cricket magazine

Australian Cricketer, The

Cricket: A Weekly Record of the Game

Cricketer magazine

Cricketer International, The

David Lord's World of Cricket

Indian Cricket

Pakistan Cricketer, The

Protea Cricket Annual of South Africa, The

South African Cricketer, The

Wisden Cricket Monthly

Wisden Cricketers' Almanack

Acknowledgements

The author wishes to thank Jon Anderson, Dr Ali Bacher, Pieter Barnard, Percy Beames, Richie Benaud, Harsha Bhogle, Andy Bichel, Ray Bright, Greg Chappell, Ian Chappell, Trevor Chappell, Colin Clowes, Malcolm Conn, Alan Connolly, Crash Craddock, Ross Dundas, Col Egar, Ian Harvey, David Hookes, Merv Hughes, Kuldip Lal, Len Maddocks, Bob Massie, Tim May, Ian Meckiff, Harriet Monkhouse, Bob Parish, Mick Pope, Brian Quinn, Ian Redpath, A. Aziz Rehmatullah, Ron Reiffel, Austin Robertson jnr, Geoff Sando, Bob Simpson, Rick Smith, Mick Taylor, Ray Webster, Don Weser and Bernard Whimpress. Also the indefatigable Ken Williams for his expert assistance with the timeline, and the many photographers who have allowed their work to be reproduced in these pages.

Index